Praise for Erin Goseer Mitchell's

BORN COLORED
Life Before Bloody Sunday

"Hers is the New Voice of the South!"

•

*"Erin Goseer Mitchell explores the intimacies of growing
up 'colored' in America during the 1940s and '50s.
She writes beautifully, helping us to understand
who we are now and who we might become."*
Pat Schneider, Author
Writing Alone and With Others

•

"The descriptions in Mitchell's Born Colored *are so vivid
that I could smell the flowers in her father's garden and
hear the sounds of her grandmother's shoes walking the
floor as they awaited the birth of her baby sister."*
LaRhonda Crosby-Johnson
Author and Health Education Consultant
San Leandro, CA

•

*"I grew up in a large city in Ohio, sheltered from 'in your
face' segregation. I truly learned from your stories."*
Helen R. Richmond
Divine Destiny Ministries

•

*"Mitchell shares a life few whites have ever glimpsed.
What makes her book so extraordinary is that whites can
see life from the other side of the mirror."*
Tim Anderson, Editor and Publisher
Fitzgerald *Herald-Leader*

•

*"I read your book and truly enjoyed every page.
You are a master of details and the English language.
Your description of every event seems so current.
The book refreshed so many memories
of yesteryears in Fitzgerald."*
Oliver L. Winkfield
Washington, D.C.

•

*"Your book gives a wonderful insight into the sacrifices
your generation made so that mine and those who come
behind can enjoy so much. You have inspired me to
continue to reach for the stars."*
Jeannine Hogg, MD

•

*"Mitchell's book is for anyone who has struggled
with living positively against the odds and for those
who have never understood the societal perils
of black people. Through it all, she sustains hope
for a better tomorrow."*
Elbert Ranson, Jr., D. Min.,
Author, Clergyman, Musician

•

*"Thank You for sharing your story with the world.
If only we could recapture that spirit of community."*
Lee Koonce, Executive Director
Third Street Music School Settlement
New York, NY

•

"Your story does/did need to be told – and now you've done so!"
Nikki Giovanni
Poet, Writer, Commentator, Activist and Educator

•

· ABOUT THE TITLE ·

When I was writing the chapter "A Year at Grandma's" I was thinking of her making soup while she did the washing. Grandma added leftovers, vegetables from her garden and hands full of odds and ends from her cabinets to make soup—a real mixture of ingredients.

My mind kept going to words related to soup like simmering, bubbling, brewing and the eventual boiling over. I could see that soup spilling all through the South. The "boiling over" on Bloody Sunday was, I feel, a result of years and years of injuries, both emotional and physical. It was the first attempt of the Civil Rights Movement to march from Selma to Montgomery to establish voters' rights. The date was March 7, 1965. On that day, 200 state troopers with tear gas, billie clubs and whips beat 500 marchers and turned them around. The terrible, bloody, violent scenes got national news coverage.

One week later, on March 15, thousands of black and white people from all over the country tried again. They marched peacefully, ending in Montgomery. Immediately thereafter, Lyndon B. Johnson asked Congress to expedite passage of Civil Rights legislation that eliminated barriers to the right to vote.

This is the story of generations of one colored family living in Alabama and Georgia prior to 1965.

BORN COLORED
Life Before Bloody Sunday
ERIN GOSEER MITCHELL

Feb. 21, 2010

Best Wishes
to
Hermene D. Hartman,

It is a joy for me to share a part of our "her-story."

Erin Goseer Mitchell

Enjoy!

AMP&RSAND, INC.
Chicago, Illinois

First Edition–February, 2005
Second Edition–May, 2005
Third Edition–January, 2006
Fourth Edition—November, 2006
13   12   11   10   09   08   9   8   7   6   5
ISBN 0-9761235-2-5

Library of Congress Cataloging-in-Publication Data

Mitchell, Erin Goseer, 1935-
     Born colored : life before bloody Sunday / Erin Goseer Mitchell
         p. cm.
     Includes bibliographical references.
     ISBN 0-9761235-2-5
         1. Mitchell, Erin Goseer, 1935-–Childhood and youth. 2. Mitchell, Erin Goseer,
1935-–Family. 3. African Americans—Selma—Social Life and customs—20th
century. 4. African Americans—Georgia—Fitzgerald–Social life and customs—20th
century. 5. African Americans—Alabama—Selma—Biography. 6. African
Americans—Georgia—Fitzgerald—Biography. 7. Selma (Ala.)—Biography.
8. Fitzgerald (Ga.)—Biography. 9. African American families—Southern States—
Case studies. 10. Southern States—Race relations—Case studies. I. Title.

F334.S4M58 2006
305.896'0730758—dc22
[B]

                                                                              2006042885
www.eringoseermitchell.com
Design: David Robson, Robson Design
Published by Ampersand, Inc.
1050 N. State St., Chicago, IL 60610
www.ampersandworks.com
Printed in the United States of America

· ACKNOWLEDGMENTS ·

First and foremost, I am grateful to God
for the gift of memory and the ability to write stories.

My Writer's Group
(who asked lots of questions and challenged me to continue):
Enid Powell, leader, whose critiques and edits were invaluable
Nancy Freyberger
Wendy Grossman
Deborah Holton
Scottie Kersta-Wilson
Rion Klawinski
Marilyn Knapp Litt
Mary Hutchings Reed
Sandy Snyder
Pam Spencer
Eric Sutherlin
Gloria Valentino
Sel Yackley

Thanks to Tim Anderson, Editor/Publisher
and Sherrie Butler, Feature Page Editor
of the Fitzgerald, Georgia *Herald-Leader*
who published my first stories and asked for more.

Special thanks to:
Barbara Berry, Pamela Bluh, Sydney Bryson,
Lillie McKinney Cooley, Mary Frances Early, Willie Lee Hart,
Minnie Haynes, Laura Knight Holland, Rev. Leroy James,
Dorothy Williamson Jones, Joseph and Cecelia Lee,
Pastor Elstner Lewis, Miriam Palm, Jessica Pettus Rankins,
Minnie Rose James Richardson, Elsie Mallory Smith,
Dorothy R. Steward, Doretha Strong*, Dorothy Tarr, Luigi Visco*,
Kenneth Williams. And finally, to Suzanne T. Isaacs and
designer, David Robson, for exceptional guidance
throughout the publishing process.

*Deceased

· DEDICATION ·

to my parents and grandparents,
who taught me to live with grace and dignity
in spite of the indignities and inequities of racial segregation

to my daughters, Audrey and Greta,
who were never forced to go to the back of the bus

to my grandsons Kyle, Jared, and Kevin
who think "colored" means
marking pens

to younger generations and others
who need to know our social history
prior to the Civil Rights Movement

As I see it, it is through the process of making artistic forms—plays, poems, novels—out of one's experience that one becomes a writer, and it is through this process, this struggle, that the writer helps give meaning to the experience of the group.

Ralph Ellison

· CONTENTS ·

• PROLOGUE •

I RETURNED TO my home in Fitzgerald, Georgia, a small town located in South Georgia's Ben Hill County, 175 miles south of Atlanta. The occasion was the town's Centennial Celebration. It was October, 1996.

The previous August, while I was visiting my mother, Mabel Blevins Goseer, I read an article in the local Fitzgerald *Herald-Leader* asking for names of present or former Fitzgerald residents who had made or were making outstanding contributions to the world. The Centennial Planning Committee was seeking ten persons to be honored with VIP Awards during the Centennial Celebration. I submitted the name of my classmate and friend since sixth grade, Oscar J. Moore, an outstanding cardiologist and surgeon who works in Beverly Hills, California. I promised "O.J." that if he were chosen to receive an award I would attend the Centennial Celebration. He was notified that he had been selected to be one of the honorees. The *Herald-Leader* carried pictures of the VIPs and I made plans to attend the Centennial Committee special activities.

I arrived in Fitzgerald on Friday. After a noontime dinner, O.J. and I went to the Centennial Flower Show in what is now the Elks Club on Roanoke Drive. During my childhood it had been a white, privately owned, ante-bellum style home. Members of the Flower Club, all white women, recognized O.J. from pictures and warmly welcomed us. We were asked to sign the guest registry and more pictures of O.J. were taken. Memories that had been locked away in my heart began to seep out. First of all, never before in my sixty-one years had I been welcomed anywhere in Fitzgerald by a white person.

After we left the Centennial Flower Show we stopped at Fitzgerald's Blue and Gray Museum that, years earlier, had been the baggage room of the train station. The other part of the station had separate waiting places for colored and white people. How many times had I bought train tickets to Atlanta or Selma at the ticket window for "coloreds," sat in the colored waiting room, and boarded the colored coach, immediately behind the baggage car of the train. The Museum was crowded so I stopped only briefly at the exhibits and then went outside, waiting for O.J. to end his visits with local people.

On Friday evening we attended a historical drama, *Our Friend the Enemy*, which depicted the founding of the "Colony City" of Fitzgerald. I entered the Grand Theater through the broad front doors under bright lights and walked on carpeted green floors, another first. The Grand was called "the picture show." We colored children had entered through the narrow side door and walked up a bare, dimly lit stairway to the "colored section"—a half-balcony. On this night I climbed wide carpeted stairs to the balcony that no longer had a wall separating colored and white patrons. I sat in the balcony, this time by choice, my adult preference for theater seating. Afterwards while the crowds exited the wide staircase, I remembered the narrow stairway to the right and chose it for my exit. It was dimly lit, unpainted, and not carpeted. The theater had been completely refurbished except for this stairway. I was glad that it had not been redone but stood as a reminder of how life was in the Old Fitzgerald.

Drip by drip the memories continued to seep out. On Saturday morning, honorees and their guests were to meet downtown for a brief reception. After the reception and a police-escort motorcade to the VIP luncheon at the Ben Hill-Irwin County Technical Institute, a building not in existence in my childhood, O.J. and I sat with other honorees. This was the first time in my life that I had shared a meal in Fitzgerald with white people.

After the luncheon, VIPs were asked to sit together on the reviewing stand on Central Avenue to view the Centennial Parade. O.J. and I preferred to mingle with the crowd along the parade route. Suddenly, memories, like a tidal wave, swept me. I could hardly keep my balance. I snapped pictures of the re-enactment of the first Parade of Unity depicting Fitzgerald's earliest fire wagon and hearse. This was followed by a group of people carrying flags representing states where former citizens now live. The United States Marine Band preceded a horse drawn wagon carrying Eulalie Woeltjen, Fitzgerald's oldest white citizen. There were colored and white children marching together in the elementary, middle, and high school bands. During my school days in Fitzgerald there was no band at our colored school. It wasn't until I received the developed film that I realized the impact of seeing the children marching and playing together had on me. There were more pictures of the school bands than anything else.

Much to my surprise there was a float in the parade for Salem First Baptist Church, the colored church that my family had attended during my childhood. The float had a sign on it that said Salem was established in 1886, the same year the town was founded. Apparently we (colored people) had been living here since the very beginning of the town. At that point I did a bit of quick arithmetic and determined that the town was only forty-four years old when I first started going to Sunday School at Salem. I hadn't known any of the early history of colored people in Fitzgerald. I had never fully appreciated the beautiful gray stone church with the magnificent Tiffany stained-glass windows and mahogany pews. Neither had I noticed the date, 1896, on its cornerstone. During my visits to the Blue and Gray Museum I saw nothing to indicate that colored people had ever lived in Fitzgerald.

As I walked along the parade route I saw the boarded-up three-story building, originally the library for "whites only" at Main Street and Central Avenue. The new library, a sprawling, ground-floor building directly across from the new Post Office, is now open to all of Fitzgerald's citizens.

Since this trip home and the day of The Centennial Parade, I hadn't had a day when I didn't recall some image or experience from my childhood. These thoughts became such a deluge of memories that I was compelled to write them down in order to get some relief. The stories begin with my earliest memories from 1938 when I was three and a half years old and continue until I married in 1956 and moved to Chicago.

When I first began writing, my goal was to share my rich family heritage with my daughters and younger family members. I wanted to record my experiences of growing up in the racially segregated South, under a system that forced on all people of my race an inferior status. I wanted them to know of the lifestyles that shaped my grandparents, parents and me, and thus shaped their lives. In all of my adult life away from the South, I had never told my husband and daughters what my childhood and youth were like. When I saw my pages grow into thick files, I thought I would compile these stories. I found the following quote by anthropologist and author, Ralph Ellison:

"As I see it, it is through the process of making artistic forms—plays, poems, novels—out of one's experiences that one becomes a writer, and it is through this process, this struggle, that the writer helps give meaning to the experience of the group."

One day, soon after the first of my stories was published in my hometown paper, Mama called me and told me that she had received many calls from friends and strangers telling her how much they enjoyed the story and how much it reminded them of their earlier lives. Many people told her to tell me to "Keep on telling our story." At that point I realized that my writing was not as much about me as it was about my people—family, neighbors, and the political and social climate of those times in Selma, Alabama, where I was born, and Fitzgerald, Georgia, where I grew up. I realized it was the story of a people—their strengths, ingenuity, and perseverance, while living under the oppression of segregation and racism in Georgia and Alabama. My mother, Mabel Alieze Blevins Goseer, and my maternal grandparents, Frank and Mabel Tate Blevins were born and lived in Alabama. My father, Stanley Goseer, his mother, Alice Glasher Goseer, and Grandmother Rose were natives of Georgia. Although segregation was a painful reality for my grandparents, parents and me, there were many very good things that happened. Today I enjoy the broader society in which I live and would never want to return to forced segregation. I have a deeply felt sense of the important values conveyed to me in my segregated community.

As I continued to write, the African proverb, "It takes a village to raise a child," began to take on new meaning. I began to realize that I was a child fortunate enough to have two nurturing, caring, supportive villages—one in Alabama, one in Georgia—which protected me and taught me to be a productive citizen.

Writing became such a compelling force in my life that I felt I would benefit from a professional critique. I joined a writers' group with Mrs. Enid Powell as leader. The members of this group have been an invaluable source of encouragement, inspiration, and support as they have listened, asked questions, and challenged me to continue writing.

It is my hope that through the stories of my life from 1938, my earliest memories, until my wedding in 1956, readers will have a better understanding of how we (colored people) lived, endured, and thrived in our southern, segregated, racist society. These were the tremors that became the earthquake of The Civil Rights Movement.

Ara Ann Amanda Clements and William P. Tate	Amelia Ann and Old Man Chisom's Boy	? ?	Rose Goseer and ?

Mabel Tate
Born
December 11, 1891
Selma, Alabama

Married
Selma, Alabama

Died
January 21, 1977
Fitzgerald, Georgia

Frank Herman Blevins
Born
December 28,1891
Perry County, Alabama

Died
May 21, 1963
Selma, Alabama

Alice Glasher
Born
1869
Boston, Georgia

Married
1897
Boston, Georgia

Died
October 6, 1921
Boston, Georgia

John Goseer
Born
1863

Died
December, 1925
Boston, Georgia

Mabel Alieze Blevins
Born
September 22, 1912
Selma, Alabama

Married
September 11, 1931
Selma, Alabama

Stanley L. Goseer, Sr.
Born
July 8, 1906
Boston, Georgia

Died
July 7, 1966
Fitzgerald, Georgia

Erin Alieze Goseer
Born
June 9, 1935
Selma, Alabama

Married
Aldus Samuel Mitchell, Jr.
August 4, 1956
Fitzgerald, Georgia

Erin Alieze Goseer
Ancestral Chart

• ACCESS AND EQUITY •

APRIL OF 1997, I shared with members of my writers' group the editorials, "Making it Happen" and "Forgiveness" by Tim Anderson, Editor of the Fitzgerald, Georgia *Herald-Leader* newspaper. They had been published soon after the centennial celebration of this small southern town. "Making it Happen" was about the diversity of the volunteers, and the positive changes that happened as the people of this town worked together during a time of common purpose. The article, "Forgiveness," was a reflection on the history of the community and closed with the idea, "We should ask ourselves if we need forgiveness. If relations need correcting in Fitzgerald or in our lives, now's the time."

I wrote a letter to Mr. Anderson thanking him for these editorials. I told him that as a child growing up in Fitzgerald, I was not allowed to use the public library. This caused me great pain.

The discussion that followed the reading of the two articles and my letter of response was lively, expressing feelings, experiences, prejudices, and reactions to prejudices. Our group leader, Enid Powell, commented that exclusion of any sort is painful. She also said that whenever any single person is judged in the context of a group, whether it is based on any other superficial judgment... it, indeed, is painful.

The word *exclusion* made my ears perk up. I thought about *exclusion* and its opposite, *inclusion*. As I reflected on the words, I realized that my feelings of growing up in a segregated society did not create feelings of wanting to be included in the white school or social activities. I don't have regrets about exclusion from the white community. But, two words have haunted me since that discussion—

Monitor School, Fitzgerald, Georgia 1947. It was one of over 5300 schools built with the aid of Rosenwald funds, 242 of which were in Georgia. Monitor had three buildings. Two were the typical seven room Rosenwald plan. In the foreground is the upper grades building and to the far left is the "old" building. The home economics building was at the back of the campus and cannot be seen in this picture.

equity and *access*—or better, *lack of access*. These words more nearly express my feelings and desires.

By the time I was in second grade I was well aware of the inequities in my narrow world of South Georgia and Central Alabama. I was born in 1935, in Selma, Alabama where my mother's family lived. I grew up and went to school in Fitzgerald, Georgia. We traveled by car or train between the two towns. There was neither equity nor access. At the service stations where we had to buy gasoline, we could not use the toilet facilities. There wasn't even a colored toilet, although toilets were provided for their white customers. We had to pull off the road and go to the bushes.

Although the distance was only three hundred miles, it was an all day trip in an old car on narrow country roads. On the way to and from Selma, we always stopped in Albany, Georgia, about 80 miles from Fitzgerald, at my Uncle Frank's house to visit, use the toilet, and get water. Other stops were usually necessary before we crossed the now famous or infamous Edmund Pettus Bridge as we entered Selma.

Another example of inequity centers on the books that we were issued at our public school. Books were brought to the colored school, Monitor Elementary and High School, in a small open truck. They had not been stacked or packed in boxes, but just dumped in the back of the truck. Our high school boys unloaded the books and stacked them in our book room—a vacant room. Later they would be sorted by grade and subject matter and distributed to classrooms. A hard cover book's inside was stamped, "Do your best to make this book last 10 years." Under that statement were ten lines for students' names and the year they had read it. We received the books; all ten spaces had been filled with white students' names, a different name for each year. Many books had pages missing as well as hand written notes and scribbles.

Our teachers taught us to make book covers from brown, kraft paper grocery bags. We personalized the book covers with colorful designs, using crayons for the book titles and our names. Now the worn, torn, dirty discards were a little more acceptable to us.

The word *access*, better described as *lack of access* as a child, is embedded in the memory of the day my mother told me that we (colored people) could not go to the library downtown. I passed it often when I went to the Post Office with Daddy to buy stamps or pick up mail from our Post Office box, one of the few places—federal property—we could use. The library available to me was at our school, housed in a combination classroom/meeting room. Two and a half walls of shelves held worn, out-dated discards. By the time I was in the eighth grade, (I was twelve at this time) I had read most of these books. My reading materials at home consisted of the daily *Atlanta Constitution* newspaper whose editor, Ralph McGill, was renowned. I also read the weekly *Pittsburgh Courier*, the *Chicago Defender*, and the *Atlanta Daily World*—newspapers that were brought in each week by the colored men working on the railroad. From these colored newspapers, I became aware of the activities of colored people that were never published in the white papers. My other reading materials consisted of books and magazines that my parents and their friends shared with me. I read everything that I could get my hands on. I was also a "comic book broker." I didn't have money to buy comic books, but I managed to collect and trade them. One day I brought home a copy of *Modern Romance*. Mama immediately took it from me and told me not to read trash like that, an instruction I follow to this day.

Occasionally, white ladies brought old *National Geographic* magazines to our house, as donations to our school library. I read them with great interest before Daddy took them to school. I enjoyed the glossy pictures of far away and exotic places. We subscribed to *Life* magazine. I eagerly looked forward to the new issues for their exciting stories and pictures. Later, when I was tested for reading placement purposes during freshman week in college, my reading level was high enough for me to be placed in the upper level track for classes.

Two very informative childhood references were huge bi-annual Sears, Roebuck & Co. catalogs and a large dictionary. The Sears catalog was absorbing reading with its descriptive details and illustrations and became my recreational reading. The Christmas Sears catalog was truly a wish book, filled with colorful pictures of toys and exciting gifts. I dreamed of owning a dollhouse, furniture, all of the dolls pictured, instead of the one doll I would get for Christmas. I imagined myself wearing the pretty sweaters and shoes. In my heart I knew I'd never have toys like these.

I lived three blocks from one of the two large parks in Fitzgerald. We walked through the park on the path that cut diagonally across it, but colored children were not allowed to use the swings and the seesaws. Since the park was not open to me, I played at my friend Agatha Jones's house. To get there I walked the railroad track one block from my home. I would place one foot in front of the other, with my arms stretched out for balance as I walked the long silver line of steel. Crossing the trestle brought thrills and squeals as I looked down into the deep gorge below. When I got to the trestle, I walked on the crossties in the center between the rails knowing that was safer. These beams were spaced close enough so I couldn't fall between them. The climax of that thrilling walk, after I crossed the trestle, was to run down the embankment from the elevated track with my arms out and pretend to be a bird. When I got to the bottom, I would complete the remaining one block with a more appropriate walk. When playtime was over I returned home through the path in the park. Mama never knew that I took the dangerous route. I knew the train schedule and never walked the train track when the train was due. I was adventurous—not stupid! If I could have played in the park, I probably would have missed that thrilling adventure, my own form of equity.

The other large park in Fitzgerald was on the other side of town. It had a swimming pool, field house, and picnic tables in a grove of towering pine trees. I did not walk through this park until I was an adult. I had never been in a swimming pool until I went to college. I did learn to swim during my college years, fulfilling requirements for physical education. But I never developed a love for swimming. Looking back, I have often wished that I had had access to swimming and lessons in a pool at an earlier age. While I was in high school, three of my schoolmates drowned while swimming in unsupervised swimming holes. I feel that those accidents could have been prevented if these boys had had access to a safe, supervised place to swim.

However, lack of access to play in the parks was not a big problem for me. We had a large yard with grass and trees. My sand pile was across the street in a neighbor's yard. I spent many hours making pies, cakes, and frog houses with the damp sand. On summer Saturday afternoons, I skated on the long, paved sidewalk at the white elementary school a block from our house. This was the only paved area in my neighborhood. A traveling roller skating rink came to town for a few weeks each year and set up on a vacant lot two blocks from our house. It was great fun skating to music on the wooden floor with my friends as partners. At other times, I skated with friends on the pavement of Central Avenue seven blocks away, near the lingerie factory, ice house, and railroad tracks.

In this same area there was a slope we slid down, sitting on opened, corrugated boxes, to protect our bottoms from the grass. We walked up and slid down many times, squealing and laughing at the thrilling rides. Roller skating and sliding the bank were our winter activities. I don't think that any of us were concerned about lack of access to formal play areas. The public segregation laws existed and were enforced in Fitzgerald as well as Selma and other parts of the South from the earliest years of segregation.

South Georgia is a mild sunny land of flowering magnolias, roses, azaleas, and moss-draped dogwood trees. It has many state parks. Chehah State Park is near Albany, a town we traveled to often to visit Daddy's family. Okefenokee Swamp Park is located about eighty miles from Fitzgerald, at Waycross, where I remember going to see Daddy's "Aunt Puddin," who owned a restaurant there. Okefenokee Swamp Park became nationally known through the comic strip "Pogo." This park became one I wanted to visit.

In December 1962, Mr. Art Hanes, the mayor of Birmingham, Alabama, ordered all city parks to be closed to prevent them from being open to blacks. He did this in response to an order from a federal judge who ruled the city's public segregation laws were unconstitutional.

We never went to the state parks even though Thursdays were designated days for colored people. My parents took the position that we did not subject ourselves to the inconveniences and humiliation of segregation when it was not essential or important to our lives. If we wanted to have picnics, family or community gatherings, we used the church or school grounds, family owned farms or our own yards.

I finally visited Okefenokee Swamp Park for the first time in 1987, when Jim Crow laws and segregation were no longer legal. To take a boat tour through the narrow passages of mirror-like water with the giant moss covered cypress trees overhead was a dream come true. The lines, "darker than a thousand midnights, deep in a cypress swamp," from the poetry of Langston Hughes, came alive for me on that visit to the swamp. I treasure the memory of the stillness of the inky water and the majesty of the ancient trees reflected in them.

The Civil Rights Movement of the 1960s did not suddenly boil over and spill into the streets in the form of sit-ins, boycotts, protests, and marches. The discontent simmered for generations, fueled by the injustice of slavery, lynching, disenfranchisement, segregation, inequities in the workplaces, and lack of equal access to public facilities. Each broken promise of:
"All men are created equal"
"Forty acres and a mule"
"Separate but equal"
"Equal protection under the law"
"With all deliberate speed"
was the fuel that kept the fires of desire for freedom burning.

The brave heroes of the Civil Rights Movement were taught, pushed, strengthened, and encouraged by generations of our ancestors, who suffered the indignities of being relegated to second class citizenship in this "land of the free, and the home of the brave."

· OUR DAILY BREAD ·

AS SOON AS the days began to lengthen, and Good Friday was approaching, our thoughts turned to planning and preparation of our vegetable garden. Mr. Nick Brantley, a neighbor who lived in the next block, owned a mule and plow. Daddy hired him to "turn the soil over" and make the rows ready for planting. Seeds from the previous year that had been dried and stored in jars over the winter—okra, various kinds of peas and beans, and corn—were taken from the pantry shelves for spring planting.

Daddy bought seed white potatoes or Irish potatoes (sounding more like "ice potatoes" when we said it in our Southern accent). The potatoes were cut into several pieces, with at least one large potato eye in each piece. That potato sprout was planted on top of the deep furrow. The plant grew during the spring and summer, developing small, thin-skinned potatoes underneath the soil. Later we dug carefully under the plant to pull a few potatoes free, placing the soil back carefully, so the others would continue growing. These tiny, boiled, new potatoes with thin skins were a springtime delicacy. In early fall, larger mature potatoes were ready for harvesting, rinsing, and a brief drying period before storage. We spread our potatoes out in a single layer, in the dark, on the black, powdery dirt under the back part of our house. I don't remember who put them under the house, but I do remember it was my job to go and get them whenever Mama needed potatoes. I remember this so vividly because this was the only chore I hated doing. According to Mama, I was small and short so it was easier for me to do. I walked under the house at the high part under the kitchen. After a few steps I had to squat and creep along because there was less head room. I carried Mama's aluminum pot with the black handle and set it down on the dirt as I filled the pot with the small red potatoes. After I filled the pot, I crept back into the daylight. I was glad to have this miserable job behind me.

Sweet potatoes were planted from slips—pieces of potato vines that were bought in the spring. Sweet potatoes also grew under the ground, but they were not harvested until fall when they were fully mature. We made a shallow hole in the back yard, about three feet square and lined it with pine needles. We put the sweet potatoes on the dried pine needles and covered them with another layer of pine needles for protection against the cold. I didn't mind getting them from their storage space, even though the pine needles stuck my hands if I wasn't careful.

Mustard and turnip greens were two of the earliest spring vegetables. We pulled up mustard greens, roots and all. Turnips were harvested by picking a few leaves from each plant, leaving the bottoms to continue to grow and develop "turnip bottoms." These were eaten later, cooked with the mature tops.

Two other early spring treats from our garden were green English peas. These days the young pods are sold in gourmet shops for stir-fry dishes and salads. We didn't harvest our peas until the round peas had formed in the pod. Because these peas do not thrive in hot weather, our season for enjoying them was short. The other treat was a vegetable we called "lady finger peas," tiny, white peas in a thin, slim, pod. Mama cooked each of these vegetables with bits of ham, creating a delicious dish. Crowder and black-eyed peas, maturing later, were two of our main vegetables for summer dinners.

We planted onions in early spring from tiny bulbs called "sets." When these bulbs grew green tops we pulled up the entire plant, scallions, to eat uncooked or to sauté. As they continued to grow, the tops became tough so we stopped harvesting them and allowed the bottoms to develop. When the tops fell over and turned brown, it was time to dig them up and let them dry out. We prepared them for storage by braiding the tops together in bunches of three and hung the bunches in a cool, dry place for our use during the winter.

String beans, pole beans and butter beans, both speckled and white, were plentiful in our summer garden. String beans grew fast and produced many beans so we planted bean seeds every three weeks to have a continuous harvest.

Tomatoes were our most bounteous crop. To eat vine-ripened tomatoes was one of the special rewards of the work of gardening. I ate them until I began scratching the itchy rash from the acid. When the rash cleared up and I stopped itching, I ate more. We kept the ripe tomatoes on the ledge of our screened-in back porch until we were ready to eat them raw or prepare them for canning. I helped Mama with the canning by washing the pint Mason jars. This was my job because my hands were small enough to put the soapy rag in the jar, to wash the sides and bottom. After I rinsed the jars, Mama sterilized them by turning the open end down on a towel that lined her roasting pan. She boiled them on top of her wood burning stove for ten minutes. While the jars were being sterilized Mama pierced and dipped each tomato into boiling water, then cold water so the skins came off easily. After she cut the core out it was my job to stuff the whole tomatoes in the jars, "with the smooth sides facing the outside, so they look pretty," Mama said. I then put one teaspoon of salt in each jar. Mama put the lids on and set them in the hot water bath for twenty minutes. Then she took the jars out of the water and set them out to cool. During the afternoon and night we heard popping sounds from the jars as they cooled, making a good seal. The next day she added these to her growing larder of canned vegetables proudly displayed on pantry shelves. By the end of summer our pantry was filled with homemade canned goods.

The "peach man" came once a week during the mid-summer peach season, selling peaches from orchards near Fort Valley and Macon. Mama bought them by the bushelbasket from the back of his truck. We ate these peaches fresh and made delicious cobblers for dessert from the large Elberta peaches. Georgia is sometimes called "the Peach State" because it has long been a leading producer of peaches. We also canned peaches using a similar canning process as the tomatoes, this time adding sugar, rather than salt. Mama used these canned peaches for making cobblers during the winter months.

Corn was our most prolific crop. During the summer we ate lots of boiled, fried, and roasted corn cooked over the open flames in our wood-burning kitchen stove. I always smile remembering the joy of eating "roshen ears" when I see people at summer fests and fairs, enjoying this treat as they hold it by the "shucks."

Summer was a time of sharing as well as a time of bounty. Sometimes when people walked past our house Mama called to them to come and get a large, brown paper sack of corn and whatever else we had in abundance.

Sometimes Mama sent me on errands to deliver cooked vegetable dinners. Miss Nancy was one of the persons I took dinners to. She walked with difficulty, with the aid of a long, slim, tree limb. Because of a birth defect, her left foot turned inward at an angle and her right foot was bent backwards. Her right leg was longer than her left leg so she walked with a severe limp. Many years later I learned that this birth defect is called severe bilateral clubfeet and is extremely painful. She was the bell ringer at Salem Baptist Church. I remember watching her in the church entrance as she pulled the strong rope leading to the bell tower. She rang it before church services and tolled it to announce the death of a church member. Miss Nancy lived in Goose Hollow, a couple of blocks from Salem, the section of Fitzgerald where some of the poorest and most deprived colored people lived. This section of town had narrow dirt streets with rows of unpainted wooden shacks. Miss Nancy's house was across the street from the city dump, with its piles of discarded furniture, boxes, papers, and garbage collected from the alleys in our town. A perpetual, smoldering fire from the heap of garbage filled the air with an acrid foul smell. Mama sent Miss Nancy's dinner in a pie plate covered with waxed paper, wrapped in newspaper and covered with a towel that I carried in my bicycle basket. When I got to the house, I propped my bike on its kickstand, and walked up the rickety wooden steps to the front porch. I went through the front room and straight to her kitchen where I transferred the food to her plate. I brought the pie plate back to be used for another meal on wheels.

Miss Aycox was another lady who received home cooked vegetable dinners from Mama. She lived behind the galvanized tin fence that surrounded the colored baseball park, a block from Monitor School. Miss Aycox was our mystery lady. She was the color of dark chocolate. She was about five feet six inches and weighed about one hundred fifty pounds. The unique thing about her was her diction and mastery of words. She spoke with no trace of southern accent or dialect. She never told where she came from or what her life had been like before she came to Fitzgerald. She boasted that she had memorized the Blue Back Speller, her only book. The first time that I took dinner to her, Mama told me to go to the front of the ball park, and then follow the outside path to the left to the back of the park. I was surprised to see a tiny one-room, wooden shack with a rusty tin roof and a rocking chair outside on the bare dirt. Her kitchen was a small area of the yard with an open fire pit. Pots were suspended on an iron stand. Large mosquitoes swarmed. They attacked me like they were her watchdogs and I was a thief, biting me and leaving large red bumps on my body. Miss Aycox's skin had no insect bites and was as smooth as velvet. She left her shack once a week, on Saturdays, to go to town to do her shopping. The colored men of our community tried to persuade her to allow them to build a house for her. She was reluctant to accept their offer. When she was eighty years old and feeble she finally agreed to their plan. Her neighbors took care of her until her death five years later.

Mrs. Logan, our white neighbor, lived across the alley from our garden with her grown daughter, Ida Mae and son, Erin. Mrs. Logan made and sold crocheted scarves and doilies. Mrs. Logan chose to share the bounty from our garden in a different way. She got up early in the morning and came to our garden to pick vegetables. Some days she returned to our yard when she saw Mama outside and would say, "Mabel, I got these peas (or whatever vegetables she had picked earlier) and I ain't got no biling meat to cook 'em wid. You know peas jes ain't good less they cooked wid meat. Can you gimme a lil' piece of meat to cook wid?" Mama gave Mrs. Logan a piece of meat, if she had it, and never let her know that she had seen her picking vegetables from our garden early in the morning.

Mrs. Logan was not mean spirited. She even praised Mama for raising my brother and me "like white folks," making us come in from play during the middle of the day, and coming back outside in the afternoon with clean clothes on. The Christmas that I got my first colored doll, she told me kindly that it was "as pretty as a white doll." My doll was one of the first store-bought dolls that was a milk chocolate color with long, dark brown Shirley Temple curls. Its facial features the same as dolls with white faces. In later years the colored dolls became more realistic replicas of colored people.

Just as we shared produce from our garden, others in our community shared the harvest from their gardens and fruit trees. It was not uncommon for someone to stop by tell us to "come and pick pears, peaches, apples, or plums," from their yards. In the fall neighbors shared peanuts that were still attached to the dried bush.

By the time I was in high school, Mama and Daddy no longer

*Sonny, age 15, and Erin, age 12 at their home on the corner of
East Jessamine and South Logan Streets, Fitzgerald, Georgia, in 1947.
My parents bought this house in 1936 and my mother still lives there.*

planted a large garden. Their garden shrank to one short row of
tomatoes and greens. Daddy turned his love of growing things into
creating a flower garden. By the time of my wedding in August of 1956,
the front, back, and side yards were lawn surrounded by flowering
shrubbery of forsythia, gardenias, crepe myrtle, hydrangea, and
camellias. There were beds of phlox, roses, delphinium, marigolds,
and zinnias. He also built a goldfish pond and a fountain.

Even after we stopped raising our own vegetables we continued to
"eat good" during the summers. It was not unusual for us to find a
"mess" of greens, peas, okra, or a bag of corn left on our porch by
some generous person.

In addition to our garden providing fresh, organically grown
vegetables, it gave us great satisfaction to have enough to share with
others. That was a good feeling when we had very little cash for store-
bought gifts. Working in the garden was a great way to exercise. It
also helped me develop a love for watching plants grow.

At home, as well as in our community, many of our social activities
consisted of gathering and preparing food. The weekly Saturday night
bread making sessions at home with Mama are among my fondest
memories. I was five years old when Mama began to let me help her

with her bread making. My first job was to color the margarine. It came in a one pound square, looking much like lard. A packet of deep yellow powdered food coloring was included in the box. We left the package on the table until it reached room temperature. I then put the softened margarine in a small mixing bowl, sprinkled the packet of yellow powder in it and stirred it with a wooden spoon until the margarine was an even pale yellow color. In later years a "new improved" way of coloring the margarine was packaged. This margarine was sold in a heavy plastic pouch with an inside button of golden yellow liquid. The instructions said to pinch the button to pop it, then knead the softened margarine until the color was evenly distributed. I thought that this was a fun job and enjoyed the kneading and turning the bag, making designs until the margarine no longer looked like lard.

After the margarine was colored, Mama allowed me to crumble the small cake of Fleishman's yeast into a bowl of luke-warm water. The temperature of the water was crucial. If the water was too hot it would kill the yeast; too cold the yeast would not grow. She taught me to get it just right, "like Baby Bear's porridge." I measured the teaspoons of salt, making them even with the back of a knife. At six years old, my hands were about half the size of Mama's and not strong enough to do a proper job of kneading. She was patient and made me feel that I had kneaded it until it was "just right." As I recall, she always did the final kneading before putting the dough in the greased roasting pan and covering it with a towel for "rest" overnight. During the warm weather she put it in the ice box. The next morning, Mama punched it down with her fist and left it for a quick, second rising. After that we rolled out the dough on the floured enamel table top, using her large wooden rolling pin. We used the biscuit cutter to make circles, and then buttered them by measuring a teaspoon of margarine and spreading it on the circles of dough. We folded them in half to make Parker House rolls. We shaped clover-leaf rolls by making three small balls and putting them in sections of a muffin pan. These were my favorite because they had more golden brown crust.

Some of the dough was saved to make cinnamon rolls. Mama rolled the dough, spread the margarine, and then sprinkled it with cinnamon, sugar and raisins. She shaped it, jelly-roll fashion, before cutting it into one inch circles. The plain rolls were baked and eaten for breakfast before I left for Sunday School.

On the way to Sunday School, Mama sent me to a neighbor's house to deliver a pan of hot rolls. I was not sent to the same home every week; so many different neighbors received the gifts of hot bread. On Sunday mornings as I walked to Salem Baptist Church, all of the neighbors had their radios tuned to the "Wings Over Jordan" Singers so I heard the entire program as I walked along. I remember learning the words to the spirituals "The Ole Ark's a-Moverin" and "When the Storm Clouds Gather" by hearing them on Sunday mornings. "Over My Head, I hear trouble in the air, there must be a God somewhere," became one of my favorites from their repertoire.

One of my Sunday morning delivery stops was to Mrs. Alice Edge. She gave Mama scraps and remnants of fabric left over from her homemade dresses. Mama used this material to make some of my clothes. Mr. and Mrs. Edge owned and operated one of the three colored dry cleaning and pressing shops in Fitzgerald. We called these businesses "pressing clubs." The Edges' brother, Mr. James, and Mrs. Georgia Lee, ran another dry cleaning establishment two blocks away from the other Edge's Cleaners on Pine Street called "up town." The fall that I was ten years old Mama worked there on Saturday afternoons doing alterations. Mr. S. T. Coffee owned and operated the colored pool hall, a cab stand, and the third pressing club, also located on Pine Street. His shop was just across the alley from Mrs. Alice Edge's shop. These dry cleaning establishments served both the white and colored community.

Some Sundays I took a pan of rolls to Mrs. Brantley. Her husband, Mr. Nick, plowed our garden plot in the spring in preparation for planting. Mrs. Brantley invited me to spend some Friday nights with her when Mr. Brantley spent the night on their farm in the country. On these Friday night visits I walked one block to her house, getting there after dinner, but before dark. Even though I had eaten dinner, Mrs. Brantley and I ate biscuits and preserves as we sat in her kitchen talking. She always asked me to play my most recent "piece" on the piano. She applauded and praised me and told me I was doing good work. I always enjoyed these evenings with her. Her daughter, Miss Irene, who by then had moved away, was my first grade teacher.

After Sunday School my friends and I had our Sunday morning treat of cinnamon rolls with confection sugar icing. Even fifty years later, when I am with these friends they remember the Sunday morning treats of Mama's homemade bread.

Every year, from as early as I can remember until I left for college, the day after Thanksgiving was the opening day of "Operation Fruitcake." It began as I cracked, shelled, and chopped pecans from the tree in our back yard. Mama measured, combined spices, and stirred them into the flour. The candied cherries, oranges, lemons and citron were chopped, measured, and set aside. When all of the ingredients were in place on her assembly line, the tube cake pan and loaf bread pan were greased, floured, and the bottoms lined with brown kraft paper. The cakes were baked at a low temperature for several hours. The baking sessions took several days because of the limited oven space, few pans and long baking times. She made at least a dozen cakes for Christmas gifts, keeping one for us. She continued making fruitcakes for many years after I finished college. One year she decided that this had gotten to be an enormous task and she wasn't going to do it any more. There were a lot of disappointed family members and friends. She gave me her recipe and said if anyone else wanted it they could have it. I tried her recipe a few times and decided that Christmas shopping in crowded stores was easier.

Food preparation in our community was also a time of visiting and sharing. On a warm Saturday afternoon in October 1945, when the sugar cane was ready for harvesting, a family friend, Rev. Pettigrew, took me to the McElhaney's farm about six miles from Fitzgerald for an afternoon and evening of cane-grinding and syrup-making. This was an unforgettable event. By the time we got there, the cane had already been cut by hand with a large heavy knife and been left to dry for a few days. We stood around and watched as the grinding wheels turned. Two horses, harnessed to a long weathered log, walked in a wide circle around a man who stood on a platform feeding the red stalks of sugar cane into a press. A stream of green cane juice gushed out the end of the machinery, through a burlap sack filter and into a barrel. The waiting men transferred the juice to a sixty-gallon iron pot that sat over a large blazing fire. The juice cooked and thickened as the water evaporated, leaving thick, golden amber syrup. This process took three to four hours of constant stirring and sampling. Some of the juice was not cooked but was allowed to ferment in an uncovered dishpan. I was allowed to drink a tiny glass of this "juice." Many years later I learned that fermented cane juice was a type of rum. As the cane juice bubbled and boiled, the men used a long large wooden paddle to skim off the scum that formed on top. They stored this scum in a small wooden barrel to ferment longer, to become a more potent drink.

One time when I returned to Fitzgerald, after I was an adult, and visited Rev. Pettigrew, we began reminiscing about the time he took me to the cane grinding. I smiled as I recalled the rum we made in the dishpan by letting the cane juice ferment. Rev. Pettigrew told me that the scum that was put in the barrel fermented and turned into much more potent rum than the drink I had sipped made from the raw cane juice. The men had thus created their supply of rum for the year. I was not aware of the work the ladies did. I was fascinated by the large fire, burning brightly in the autumn twilight, the horses walking in a circle and the constant attention being given to the bubbling pot.

When the syrup cooled it was poured into sterilized whiskey and wine bottles and other jars that all of us had collected the previous year. We washed and saved these containers to use for storing syrup in the fall. From the evening of fun and fellowship we came home with our year's supply of syrup for gingerbread and Saturday morning flapjacks. During the summer Daddy made a drink he called "sweet water," prepared by pouring cane syrup over water and ice, and stirring it until it was the color of iced tea. It made a refreshing summer drink.

On one occasion, in Selma, I had the unforgettable experience of "hog-killing day." This was another time when neighbors cooperated in food preparation. A fire was made under the large, black pot, usually used for washing clothes. I remember seeing the slaughtered hog hanging up by its hind legs. I hurried into the house and stayed there until the animal had been cut into pieces that I recognized as uncured bacon, hams, roasts, and ribs. The tasty pieces of tenderloin that Grandma fried helped to ease the horror of the earlier part of that day. I also learned that day that chitlins were the hog intestines. I refused to eat them then and even now I don't want to be in the same room where they are being served. That aroma still reminds me of hog-killing day.

At home in Fitzgerald, Daddy bought a pig "on halves" with a farmer. Daddy paid for the pig, and the farmer did the butchering giving Daddy half of the meat. The hams, shoulders, and sides for bacon were rubbed with salt and a special spiced curing mix to preserve it. After a few weeks meat was hung in the smoke house to continue preserving winter meat. Mama ground and seasoned some of the meat to make sausage. Right away we enjoyed fresh pan sausage.

The remainder was stuffed into casings, smoked, and eaten later. We ate roasts and chops for a few days. I was never curious or wanted to be a part of hog killing time again after that experience in Selma.

Looking back, it seems that we spent a lot of time in summer and fall growing, gathering, and preparing food. Years later in my college French class I memorized a poem about the ant who worked all summer, storing food for winter, while the grasshopper chirped away, and had no food when winter came. I think we were more like the ant in our efforts to have food and survive the winter. By the end of the summer Mama proudly showed off her pantry shelves filled from top to bottom with canned fruits, soups and vegetables. I looked forward to the apple and peach pies she made after work on Friday afternoons in the winter.

Daddy's favorite grace before meals was, "For food, for friends, for loving care, we thank Thee, Lord. Amen." Over the years it has become one of my favorites. It is brief and to the point. It also summarizes for me my early experiences of planting, harvesting, preserving, and sharing food. When I had my own small family, I picked vegetables and fruits from farms in Indiana and preserved them by making frozen food packets. I continue to have a small garden each summer. I have enough tomatoes, basil, mint, sage, tarragon, rosemary, and parsley to share with friends. The joy and pride of growing and sharing "home grown" is still an important part of my life.

· DESIGNER ORIGINALS ·

ONE DAY AT the airport in Dallas, Texas, a regal, attractive, and exquisitely dressed woman attracted my attention. She was impeccably groomed and was wearing a striking dress of soft flowing fabrics of complementary colors and patterns. When I returned home I told one of my fashion conscious friends about this woman and her impressive dress. From my description, my friend told me that the dress was probably a Diane Fres original.

I smiled when I saw this dress because it brought back memories of dresses Mama made for me when I was young. Many times my outfits were made of coordinating fabrics and harmonizing colors, blending prints and plaids in unique and striking combinations. Mama was artistic and made these original creations from inexpensive remnants and scraps of materials given to her by family and friends. Mama also combined dress patterns to create new patterns, gathered ideas from magazines and catalogs, or copied designs that she saw in the finest department stores. Occasionally ladies from the white churches brought boxes of clothes to our house for Mama to use or to distribute to colored people. She took the least worn material from long full skirts and made vests, skirts, blouses or party dresses. The finished garments were good looking and I wore them with pride. I didn't mind that my clothes weren't store-bought. Even at a young age, I reveled in their special flair.

Another source of fabric for my clothes were feed sacks that Aunt Jennie and Uncle Clarence gave us. Their farm was in Marion Junction, fifteen miles from Selma. Corn for chicken feed and food for some of the other animals came in brightly colored, floral cotton sacks that held fifty and one hundred pounds of feed. Mama always asked Uncle Clarence to buy at least two sacks of matching print so that there would be enough material for a dress. We saved the thread from the feed sacks. By pulling at a certain point it unraveled easily and made one continuous thread. We wound the thread around a piece of folded paper to save and reuse. After washing and ironing the sacks, Mama's creating began. With a bit of rick rack, seam binding, ribbon, or buttons another unique outfit was born.

The people in our community knew what a magician Mama was at recycling, working her magic with used men's suits. She ripped these garments apart, discarding the badly worn sections. She used the remaining fabric to fashion a new coat, jacket, or skirt. One of my favorite coats was brown tweed trimmed with red velveteen and sporting a matching bonnet and muff. Another favorite coat, created from a recycled man's suit, was navy blue tweed, trimmed in blue velveteen. I did not have a ready-made, store-bought coat until I was eleven years old. I remember it so well because it was a first. This coat was a tan, swing-back style with three large brass buttons and a large pointed collar. We bought it at Friedlander's Department Store, Fitzgerald's largest department store, located in the five story building, the tallest building in our town.

When I was a little girl in the late 1930s and early 1940s, flour and sugar was sold in five and ten pound sacks of fine white material. Family members saved the sacks for Mama. We opened them at the seams, washed and ironed them, and used them to make my slips and blouses. Mama used white embroidery thread to make blanket stitches around the neckline and armholes as an added creative touch. These were always cut wider and longer so that the seams would be large enough to be let out, insuring at least two years of wear.

I didn't have a big sister or cousins as a source of hand-me-downs so my "new/used clothes" were usually redesigned from recycled fabrics. Occasionally I had a few store-bought dresses, but these don't stand out in my mind because the ones that Mama made were much prettier. Not all of my dresses were from recycled materials. Mama bought organdy, taffeta, and other fancy fabrics to make my dresses for special occasions. One year my Easter dress was made of light blue taffeta with a shirred neckline, short puff sleeves, fitted bodice, and a tiered skirt with two pink taffeta rosettes at the waist. I wore this exquisite creation once the year that it was new and two times after that. I remember it as the dress that was too pretty to wear. One

Erin's 9th Grade Monitor School Spring Recital.
Salem Baptist Church. Fitzgerald, Georgia.

of my favorite dresses was a two piece, button-down-the-front, madras plaid dress. Another favorite was a dark green, floral print, voile, trimmed with pink organdy. The only dress I ever disliked that she made for me was a dark paisley print. I told her when she selected the material that I didn't like it but she bought it anyway. It was a waste of her time and money because I wouldn't wear the dress.

When I was about seven years old I began making slips, panties, and dresses for my dolls, doing hand sewing. Mama helped me with these projects. I was in the seventh grade when I began to make some of my clothes. The first item I made for myself was a floral print broomstick skirt—a tightly gathered skirt with a two inch waistband. I made it without using a bought pattern by cutting the thirty-six inch wide material into two even pieces, allowing enough material in each piece to make a three-inch hem. The following year I began formal sewing lessons, a requirement for each of my four years at Monitor High School. This was the beginning of me learning to read patterns and following the guide sheets. The first class project Miss Pierce, my home economics teacher, had me make was an apron. My second sewing class assignment was a pair of pajamas. I chose a bright pink cotton fabric with tiny flowers. It was good that only my family saw these pajamas. I wore them until I outgrew them even though the workmanship was poor. After I mastered the basics of sewing and using patterns I began to combine and modify patterns to make more interesting dresses by adding a ruffle, flounce or changing the style or length of the sleeves. By the end of four years of sewing classes I was making most of my cotton dresses. Mama continued to make my suits and coats. One of my original creations was a pale blue, tissue chambray dress with tiny white flowers. I chose to put a deep gathered ruffle at the bottom. By then I guess I was "a chip off the old block," not satisfied to follow the pattern, making one-of-a-kind dresses. I learned my lessons well. In later years I began shopping at rummage sales searching for clothes with unique buttons and trims. I used these found treasures to embellish my dresses or to upgrade an inexpensive store-bought suit.

I have an old cookie tin filled with an interesting collection of buttons. My daughters enjoy sorting through my treasures looking for "gems." Recycling became a way of life. This creating one-of-kind clothing has not only saved a lot of money but has been a source of pride and joy in creating and wearing designer originals.

· SCHOOL DAYS ·

MONITOR ELEMENTARY AND High School, the only school in town that colored children could attend, was the heart of and the strongest unifying part of our community in Fitzgerald. This was the early 1940s when many colored children passed at least one white school as they walked to Monitor, during the years of legally segregated schools. My family lived on the corner of Jessamine and Logan Street, one block from the Third Ward elementary school, and five blocks from Monitor. Our school was located on South Monitor Drive, on a campus that was one block long and one half block deep. There were three red brick buildings and a wooden shack that served as the storage house for the coal that was fuel for the iron pot-bellied heaters in each classroom. The "old building," as we called the first building constructed, housed the classrooms for grades primer (the equivalent of kindergarten) through fourth grade.

The center front entrance of this building had wild rose bushes that grew as high as the window ledges and in spring bloomed profusely with deep pink roses outside Miss Ida Cook's primer classroom. Miss Cook was my first teacher when I began school at Monitor in September of 1940. I was five years old, one year younger than the legal age for starting school.

The original plan was that I would stay with Miss Cook until I was old enough to be officially enrolled in school. Early in the school term when I was lonely for Mama, Miss Cook would allow me to go for a brief visit to Mama's second grade classroom.

At that time Miss Cook appeared to me to be a giant. She was probably no taller than five feet seven inches and weighed no more than one hundred fifty pounds. She had long, narrow feet and always wore black, laced-up, medium-heeled Oxfords. Her skin was the color of vanilla wafers and her thin lips were always covered with bright red lipstick. Her wispy, straight hair was as black as coal and was still just as black when she attended my wedding nineteen years later. It was then that I realized the magic of Miss Clairol.

Miss Cook's classroom was a large, open room with homemade wooden benches around the walls. She designated a small section of one bench as "the bad bench," where she had disobedient children sit. On the first day of school, Miss Cook warned us of her "mean left hand" and how it would spank us if we didn't behave. She spoke of it as though it was not a part of her body. I don't ever remember seeing her spank a child. I do remember getting beat up on the first day of school by the Dukes twins, Iris and Irma. I had been taught it was not nice to fight so I didn't hit them back. They had to sit on "the bad bench" for the remainder of the day. More than thirty years later, at one of Fitzgerald's Grand Homecoming Celebrations, Iris and Irma told me that they too hadn't forgotten their first day at school, and apologized for fighting me.

Blackboards covered our classroom walls. We had the large chart-type book about "Dick and Jane." At reading time we sat on the floor as Miss Cook pointed to the pictures and words using a long, wooden pointer. At story time we also sat on the floor close to Miss Cook as she sat in her big chair and read to us. In an open area of the room she also played games with us. At the end of the school term she told my parents that under no circumstances would she keep me a second term because I had learned everything that she had taught at that level.

When I was eight years old Miss Cook began inviting me to spend some Friday nights at her house. She lived two and a half blocks from us in her large, white wooden two-story house with a narrow front yard enclosed by a low, white, picket fence and gate. We sat on the front porch in her swing and talked until bedtime. She told me about her nephew, "Piano Red," who played jazz piano at The Royal Peacock Club on Auburn Avenue in Atlanta. During the course of our conversations, she asked me to tell of my school activities. I slept in the front room, her guest room with its four poster bed and high mattress. Her bedroom was in the middle of the house opposite the dining room. I never went upstairs to the second floor where her roomers lived. They used the back stairs as their entrance. In retrospect, I feel that my spending the night with Miss Cook was

Erin, age 6. I loved being dressed up in my favorite dress.
It was made of white sheer cotton with red dots and red rick-rack.
The large red bow and red sandals completed the outfit.

another example of the caring spirit that my community showed their children. Mrs. Faustine Boyd, my third grade teacher, in a conversation many years after Miss Cook's death, said that many days Miss Cook had as many as eighty-five children in her classroom because parents knew that in an emergency they could bring their potty-trained children who were not yet enrolled in school and she would take care of them. She never refused to help a parent.

The beginning of my second school year, when I was six, I went to first grade with Miss Irene Brantley as my teacher. My most vivid memories of first grade were the stationary wooden desks with tops that could be lifted to house our books. Each Friday afternoon we had spelling bees. We children lined up along the wall by the windows and took turns spelling words Miss Brantley called. Looking back, as an elementary teacher myself, I've often wondered how we knew how to spell enough words to have a weekly spelling bee.

Mama was the only second grade teacher for all the colored children in Fitzgerald. When I was promoted to second grade, she became my teacher. I remember sometimes her classroom was so crowded that we sat two at a desk that was built for one student. I was unhappy sitting next to another student. That was a very difficult year for me. I felt that Mama was stricter with me than she was with my classmates. As a parent, I realize now that it must have been a difficult year for her as well, with her never having a break from me either.

There were no paved sidewalks or walkways on our campus. The basketball court, behind the old building, was bare dirt. On the days we had games with a visiting team, the lines of the court were marked off with lime. The nets were attached to rusty hoops on the homemade backboards.

I remember the three majestic oak trees on the front of our campus. Mama brought the chair from her desk outside and sat under one of the trees with her partner as they served their appointed supervising duty. Two teachers were assigned to this post at the ten o'clock, fifteen-minute morning recess for elementary students. They were also on duty for the hour-long lunch period for the entire school. We were allowed to go to Mr. Sam Chester's at lunchtime, make our purchases, and promptly return to campus.

Sam Chester's store was a colored owned store two doors from our campus. It was a small, unpainted frame building with four steps leading up to the front porch. Mrs. Mary Chester, Mr. Chester's wife, a tall plump, pecan-colored, soft-spoken woman, also worked in the store. She made the most delicious sandwiches of tomatoes, onions, sautéed ground beef and pork, highly seasoned with spices. They were individually wrapped in waxed paper and kept warm in a large roasting pan on her black, wood-burning stove, until lunch time. Each school day at noon students made a mad dash to the store to buy these hot, greasy, delicious sandwiches at a dime each. They always sold out. Mr. Chester sold crackers, candy, potato chips, and souse meat (a spicy, congealed meat loaf that was made from the hog's head). We bought bottles of pop that had to be opened on the side of the red metal Coca-Cola cooler.

Mr. Chester, a dark brown man from the southern coast of Georgia, spoke rapidly in what we called a "geechee" accent. He frightened me as he waved his arms and shouted at us, insisting that we rush in making our selections and paying him. We called him "Mistersamchester," without making it three words.

Most days I brought a sandwich from home. My weekly allowance was a handful of pennies Daddy gave me on Friday nights. When I had enough pennies, I rolled them in a penny wrapper. I took them to the store the next day and changed them into nickels and dimes. Daddy was always amazed that I was able to save some of this meager allowance. Sometimes I had as much as two dollars saved. Most days, at lunch time I preferred spending only a nickel for a half-pint bottle of chocolate milk, a Grapico pop or my favorite drink, an Orange Crush sold in an amber bottle. I waited until the rush was over before going to the store. Sometimes three of my friends and I would pool our money and buy fifteen cents worth of lunch meat and a small box of Saltine crackers. We sat on the school steps and ate lunch together. On days that we didn't pool our money, I would eat hurriedly, standing up, so I could join in playing jump rope, Hide and Seek, Hopscotch, Little Sally Walker, or Shoo Lou. Some of the larger children played Pop the Whip. I joined in that game once, got thrown to the ground, and never played again.

During my time in elementary school I remember days when we had special treats of food, when commodities were served. Commodities were government surplus food that was delivered to our school. Among the food items that I remember were yellow grits, cheese, cocoa, powdered and canned milk, assorted dried beans, canned tomatoes, and prunes. Parent volunteers with their skillful and loving hands, came to the home economics kitchen, prepared and served delicious dishes for the entire student body of about five hundred students. The day before we were to be served our teachers told us to bring a cup and spoon from home. My cup was white enamel with blue flecks and a blue rim. When the food was ready, we lined up by classes and went through the line to be served. I don't remember any of my friends or me eating the cups of prunes. As soon as we were far enough away from the adults, we had prune fights, throwing prunes at each other, running away and trying not to get hit.

Elementary children were not allowed to go to "The Park," the colored baseball diamond one-half block from school, where the high school boys played baseball. At a quarter to one, when lunchtime was almost over, Daddy walked around the schoolyard ringing the medium-sized brass bell. Some primary children ran to be first in line at their assigned class places, as others crowded around Daddy pulling his pants legs, and touching him on the shoulders asking, for a turn at ringing the bell. He would pass the bell to a child as he watched the big smile on the ringer's face. Daddy loved the children and they knew it.

My most outstanding memories of elementary school were May

*Stanley L. Goseer, Sr., Principal Monitor High School,
Fitzgerald, Georgia. "At recess, students often came
to Daddy for a hug or an opportunity to ring his brass bell."*

Day activities, one of the high points in our school year. It was a day when all classes were suspended and we had a full day of outdoor festivities. The activities included relays, square dancing, and contests. In the three-legged races, two children shared one croker sack, (a large burlap bag). Each child with one leg in the sack, raced to a finish line. Another fun race with croker sacks was the one where each contestant stepped into the sack with both feet and hopped, ran, stumbled, or fell. There were many laughs as they struggled to stay upright while trying to get to the finish line.

Plaiting the May Pole was also an exciting part of the pageantry of that day. A tall pole was erected in the center front of the campus on which pastel fabric streamers were attached at the top. It was graceful and beautiful to see the girls in their full-skirted Sunday dresses, as they held the streamers, weaving in and out of the circle to recorded waltz music. Mama's contribution to May Day was supervising the set up and teaching the May Pole Dance.

The funniest part of the day for me was "the suitcase race." Contestants stood at the starting line carrying a suitcase containing a change of clothes. They were instructed to race to a marker, open the suitcase, put on a hat, dress, high-heeled shoes and a purse on top of the clothes they were already wearing and return to the starting line. The first contestant back was the winner. I don't remember if prizes were given but I'm sure the fun of winning had its own rewards.

Parents participated in the May Day festivities by running the concession stands where sandwiches, peanuts, popcorn, candy and drinks were sold. The profits from the sales went to the school to fund duplicating fluid, paper and sports equipment.

At the end of my third grade term I went to Selma for the summer and lived with Grandma and Grandpa. My little sister, Alice Rose, was born that summer, when I was nine years old. (More about that later.) The following September I was enrolled and continued grade school at Selma University, a Baptist sponsored first-grade through junior college school.

I was ten years old when I returned to Fitzgerald in September of 1945. I had completed the fourth and fifth grades in one term, so when I returned to Monitor I was in the sixth grade. I was now in "the new building," that housed fifth through eleventh grades. The new building, with its eight classrooms was basically the same architectural design as the old one, except the inside spacing was different, allowing for a combination library/classroom/meeting room, in the center of the building. The principal's office, Daddy's office, located at the center entrance, was a narrow room with a desk, chair, duplicating machine and shelves.

Mrs. Otha Pettigrew was my sixth grade home-room teacher. She and Miss Agnes Gordon (later Mrs. Riggs) worked together using a new concept called team teaching. We changed classes every day, walking across the hall and spending two class periods away from our homeroom.

Our neighborhood and school population had always been so stable that it was pleasant to return to Fitzgerald and meet new children in our community. Mama had written when I was in Selma and told me that a new family had moved to Fitzgerald. Rev. and Mrs. Oscar Moore, Sr. and their four children came from Atlanta after Rev. Moore was appointed president of Bryant Theological Seminary. In a school where everyone had always known each other, I had the rare opportunity of meeting new friends. O.J. was my classmate. His sister, Benolia, was a grade ahead of me and their younger brother, Marcellus, was in the third grade. They had a baby brother Ralph, who became my baby sister's classmate and friend. I liked O.J.

Monitor School, Fitzgerald, Georgia, 8th Grade Class.
I am in the first row, second from the right.

immediately and thought that he was cute. In December, when it was time for pulling names for Christmas gift exchanges I told Mrs. Pettigrew that I didn't want to pull a name. I wanted to buy a gift for O.J. She told me that it was not proper for a girl to buy a gift for a boy. I don't remember what happened with the gift exchange that year. Since then I've never wanted to be a part of a grab bag. I prefer to select gifts for friends at Christmas and other times during the year, as I see items I think they will enjoy.

The next term I went to seventh grade and to another unusual circumstance. My seventh grade teacher, Mrs. Ella Bryant, didn't live in our community. She lived in Tifton, twenty-nine miles away, and drove to Fitzgerald each day. All of my previous teachers were long time residents of Fitzgerald and taught the same grade in the same room for many years. Mrs. Bryant brought her elementary-age son with her every day. She was my first introduction to the working, commuting mom. I remembered her when I taught in Chicago and took my older daughter to school with me every day.

Eighth grade, when I was twelve years old, was my first year of high school. How exciting it was for me having five teachers and changing classes for each subject. That was the pattern for the next four years—mathematics, English, science, civics, and for the girls, two class periods each day in home economics.

The third brick building on campus was the home economics building, a four-room, red brick building behind the new building. Home economics was the strong focus for teaching colored girls because we were being trained to be cooks, seamstresses, baby-sitters, and housekeepers for white families. We had a large sewing room with long tables that were used as desks and also as cutting surfaces. There were adequate storage cabinets for our books and supplies. We had enough sewing machines that were kept in good repair so we never had to wait to use a machine. The adjoining room, the laboratory/kitchen was large and well equipped with stations for planning, preparing, and serving meals. There were adequate funds available to purchase food and supplies for our cooking classes. Our sessions in this building rotated from meal planning, cooking, sewing and childcare. We were also taught efficient ways of cleaning. This, in addition to my cooking and sewing lessons from Mama and Grandma, allowed me to become an excellent cook and seamstress.

My favorite teacher during freshman year was Miss Minnie Pierce, my home economics teacher. She came to Monitor on her first teaching assignment after finishing Fort Valley College in Fort Valley, Georgia. She grew up in near-by Perry, Georgia, and was the daughter of the colored funeral director there. She insisted on our being accurate in measuring, layouts, cutting and sewing, and maintaining high standards of cleanliness during our cooking sessions. It didn't take me long to become one of her great admirers. She became my role model. She was tall and slim and had a beautiful smile. She was gracious and walked with a regal gait. I was not her only admirer. Robert Butts, the handsome, older brother of one of my classmates, courted and married her. At the end of the term they moved away and I never saw her again. Years later both were killed in an automobile accident. When Princess Di was killed I was reminded of Miss Pierce, "my regal princess" who I thought was as affable and charming as Princess Di.

We were not as fortunate in our allocations of funds for subject areas other than home economics. Our science, math, and English classes, and library space had sparse, old, equipment and teaching aids. The front of our books had labels in them that said, "Do your best to make this book last ten years." When we received books at Monitor they already had ten names of white students who had used them previously. I remember receiving my first and only new public school book, a civics book, in my senior year.

The third room in the home economics building served as a receiving, sorting, and storage room for the used books that we received from the white schools. The forth room in this building had a dirt floor with large doors that opened to the outside like garage doors. I never knew the use or purpose of that room.

My favorite subject in high school was English. I remember being given homework assignments to conjugate verbs. We would have to stand in class to read the assignment aloud. We had fun laughing if anyone "split a verb" as they read their assignment. We studied parts of speech and were given long lists of words to identify. We had lots of practice diagramming sentences, as a way of analyzing the relationships of words. A lot of this work was done at the blackboard. I'm not sure if I would be able to diagram a sentence now, but it's not because I didn't have enough practice. We were also required to read, write book reports, and memorize poetry and famous speeches.

My English teacher during my senior year was also a new teacher. Agatha Jones, my childhood friend, who was five years older than I, finished Spelman College in 1951 and returned to Monitor to teach. She required us to do lots of reading and writing of essays. She gave me even more assignments than she did my classmates, returning my papers for rewrites until she considered them excellent. She dismissed my complaints by saying that I must do as I was told. In addition to that reprimand, she would say, "Good, better, best, never let them rest, until your good becomes better, and your better, best." At the time it didn't occur to me that she was keeping my final rewrites. She returned all of the rewrites at the end of the term and said, "Take these to Spelman with you in the fall. You will need them for freshman English classes." I took them with me and was able to use many of these essays, making only minor changes.

My classmate, O.J. Moore, recalls a similar experience with our biology teacher, Mr. Emmitt Jones. He coached and tutored O.J., giving him extra assignments and teaching him how to make biological drawings. At the end of the year, Mr. Jones told him that he had notes, charts, and plates that he would be able to use in his freshman biology classes at Morehouse College. O.J. finished Morehouse and Howard University Medical School in Washington, D.C. He became a medical doctor and is, at present, a cardiologist in

Beverly Hills, California.

In spite of our limited supplies, books, and resources, our teachers provided us with many opportunities for enrichment. We were taught the art, history, and literature of colored people that was not included in our textbooks. The works of Langston Hughes, James Weldon Johnson, George Washington Carver and Booker T. Washington were not strange to us.

Our dedicated and ingenious teachers provided many opportunities for us to participate in extracurricular activities. These school activities were the most important parts of my social life. Our teachers volunteered to coach girls' and boys' basketball teams. I tried out for the team but team members took it as a big joke, saying I was too small to even try. After I didn't make the team, I watched the game closely and learned all of the plays and rules. During my junior and senior years I was expert enough to become the official scorekeeper for our teams. I was happy with this position because I was able to travel with the team to nearby towns and district and state playoffs.

After each home game we served our visiting teams hot dogs and hot chocolate. We pushed the tables in the sewing room against the walls and danced to music from the record player until it was dark and time for the visitors to leave. I enjoyed dancing with our cute basketball players and visitors.

When we had out of town games, our teachers and community volunteers provided transportation, using their cars to take us to the games. The saddest time of my high school days was when two of my classmates, Evelyn Roberson and Bernice Whipple were injured in an automobile accident while returning home from a basketball game. Lola Roberson, who was a class under me, was killed in this accident. I've never been able to erase the scene from my mind of Lola, lying in a coma, in the colored wing of the Fitzgerald hospital. Her death was my first experience of the death of a peer.

Each spring, high school students presented a play directed by our teachers. We learned our parts and practiced in our classrooms until five days before the performance. Salem Baptist, Mount Olive Baptist, and Bethel A.M.E. Churches allowed us to use their sanctuaries. With borrowed props of sofas, chairs, tables, and whatever else we needed, we set up the stage on the church pulpit on Monday and began rehearsing there for Friday night production. We strung a strong wire and hung white sheets across the front of the church to conceal the stage before curtain time and between acts. The plays were always humorous. We played to a packed house with an appreciative audience. These plays were the talk of our school for the next months, with many of the students quoting funny lines from the play. I put my whole soul into every part I was given. Many times I was told the character was "just like you." I took it as a compliment, even if the character was a "dizzy dame," because I knew I had taken the role and played a convincing character.

Our school participated in the district and state Fine Arts Festivals for colored students. We competed in solo and choral competitions, poetry, and oratorical contests. Our mixed chorus and drama group won in our district and went to state competitions at Savannah State College. James Arthur Maultsby and Henry Mott were our outstanding orators. James Arthur became an officer in the armed services and Henry became a high school teacher in Florida.

For juniors and seniors, the prom was the big social event of the year. It was held in the center hallway of the new building and one classroom that had been cleared of furniture. We decorated the area with green and white crepe paper streamers and balloons to give the area a festive air. Punch was served and we danced to live music by "Smiling" Ben Shorter's Band. This was the time for floor length taffeta, chiffon or net dresses. Mama was creative and used the material from dresses that white ladies had brought to our house in give away bags. Mama and I redesigned the dresses and made them small enough to fit me. I was fourteen years old my junior year and fifteen my senior year. My parents thought I was too young to have an escort to the prom so Daddy took me and brought me home both years. Many parents came to the prom and stood along the walls as chaperons.

Soon after the prom, the long awaited graduation came. On the Sunday night of graduation we proudly marched down the aisle of Salem Baptist Church as Mrs. Gwendolyn Jones played "War March of the Priests," on the piano. Our shoulders were proudly erect, our graduation caps perfectly flat on top and all our gowns carefully measured to be the same length from the floor.

It was tradition that the valedictorian and salutatorian of the senior class give graduation speeches. O.J. Moore was our valedictorian and I was the salutatorian. After O.J., it was my turn to speak. It was May 1951, three years before the Supreme Court's decision that "separate but equal" was declared inherently unequal. As a fifteen-year-old child, born and raised in the South, school integration was a foreign concept to me. In my graduation speech I made a plea to the powers that be to make good the earlier promise of "separate but equal." That "Negroes" (as we were called then) would be provided with equal educational opportunities, accommodations, adequate books (not torn, dirty, and old), supplies and equipment, and that our teachers receive the same pay as white teachers for the same experience and expertise. The idea of not being separate was not even a slight desire or concern for me, as long as we were treated equally.

Our separate and legally segregated school was far from ideal, with its physical limitations, inequities, and with an educational philosophy that tried to groom us to be second-class citizens. In spite of all of this, our teachers prepared us to grow and move beyond the narrow confines of Fitzgerald. Their efforts were not in vain. The curriculum provided the minimum course work for college admission. With good grades I had no problems meeting the entrance requirements for college. I am forever grateful for their dedication and commitment.

· LIKE MY "OLD PA" ·

My father, Stanley L. Goseer, Sr. (1906–1969).

My paternal grandfather, John Goseer (1863–1925).

THE SUMMER THAT I was eleven years old an adult family member said to me, "You 'jes like your old Pa." I don't remember what I had said or done to elicit that comment. I do remember that by the tone of the person's voice it was intended to be an insult. I smiled and took it as a compliment because Daddy had many fine qualities that I admired. He also told me that I was smart and cute, and he took me many places with him.

My daddy, Stanley Goseer, Sr., the youngest of five children of John and Alice Glasher Goseer, was born July 8, 1906, in Boston, Georgia. Daddy never talked to me about his parents. He did tell me that his father's mother, Ma Rose, lived with them.

The only picture we have of my grandfather, "Father John," is one that was taken after his children were born. In that picture he appears to be about forty years old. He had short curly hair, a heavy mustache, and hazel eyes. The only picture I've ever seen of Daddy's mother, Alice, is one where she is standing by a large tree, wearing a long dark skirt, a lighter colored apron with one pocket, a blouse with long sleeves that are rolled up to her elbows. She holds a hoe with both hands. In this black and white photo she appears to have a dark brown complexion and long, thick black hair. She is thin and gaunt. Her face, arms and hands depict a life of hard work. She died in 1921 when she was fifty-two years old, after living in south Georgia all of her life. The background of this picture shows a tree that is surrounded by lush foliage and blooming flowers in pots and buckets. Some of the plants are on crudely made stair-step like structures. The

My paternal grandmother,
Alice Glasher Goseer (1869–1921).

others are set on bricks placed on the ground. I can identify some of the plants as varieties of begonias, hibiscus, and ferns.

Is a green thumb hereditary? If so, Daddy inherited it from his mother and I inherited it from him. Daddy loved working in his yard, growing flowers that were native to South Georgia and experimenting with others that were difficult to grow in that area. One year he decided to grow delphinium, a flower that grows best in a cold climate. He kept the seeds in the refrigerator all winter. When spring came, he sterilized soil in the oven of our kitchen stove. What a stinky mess that made! When the soil cooled he took it outside and planted the seeds in it. That summer he had strong, tall spikes of the most beautiful deep-blue delphiniums I have ever seen.

From my earliest years I always enjoyed following Daddy around the yard like a little puppy. When I was large enough he allowed me to help him dig, plant, pull weeds, and prune the plants. I was probably more trouble than help. He always referred to his flowers by name and had me repeat after him until I learned each one. I enjoyed pronouncing names like camellia japonica, delphinium, pyracantha, rhododendron, hydrangea, and the many other flowers that bloomed in profusion in South Georgia. As a child I always had chores to do inside but I preferred gardening. I still prefer gardening to housework.

Another of Daddy's hobbies was writing. He spent many happy hours at his heavy, black manual Royal typewriter. He was a champion two-index-fingers typist. He wrote fiction but never got any of it published. For as long as I can remember I've been fascinated by the sounds, rhythm and power of words. Looking back, I feel that Daddy influenced my interests in reading and writing. He was an avid reader and shared his readings with me. I remember him telling me that he enjoyed savoring details and full descriptions.

Daddy was fifteen years old when his mother died. His father, "Father John," died in 1925. His mother had always told him that she wanted him to finish college. After his mother's death he left his small hometown of Boston, Georgia, and enrolled at Paine College in Augusta, Georgia. During the 1920s and 1930s many of the colleges also enrolled high school students. Daddy finished high school there and graduated from Paine College in the class of 1930. Daddy's oldest brother, Frank, lived in Albany, Georgia. He worked on the railroad as a Pullman porter. Although Uncle Frank was not able to offer Daddy any financial assistance, Daddy visited him during Christmas vacations and lived with him for brief periods between school sessions and summer jobs.

While Daddy attended high school he lived "on premise,"—the servants quarters—as a house boy for white ladies—cleaning floors and windows, washing dishes, gardening and chauffeuring, earning money to pay his tuition. His summers were spent working at a resort in Bar Harbor, Maine doing similar jobs. During his senior year he lived on campus at Paine and continued to work. I benefited from his early experiences because he developed a strong work ethic and was a perfectionist in his cleaning jobs. When I was growing up he didn't wash dishes often but supervised my work to see that I did a good job. The only times he helped were when we had company for dinner. He used water that was too hot for my hands so I didn't have to wash dishes on those occasions. He dried plates and glasses with a lint free cloth, held them up to inspect them, and polished them until they were sparkling. I continue to enjoy gleaming plates and glasses, even when I eat alone. Thanks to electric dishwashers and spot free detergent I can enjoy spotless dishes without the extra work.

Part of Daddy's work as houseboy was to clean wood, tile and linoleum floors. He liked smooth, clean, dust-free, highly polished floors. When he could afford it, he hired high school boys to clean our floors. When he didn't have money to pay workers he did the work himself. As a child I never had to mop floors because Daddy didn't think this was work for ladies or girls. After Daddy cleaned our floors he took off his shoes to enjoy the feel of walking on smooth clean floors. I still don't like to clean floors. My earlier conditioning for clean floors is stronger than my dislike for the task. So, with reluctance I clean my floors. I was happy when the new wringer mops were invented, making it unnecessary to touch the mop head or dirty water. The work is worth the satisfaction I get after the floors are cleaned and polished. I take off my shoes and enjoy walking around barefooted.

I never had a job away from home until I was a sophomore in college. Sometimes I got paid for special jobs at home. We had a fig tree in our back yard that was loaded each June with sweet, deep burgundy figs, one of my favorite fruits. I had to compete with the bees and June bugs for the ripest figs. I wasn't afraid of the bees and never got stung. When I picked figs, peeled and served them to Daddy in a large bowl I got paid a quarter, a lot of money for me. I was happy to pick the figs and earn a quarter, even though I knew Daddy might come back to me for a loan to pay the newspaperman.

Even though Daddy was the principal of Monitor Elementary and High School, and Mama was the second grade teacher, their combined incomes brought in very little money. The salary scale for all teachers was low, but colored teachers were paid less than white teachers with the same training and experience. The summers that Daddy didn't have to attend summer school at Atlanta University he supplemented his income working as a painter. He was meticulous and took great pride in his work. He developed a reputation as a good craftsman and was sought after for painting jobs. One of the jobs he was proudest of was painting the outside windows, doors, and columns of Central Methodist Church, the large church on Central Avenue, the white people's church. When he finished this job he took me to the church to show off his good work. He pointed out how he had been so careful that not a drop of paint was where it should not have been. He also explained the advantages of using high quality paint that does not run or spatter easily. I'm not a painter, but I'm annoyed at painters who do

My maternal grandparents, Frank H. Blevins (1891–1963) and Mabel Tate Blevins (1891–1977) on the porch of their home, all dressed up for church.

careless work. I will check them and point out places that need retouching or cleaning up. Daddy always told me that any job worth doing should be done with pride.

Sometimes Daddy hired people to help him with the yard work. Our yard and house covered one fourth of the city block, except for one small house that was adjacent to our back yard, where Mr. "Barber" and Miz Goshea lived. Our back yard had a large pecan tree, an apple tree, a peach tree, a weeping willow, dogwood trees, a grape arbor, a fig tree, a magnolia, and chinaberry tree in the front yard. Hydrangea and camellia bushes, sweet shrub, honeysuckle vines, forsythia, azalea and rose bushes, a lawn of Bermuda grass, and a vegetable garden covered about half of the side yard and extended to the alley. When Daddy hired help, he always invited them in to wash up and sit at our table to eat lunch or dinner. When some of the same people worked for white people, if they were offered food, it was handed to them from the back door, and they ate on the back steps or in the back yard. Daddy treated people who worked for him with great dignity and respect. Whenever I have anyone helping at my house I always offer food or drink. I always express appreciation for their help.

Daddy always paid fair wages. One day he said to me, "The food

My maternal grandfather's mother,
my great-grandmother, Amelia Ann Tucker.

and items they have to buy at the stores cost the same as I have to pay, so I must be fair with them." In the late '40s and early '50s colored ladies worked as domestics in white homes, doing all of the cleaning, cooking, laundry, and child care for wages averaging $7.50 a week. Some were paid as little as $2.50 per week and rarely was anyone paid as much as $15.00. Daddy said that this pay scale was unfair and did what he could to correct this injustice whenever he could afford to hire persons to help him.

I've been told that I was an absolute knockout from day one as I entered this world Sunday evening, June 9, 1935, at my maternal grandparent's home on Lapsley Street, in Selma, Alabama. My great-grandma, Grandma Tucker, Grandpa Blevins' mother, was the midwife and Grandma Blevins was helping her. Daddy was also there for the delivery but fainted. Grandma Blevins had to stop helping Grandma Tucker to revive Daddy.

Despite my "knockout" beginnings I was not one of those little girls who caused people to coo, "Oh, isn't she cute!" I was scrawny and pale with soft, fluffy sandy hair, crooked teeth and a long nose that dominated my thin face, a real ugly duckling. I didn't look like either of my parents. My hair and hazel eyes were more like Daddy's father, John Goseer. From the first day that Daddy told me that my eyes were

My mother,
Mabel Alieze Blevins Goseer.

pretty, I believed him, and it no longer mattered when I was called "cat" eyes. Sometimes unkind or unthinking adults asked "Are those your real parents?" or "Where did you come from? You sure don't look like them." I never responded to their questions. My schoolmates were many shades of brown. I was sometimes called "yalla gal," which always caused me pain because I wanted to be brown like everyone else. Comments like, "You too yalla to have all dat nappy hair," caused me to hang my head. Daddy frequently rubbed me on the head and said, "You're a pretty little girl and you have such beautiful eyes." That helped ease the pain, but peer acceptance was important to me. Sometimes schoolmates teased me as they called me "cat" eyes, referring to my hazel eyes that sometimes changed colors. I handled the comments from children better. When I was called this, I smiled and responded with, "Meow?" I have continued to be happy with my pretty eyes. All of my life, through the best and worst of times, I've looked in the mirror and said to myself, "What pretty eyes you have!" That was a great gift from Daddy.

I was twenty-seven years old when Grandpa Blevins died. At his funeral my family realized that I looked more like him than any other member of the family, including his own children. The mystery of the long nose and pale color was finally solved.

I think that for most little girls their concept of a beautiful woman is their own mother. This was certainly true for me. Mama is caramel-colored with dark brown eyes. When she was young she had shiny, soft, black hair that flowed to her waist in large waves. The ladies in her family who lived in and near Selma had similar physical characteristics. Until I matured and developed more self-confidence, I just lived with the fact that at least I had pretty eyes. I wore braces on my teeth when I was a teenager. I began getting my hair straightened so I no longer had to wear braids to keep it manageable. I was at least thirty years old before I accepted my complexion, the texture of my hair, and my long nose as unique and beautiful.

I was thirty-two years old when Daddy was diagnosed with cancer of the liver. He had surgery and received a prognosis of about two years to live. He accepted the report bravely and considered the time his "reprieve," as he called it. He continued to work, even though during the final few months he was not able to drive, and was only strong enough to stay at school a half day. He loved his work with children, a trait that I think I inherited. He received chemotherapy treatments, but in early spring decided to discontinue them. He was able to complete his school term in May 1969. My school term was not over in Chicago until June, but I felt compelled to go home and not wait until the end of the month. I followed my intuition and went home to spend a week with him.

On my last day at work before this trip my principal gave me my "efficiency rating" for the school term. This was the first time that the Chicago Board of Education had issued this printed form and delivered it to teachers. In previous years they were put in our files at the central office and were available for our inspection. I had never gone to check my files. This year I proudly shared my rating of Superior with Daddy. He told me how proud he was of me. That was the only time in my teaching career that the formal rating ever meant anything to me. My satisfaction always came from the achievements of my pupils.

Mama was still working so Daddy and I spent a lot of time talking. I fixed whatever he wanted to eat or drink, which was very little. When I left at the end of the week, I knew that this visit would be the last time I would see him alive. In the meantime, he told Mama that I must not come back until the time of his funeral. He died three weeks later, on July 7, 1969, one day before his sixty-third birthday.

During our final week together he told me that he was proud of his three children, Stanley, Jr., Alice Rose, and me. He said that we were good citizens, independent, responsible adults, and had caused him no problems. To him, this was the essence of successful fatherhood and a meaningful life.

He planned his funeral in great detail; even to the time of day the service in Fitzgerald was to take place. He wanted it to be brief, at ten o'clock in the morning, so we could make the five-hour drive to Selma for burial in Mama's family burial plot.

I still smile as I remember Daddy when I'm working in my yard. The work hasn't gotten any easier. I'm still dirty, tired, and aching, but satisfied when I finish. Thanks to electric dishwashers and modern mops, I can enjoy sparkling dishes and clean floors without a lot of hard work. The principles of excellence and fairness that Daddy instilled in me are still an important part of my life. I continue to feel proud as I remember being told, "You jes like your old Pa." What a wonderful compliment that is!

· AN ABORTED VISIT ·

WHEN I WAS six years old my daddy took me on our first trip with just the two of us: a planned bus ride during the Christmas season. We were on our way to Albany, Georgia to visit my daddy's brother, Uncle Frank. I was excited and feeling like a big girl to be going away just with Daddy.

I was all dressed up in my new designer coat that Mama had made me. It was gray tweed with a red velveteen collar, a matching red velveteen muff, and a bonnet that tied under my neck.

When we got off the bus in Tifton to change to the bus for Albany, a white lady asked Daddy "Whose pretty little girl is she?"

Daddy very proudly answered, "She's my daughter."

I still remember the look on the white lady's face as she huffed and turned away with a look of disdain. She had mistaken me for a white child, because the color of my skin was lighter than the outer shade of an almond shell. By the end of December my suntan of the summer had completely faded. Daddy was the color of the inside, edible part of the almond. The white lady could only see my hazel eyes. My red bonnet covered my dark hair.

We didn't get to Albany that Christmas. When the bus arrived and the passengers boarded, white people first, there was no room on the bus for us. We returned to Fitzgerald on the next bus. I don't remember Daddy and me talking on the way back.

Mama was surprised to see us back so soon. Daddy told her about the incident with the white lady. He also told her about not being able to board the bus to Albany. I never heard my parents discuss the incidents of that day again.

In retrospect, the fact that my parents and I never talked about this trip that started out with so much anticipation and joy and ended in such disappointment, is just one example of many painful experiences that never got discussed. I recall one of the slogans Daddy had in his office, "That which cannot be changed must be endured." In the mid '40s—before the Civil Rights Movement—I suppose Daddy adopted this philosophy, while quietly planting seeds of protests in his students and me. The next generation initiated the change and were the active participants in sit-ins, protests, marches and boycotts.

· PIANO LESSONS ·

WHENEVER I HEAR or read about programs seeking volunteers, I recall kind, unselfish persons of my childhood who were a major influence in my life. Mr. Isaac Dukes worked as an agent for the Atlanta Life Insurance Company, making collections in Fitzgerald, Georgia and neighboring towns. He was a dedicated member of Holsey Chapel C.M.E. Church, where he served as superintendent and teacher of the Sunday School. In spite of his busy life he found other ways to share his life.

The time came in my piano study when I needed another teacher to keep me advancing in skills. Mr. Dukes volunteered to drive a group of us to Mrs. Gladys Jones in Douglas, Georgia—a town thirty miles from my home in Fitzgerald. There were six children who benefited from this caring man. His three daughters, Yvonne, Iris and Irma, their cousin Barbara, a boy named Edsel, and I all crammed into his two-door car. Four of us sat in the back seat and two were in the front with Mr. Dukes.

Although Douglas was only thirty miles away, he picked me up on Saturdays at eight a.m. for lessons that began at nine o'clock. He drove very slowly, much to our dismay. I smile as I recall him driving, leaning forward with both hands on the steering wheel. He not only picked us up and drove us, but he sat with each of us during our lessons. We could play outside until it was time for our lesson. How could we not practice all week in order to have the best lesson possible? He encouraged and complimented us when we had good lessons. If a lesson was mediocre we had to listen to a lecture on "doing your best." He was an amber colored, soft-spoken man with expressive hazel eyes. I never heard him speak in a loud or angry voice.

He also encouraged us by providing opportunities for us to play for an audience in Sunday afternoon programs, where we gained experience and confidence. When no programs were scheduled, he gathered us around the piano in his living room to play and sing together. This was not one of my favorite activities. The good part was that his wife, Mrs. Ruby Dukes, made delectable cakes. She took great pride in making many different kinds—chocolate, lemon, coconut, cherry, and my favorite, pineapple. On Sunday afternoons I wanted to visit with my friends and sample some of Mrs. Dukes' delicious cooking. She prepared baked chicken, dressing and collard greens every Sunday. It didn't matter that I had eaten dinner at home. I always got a saucer and fixed a "mini" dinner of a slice of chicken breast, a spoonful of dressing and some collards. Then I ate my slice of cake. After our music and eating session there was always time for our weekly walk to the dairy store for an ice cream cone. "Be back before the street lights come on" was a strictly enforced rule. If for some reason I changed my Sunday routine, Mrs. Dukes told me that she missed me. Years later, whenever I returned home she always invited me over to have some of her scrumptious food. The sharing of food that I learned from Mrs. Dukes is an important part of my life. I enjoy cooking and having friends visit my home to share a meal.

Mr. And Mrs. Dukes are no longer with us, but they both lived long, fruitful lives. Mr. Dukes' generous spirit lives on as I continue to study, perform and teach music. I continued to play the piano but the pipe organ became my favorite instrument. For me, Mr. Dukes captured the essence of the spirit of volunteerism. The Dukes family continues to represent the epitome of caring neighbors.

• LESSONS FROM THE LIZARD
AND THE POSSUM •

MAMA HAD TWO large potted ferns that were her pride and joy. During spring and summer she kept them on the front porch where they could get the proper amount of sun and shade. It was my job to water them every day. I was told to save the tea leaves from dinner to spread around the base of the ferns because "it was good for them." I suppose that was my earliest lesson in organic gardening. In winter Mama brought the ferns in the house and kept them in the living room to protect them from the cold weather. I learned later that cold weather is a relative term. The temperature in Fitzgerald rarely dropped below forty degrees. Our living room was not heated except on the rare occasions when Daddy made a fire in the fireplace. The ferns stayed green all winter. By April they were again placed on the porch and began putting out new fronds. In May these plants went out on loan to our high school for the graduation exercises held at Salem Baptist Church. (Our school didn't have an auditorium.)

One summer as I watered the ferns, I noticed small lizards crawling on their leaves and nearby. I watched more closely and saw that the lizards changed colors as they crawled from the ferns to the porch and to the azalea branches. When they were on the ferns they were bright green, on the porch they faded to gray like the painted wooden porch. When they crawled on the azalea branches they turned brown. I ran to tell Mama about my observation. She explained it was "protective coloration"—that some animals were able to do this. I experimented by putting a blue pot cover out and watched the lizard crawl on it and change color again. I entertained myself many times watching this phenomenon. Daddy liked to tell me animal stories. One of the ones I remember was how "Brer Possum" protected himself from predators by turning on his back, lying perfectly still, playing dead until he was out of danger.

I don't know if I was "carefully taught," as the song from *South Pacific* states, or I instinctively developed a mask or protective cover in order to cope with the "predators" in this small southern, racist town. Probably both.

When I was about ten years old Mama began allowing me to walk to MacCellans Ten Cents Store on Pine Street to buy my socks, hair ribbons, small toys, and sheet music. Before she let me go she told me to always speak to all of the colored people that I passed, but not to say anything to white people unless they said something to me. The instruction that I understood to be the most important was that I must not allow any white man to "catch my eye"—meaning that I should not make eye contact with them. She told me that they would wink at colored girls and ladies, a form of flirtation and some encouragement for conversation. There was a double standard of behavior for white men with colored females, and black men with white females. White men often made flirtatious, even lewd comments, which colored women had to ignore, having no protection from their inappropriate behavior. On the other hand, a colored male who made any sexual overture or was even accused of such was subject to a severe beating or lynching by white men.

Although Fitzgerald proudly boasts that it never had a Ku Klux Klan chapter, and there is no record of a lynching ever being committed there or in Ben Hill County, we lived separate lives with no more interaction with white people than was absolutely necessary. We received colored newspapers that were brought in by colored train porters. *The Atlanta Daily World*, weekly *Pittsburgh Courier*, and *Chicago Defender* reported police brutality and mob action against colored people that was not printed in the white newspapers. We also subscribed to *The Atlanta Journal and Constitution*, a white newspaper, where Ralph McGill served as a fair and honest editor. The information from the newspapers confirmed our knowledge of the subtle economic, social, and psychological pressures white people exerted over colored people; always we had to be cautious.

Mr. Fred Ayres was superintendent of the Fitzgerald School System and Daddy was Principal of Monitor Elementary and High School, the colored school. Mr. Ayres would drive up to our front door and blow his horn when he wanted to see Daddy. When I went to the door he would say, "Is Stanley at home?"

If I answered, "No, Sir, Mr. Ayres, he is not here," he would say to me, "Tell Stanley I said to come to my office when he gets back."

Mr. Ayres never referred to Daddy, or addressed him as Mr. Goseer, but always as Stanley. Daddy always called the Superintendent, Mr. Ayres. His visits to our school were rare and brief. Those experiences with Mr. Ayres were my first lessons in the power of white males.

The Gulf Oil Distribution Center was across the street from our house. Only white men worked there. Sometimes Mama would send me there to get change for a ten or twenty dollar bill. I was instructed to speak softly and politely when I asked for change. I practiced my lessons in avoiding eye contact and never had any uncomfortable times during my trips to the oil company.

In 1946, I was twelve years old and started eighth grade, my first year in high school. At that time we graduated from high school in the eleventh grade. Eighth grade was a happy exciting year. I loved changing classes and having a different teacher for each subject. I began noticing boys and deciding which ones were cute or nice. I enjoyed watching them play baseball or basketball as I ate my lunch, which I brought from home.

My freshman year in high school was also the year that I started to wear braces on my teeth. My family made the great financial sacrifice to pay fifteen dollars a month to have my teeth straightened. We didn't have a colored dentist in town and Dr. Tuggle was the only one who did orthodontic work. Mama accompanied me to Dr. Tuggle's office for all of the initial work of making impressions and applying the shiny metal bands and wires. After all of that was in place, Mama began allowing me to go alone for the frequent adjustments that followed.

During my visits to Dr. Tuggle's office, I began using my lessons from the possum. Dr. Tuggle began to schedule my appointments on my lunch hour, which was also the lunch hour for his assistant, a white lady. When I arrived, his assistant would get me set up in the chair and put the bib on. He would tell her that she could go to lunch, that this would only take a few minutes. As soon as she left, he stuffed the cotton rolls and evacuator in my mouth. He then began conversations that were clearly inappropriate, commenting on my getting to be a "big girl" or a "sweater girl." He got absolutely no response or reaction from me; no excitement, anger—nothing. He began putting his right hand up my skirt high on my left thigh and began to rub my inner thigh with his thumb. During these times he continued to talk about me being "a big girl now." I instinctively acted in the manner of a possum when it sensed danger. I must have known that if I had responded with anger or resistance he would have gotten some satisfaction.

When school was out for summer vacation he began scheduling my appointments at the end of the day when it was time for his assistant to leave. He told Mama that he would bring me home in his car, since I was his last patient. Mama refused his offer and told him that I would ride my bicycle. I never told Mama or Daddy about his inappropriate conversations or behavior. What good would it have done when they were unable to do anything about it? All of this happened when there was no "equal protection under the law." I wore my mask and bore my pain in secret, not giving any visible reaction, blending, one could say, into the chair as if I were a lizard, willing myself to be invisible. He might as well have been talking to a wall or touching a stone.

When he couldn't get me in his car, Mama began to call to see if I were still there or "how long will it be?" After a while he finally stopped his inappropriate behavior. I wore braces until my senior year. What a glorious day it was when the braces came off! I had straight teeth and no more visits to Dr. Tuggle!

After my senior year in college I returned home for a brief visit. I saw Dr. Tuggle in Friedlander's Department Store. Dr. Tuggle's office was upstairs. I "caught his eye," going against what I had been taught earlier. He didn't wink. I didn't speak, but, instead, glared at him until he hung his head. If looks can kill, I became a murderer that day. I never saw him again.

When I came home I told Mama that I had seen Dr. Tuggle. I called him a dirty bastard (strong language to use in front of Mama) as I told her how he had treated me at his office when we were alone. I felt a sense of relief and triumph when I told her that I had glared at him until he hung his head. She asked me why I had never told her about his behavior before that day. I explained that I felt there was nothing she could have done to help me, given the racial climate of the times. I had seen how helpless Daddy was in his relationship with Mr. Ayres and other white people in our town. I felt that if I had told my parents what was happening, they could have lost their jobs or been harmed in other ways. In the white community I was nothing but "a little nigger gal" and in no position to complain about the actions of a white professional man. Mama didn't respond; her silence was admission that I was right. I am sure that it was an extremely painful moment for her. We never discussed it again.

I returned home for a brief visit in May of 1998. While I was there I visited one of Mama's contemporaries, Mrs. Mamie Grant. Our conversation turned to the old days in Fitzgerald and some of my experiences as a child growing up there. I told her of my experiences with Dr. Tuggle. Finally, the silence that women unfortunately had always kept was broken. As I spoke about these incidents, she nodded her head. When I finished, she told me that he had also dismissed his assistant and as soon as she was gone he would fondle her breasts and make lewd remarks. She would push his hands away in anger. During this time she also never told anyone about his behavior, living in fear of his retaliation. I realized I must have been one of many victims of this vile man, not that it makes it any less painful.

Ever since I became an adult I've had a sense of Divine Guidance, or as I sometimes call it, "protective custody," just as the lizard has protective coloration and the possum, the instinct to play dead. I think the way I faced that potentially explosive situation was one of my early experiences of Divine Guidance.

I still feel that I handled it in the best manner under the circumstances to protect my family and community from a racial outburst. But my heart goes out, belatedly, to all those, especially children, who bore their trials in silent dignity.

· GRANDMA'S COW ·

*My brother, Stanley, Jr. (Sonny), age 12, and me, age 9, during the year
we spent with our grandparents in Selma, Alabama.*

THE ONLY MEMORY I have of my maternal great-grandfather,
Grandpa Will Tate, was on a summer's day before I was old enough to
go to school. He was sitting in a chair on the front porch of his two-
story log cabin. I remember his black suit and tie, white shirt, long,
round-toed shoes and spats. He pulled me close to him, held my arm
with one hand and cupped his other hand over his ear, continually
repeating, "What say? What say?" I don't remember what I was trying
to tell him, but I don't think he ever heard me.

My great-grandmother, Amanda Tate, "Grandma Manda," died in
1934, one year before I was born. Grandpa Will Tate died seven years
later. When Grandpa Will Tate died, his two sons, Uncle Arthur and
Uncle Stanley, and their families continued to live and work on the
farm. At the time of his death, his daughters, Aunt Willie, Aunt Jennie,
and Mabel (Grandma), had already married and moved away.
Grandma's legacy from her father was a cow that she named Alice.
She was a Guernsey, the color of a kraft paper bag. She had white
markings and a long head with a white shield on her broad forehead.
Her eyes were large and her horns curved upward and forward. I liked
to stand by the fence in the back yard and look into her brown eyes.

Grandma treated Alice as if she were a pet, grooming her and talking to her. Grandpa helped in her care by taking on the responsibility of feeding her and scrubbing her wooden trough so that she always had clean fresh water.

Lapsley Street was one of the few streets where colored people lived that had paved streets, sidewalks, curbs, and walkways. Most of the streets in the colored neighborhood were dirt, because the city required the residents to pay for their own paving. Lapsley Street ran parallel to Broad Street, the main street in town, that began at the Edmund Pettus Bridge—the site, where in March, 1965, the Civil Rights March from Selma to Montgomery originated. Lapsley Street was a main thoroughfare that intersected with highway 80 West to Mississippi. Even though it was a main route in Selma in the 1930s and 1940s, there was no city ordinance against owning and keeping cows and chickens in this neighborhood.

Lapsley Street and First Avenue, another paved street in the colored community, were streets of single-family wooden homes, painted white, gray, or cream. All of the houses had front porches with swings and chairs. Some of the homes had side lawns and driveways. The street was also lined with chinaberry and majestic oak trees. When the oak tree in front of our house was cut down in the mid 1990s, according to the growth rings, it was estimated to be more than one hundred and thirty years old. The chinaberry tree didn't live as long and had to be cut down in the early 1950s.

Selma University is also located on Lapsley Street. When I was a child, living in Selma, it was a primary school through junior college for colored students. The year that I went to school in Selma I attended Selma University. My mother and her brother Frank also attended school there. Daddy came to teach at Selma University immediately after graduating from Paine College in 1930. He met Mama, who was then a freshman in college. They were married in September of the following year and moved to Georgia.

My grandparent's home was typical of the homes on the street with its front and side lawn, an oak and chinaberry tree, white exterior, front porch extending the width of the house, hanging swing, glider swing and chair, and a wooden bench. There was a stone bench under the chinaberry tree where my friends and I often sat on summer afternoons and evening, talking and playing games.

Alice lived in a fenced off portion of the back yard that she shared with several hens, young chickens, and one mean rooster. Her shed was attached to the chicken house and her salt lick was mounted on a pole near her shed. I wasn't afraid of Alice, but I didn't go inside the fenced off portion because the rooster would attack everyone except Grandma and Grandpa.

Alice kept cool under the huge pecan tree that towered over the second floor roof of the house. The back roof didn't have gutters, and in the fall when the pecans hit the slanted roof they rolled to the ground. We harvested and kept enough of the nuts for our family's use. Grandma told me that the money from the sale of the remaining pecans was enough to pay the annual property taxes.

When Grandpa came home from work at the Post Office, he would eat his supper of leftovers from dinner, and then take Alice for a walk and grazing. He put on his wide brimmed hat, put a rope around Alice's neck and led her across Lapsley Street, down the side of the railroad tracks to the grassy banks of Valley Creek. When he brought her back and put her in the back yard he would sit in the glider swing and smoke his pipe. Some evenings his neighbors and friends Mr. Vassar, Mr. Houston Reid, or Mr. Jefferies joined him for a visit.

The Buckeye, a large cottonseed processing plant at the railroad tracks that crossed Lapsley Street, pressed cottonseeds to extract the oil. The residue from this process was used for cattle feed. Some of the railroad tracks ran through the Buckeye where their products were loaded to train cars from the enormous silvery gray storage tanks, to be shipped away from Selma. During the week when the plant was in operation our neighborhood smelled like roasted peanuts. We didn't need clocks on weekdays because Grandma's rooster woke us up early in the mornings and the whistle at the Buckeye was our timekeeper for the remainder of the day. The whistle blew at eight o'clock to start the workday, at noon for the beginning of lunch, one o'clock for the end of lunch, and at five o'clock for the end of the workday. The trains also came on a regular schedule. One of my summer time activities was counting the cars and tanks of the freight trains and counting the many states printed on the cars. Many times after more than fifty cars had passed I would tire of counting or reading the state and company names.

On Sunday afternoons Grandpa always took us for a drive in the country to visit relatives. On our return trip he stopped by the side of the road, cut tall grass with his scythe, and filled the trunk of the car with fresh grass to bring home to Alice. In the fall he stored bales of hay in the garage so that Alice would have food during the winter.

Grandma got up early each morning to milk Alice, as she stood still, peacefully chewing her cud. Grandma held two teats at a time, alternating milking each as the warm milk streamed into the pail. One day Grandma tried to teach me milking, but my hands were not strong enough to squeeze and pull the teats firmly enough to have the milk flow down. Alice must have realized that I didn't know what I was doing so she began to swish her tail and toss her head. I gave up trying to learn to milk Alice. I didn't like the feel of the long, soft teat in my hand. I never tried to milk her again.

Grandma's cow was her pride and joy as well as a source of income. Grandma never had a job outside her home. The money that she earned selling milk and butter was a welcome addition to the family budget. Alice provided sweet milk and cream, as well as butter and buttermilk for us. There was also enough butter and buttermilk for Grandma to sell. She milked Alice early each morning and put some of the milk in the refrigerator. The remainder was left out to turn into clabber, a yogurt-like texture of sour milk. When the milk got to the clabber stage, she put it in her gray earthenware churn. The round wooden top had a hole cut in it to insert the dasher, a long wooden pole with an "X" cross bar at the end of it, that was moved up and down to churn the milk. Grandma got an even rhythm going as she churned the milk. Sometimes she let me help her. She took the top off periodically to see if the butter had formed. When she determined that all of the butter had come to the top, she used the dasher to pull the butter out of the churn, squeeze it with her wooden paddle, stir cold water into the butter, and pour off the milky liquid. She called this "washing the butter." When the water was no longer milky she would put the butter into half pound and one pound wooden butter molds that had interesting shapes of fruits and vegetables carved into the wood. The butter-filled molds were put into the refrigerator to chill until the butter was firm enough to be pushed from the molds. For the final step, she wrapped the molded butter in waxed paper, and returned it to the refrigerator. On Saturday mornings she filled orders for buttermilk and butter.

My job in this enterprise was to make the deliveries to Grandma's customers. The buttermilk was put in quart glass bottles and capped with special cardboard disks that she bought. Each order was put in a brown paper bag with the customer's name on it. My wire basket was lined with a large towel to pad and cover the bags. Then I was off to make my deliveries and to collect the money. I was nine years old during the school year that I had these responsibilities. I brought the money back to Grandma. She counted it and left enough on the table to pay for my piano lesson on Saturday afternoon. I don't remember the price of the milk or the piano lessons but I took pride in having the responsibility of making the deliveries and collections. Later her customers told her what a fine job I had done.

· A YEAR AT GRANDMA'S ·

WHEN CHRISTMAS VACATION came, Grandpa and my brother Stanley, "Sonny," had to stay in Selma to take care of Alice, the cow, and the chickens. Grandma began making plans to go to Fitzgerald because Mama had influenza and was extremely ill. My baby sister, Alice Rose, was there with Mama and Daddy.

Grandpa took Grandma and me to the bus station on Broad Street about four o'clock a.m. to get a bus for the fifty-mile trip to Montgomery. From there we would go by train to Fitzgerald. It was still dark when we arrived at the bus station in Montgomery. We took a taxi to the train station. In the dim light of dawn the taxi driver had mistaken us for white and took us to the entrance of the white waiting room. Grandma's complexion was the color of vanilla wafers. Her hair was thin, straight, and snowy white. My complexion was lighter than hers. When Grandma asked him to take us around to the colored waiting room in back, the driver began shouting, "I ain't 'sposed ta ride no niggers in my taxi. You gonna havta pay double."

Grandma paid him in silence and struggled to get our two pieces of luggage and lunch box out of the taxi. Once our suitcases were on the sidewalk, Grandma wiped away tears, with the back of her hand; I had never seen her cry before. As she continued to wipe away the tears, she stood still and sighed, "He didn't have to do that. He didn't have to charge us double. No one else would've known. He didn't have to be that mean. I didn't know we weren't supposed to ask him to take us to the train station." We stood there for a few minutes trying to regain our composure before gathering our luggage to walk into the colored waiting room.

We sat quietly, alone, until the train came. There were no other colored people in the waiting room at that early hour. When the conductor called "All aboard," we boarded the train at the coach designated for the colored passengers, directly behind the coal and luggage car. The newer, cleaner, and more comfortable coaches were for white passengers.

Once inside the coach we found there was enough empty space for us to take two double seats facing each other. Soon after the train departed, the white conductor made his rounds punching holes in our tickets and putting a color-coded slip on the window shade by our seats to indicate our destination.

When we were comfortably settled, Grandma opened our lunch box of fried chicken, store-bought Sunbeam light bread, cake and fruit. Grandma made the best chicken ever! She marinated it with salt, pepper, paprika, and buttermilk, and left it in the refrigerator for a few hours. When she was ready to cook it, she dipped the moist pieces of chicken into flour that formed a batter. She fried the pieces of chicken in hot oil, turning them often, until they were crisp and golden brown on the outside, but juicy on the inside. Family members try to duplicate her recipe but we never feel that ours is ever as good as hers. We enjoyed our breakfast/lunch despite the taxicab incident. I walked back and forth a few times to the water dispenser for the tiny, cone-shaped paper cups that I pulled out with a gentle squeeze. The water wasn't cold, but I enjoyed the walk and filling the cup. Later in the trip, when we came to a stop in a large town, a man boarded the train selling drinks and snacks. We bought an Orange Crush and RC Cola from him.

The colored train porter spent as much time with us as his other duties allowed, telling us jokes and funny stories. Daddy's brother, Uncle Frank, was a train porter and had told me how much he enjoyed visiting the colored passengers. Although the trip was only three hundred miles, it seemed very long. We finally got to Fitzgerald, mid-afternoon, tired and dirty from the black soot blowing on us from the furnace and coal car in front of us.

When I arrived home Mama was in bed, too weak to sit up. Grandma began cleaning, cooking and taking care of her and my baby sister, who was now four and a half months old. I had the pleasure of playing with Alice Rose. She was large enough for me to hold and rock in Mama's large rocking chair. Her hands were large enough to grasp my index finger. I stroked her soft legs and little long feet. She smiled and cooed at me.

After a week of Grandma's tender loving care Mama was feeling better and began asking me about school. As she questioned me and made up tests for me, she found that I didn't understand beginning long division, which I should have known by the middle of fourth grade. She worked with me from her bed because she was still not strong enough to be on her feet. We were both happy when I improved my skills.

After spending Christmas of 1944 in Fitzgerald, Grandma and I returned to Selma after the holiday break. I don't remember any details of that trip. Evidently it was uneventful with no more encounters with mean taxi drivers. Or was it that we stayed "in our place," according to southern Jim Crow laws?

When I returned to school in Selma after the holidays and my visit home I was more content at being there. I had been very lonely and miserable at the beginning of the school term. I wanted to be at home with Mama, Daddy, and Alice Rose. I wouldn't have minded if Sonny had been the one to stay in Selma, because he was thrilled over learning to play the coronet. My grandparents were good to me but Selma wasn't home, at least not during school time.

In addition to missing Mama, Daddy, and my friends in Fitzgerald, I had to make adjustments to a different school system. The elementary school of Selma University was structured on the old English system of standards, rather than grades. First through fourth standards were supposed to be the equivalent of grades primer through sixth grades in the public schools. I was nine years old and had just completed third grade in Fitzgerald when I was enrolled at Selma University. I was placed in the third standard without being given any placement tests. I complained about everything that had to do with school—the children in my class were too young, there were too many children in the class, and the work was too easy. I liked my teacher, Miss Lucille White, but I gave her a hard time with my negative attitude. She was sensitive enough to know that something was wrong and requested a conference with Mama at the beginning of the term, before she returned to Fitzgerald. That was the first and only time a teacher requested a conference with Mama because of problems I was having at school. When Mama and Miss White asked me what was wrong I told them that I was bored because I already knew all of the things Miss White was teaching. The truth was that I wanted to go home with

Mama and Alice Rose, but I didn't tell them that. Miss White and Mama decided that I should be moved to the fourth standard where the work would be more challenging.

Miss White's classroom was in a red brick building with one other classroom next door. Miss Burroughs taught the fourth standard in a small, one room, white, wooden building next to the brick building. The class size was smaller; not more than fifteen children. We sat in straight chairs around a large black, pot-bellied, coal-burning stove. Miss Burroughs gave out assignments verbally and remained seated at her desk and wrote while we either did our assignments or talked. It seemed to me that it didn't matter to her what we did as long as we were not disruptive. My classmates and I laughed and talked about her; we decided that she sat there all day writing letters to her boyfriend. Once a week, we were marched single file up to the top floor of the three-story high school and junior college building to attend convocation. That year recess and lunch times were the best parts of my school days.

At noon we were dismissed for a one-hour lunch break. I walked the two blocks home to eat. Early in the term a classmate, Erin Hampton, began walking home with me every day. She was the first and only classmate I ever had with the same first name as mine. We became great buddies and called ourselves "the two Erins." Grandma never questioned the fact that she came to eat every school day. Grandma fixed her plate along with mine.

Grandma had an electric stove in the kitchen and a small coal-burning heater in the bedroom next to the kitchen where she kept a fire burning all day, every day, during the winter. This heater had a front apron and a bottom grate that held the ashes. When Grandma baked sweet potatoes she put them in the hot ashes from the heater, turning them with the iron coal poker. She baked cornbread in a black iron skillet that she placed on the apron of the heater near the glowing coals. At noon the house was filled with the aromas of good food.

Erin and I ate quickly so that we could get back to school to play Tag on our large playground. The high point of my school day was to see my play "Mama," Mattie Hopson. It was a tradition at Selma University that high school girls adopt a "baby daughter." I don't remember how I became Mattie's "baby," but it made me very happy. I met her every day as soon as I returned to campus after lunch. I got my daily hug and gave her a love note that I had written in class that morning. She also wrote notes to me that I kept and read many times. Mattie had a sister, Betty, who became my "aunt" and another person to hug me. Her twin brothers smiled and spoke whenever they saw me. They told their friends that I was Betty's "baby." In retrospect, my relationship with Mattie and her family was a blessing. I was lonely for Mama and missed being in Fitzgerald with my friends.

Grandma was a great storyteller. By bedtime, the fireplace in the room where I slept would have the room warm and comfortable. Grandma, Sonny, and I would sit around the fire after we had finished our homework. Grandpa would stay in the room across the hall where the heater had been burning all day. Grandma would pull the string to turn off the light that came from the single bulb in the ceiling and tell ghost stories as the flames flickered from the coals in the fireplace. The stories that I remember most vividly were about Ichabod Crane and the headless horseman. It was not until I took American Literature in college that I learned these stories were by Washington Irving and came from Knickerbocker Tales. As I listened to Grandma I would be thrilled and frightened at the same time, but never discouraged her from telling these stories. She also knew many poems from memory. She had fond memories of her teacher, Professor Hudson, who fostered her love of literature.

Grandma's favorite poem was "The House by the Side of the Road" by Sam Walter Foss. I learned the entire poem by hearing her say it so often. I believe it was her favorite because it expressed her philosophy of life. Their house on Lapsley Street became "home away from home" for all of our relatives who needed somewhere to visit or live. Before motels and hotels were open to colored people in Selma, cousins, nieces, nephews, and friends up North would write and tell her when they were coming to visit. They were always welcome. Grandma was running a Bed and Breakfast—and Dinner— and didn't even know it. Many of her guests called her Mama Mabel or Aunt Mabel and Papa Frank. When I was a teenager I remember Grandma telling me, "Don't love nobody." I suppose that was her way of trying to protect me from the pain that sometimes comes with loving people. By the time she told me this it was too late. I had already learned from her the joy of loving and sharing. I enjoy having friends and family in my home and almost always can prepare a quick meal for a sudden guest.

The "vegetable" lady, a statuesque dark-chocolate-colored lady, came by early on summer mornings calling, "Get your nice fresh vegetables, Crowder peas, speckled butter beans, okra, nice fresh roasting ears!" She carried her vegetables in three baskets. In each hand she held the handles of a large basket. Walking with a regal gait, she balanced a large, bowl-shaped basket on her head. If someone wanted to make a purchase she would lower her body slightly to set the hand-carried baskets on the sidewalk. Keeping her balance, she then lifted the third vegetable-laden basket from her head. She measured and sold the produce using a tin quart-measuring cup. Grandma put the vegetables in her own containers. These purchases from the vegetable lady supplemented the harvest from our small backyard garden and the vegetables Grandma's brother or sister gave her when we went to the country on Sunday afternoons.

Before Grandma got her new wringer washing machine in 1946, Monday mornings, after milking time and breakfast, was washday. The leftover pot roast from Sunday's dinner was put into her large soup pot with water, fresh tomatoes, and onions from the garden, and some of the vegetables she had bought that morning.

While the soup was simmering, Grandma made a fire under her large black iron wash pot. She filled it with water from the spigot near the back door. White clothes and linens went into the wash pot, along with soap powder, and were left to boil. Meanwhile, three galvanized tin washtubs, hung by nails on the back wall of the house, were set up on a wooden platform that Grandpa had built under the pecan tree. Grandma used a wooden ax handle to lift the clothes and put them in the first tin tub that had been half-filled with cold water, so it wouldn't burn her hands. She'd use the rub board and P&G soap to rub out any remaining soiled spots. Then she'd wring the soapy water out of the white items and put them in the second tub for their first rinse. The third tub was also a rinsing tub but with "blueing"—a royal blue powder sold in a cylindrical wooden container and used to make the white clothes appear brighter. The colored clothes were washed and rinsed in the same water. The very soiled work clothes were put in the iron washtub with the hot water and rubbed. They were the last clothes rinsed and hung to dry.

Wire clotheslines were strung from the pecan tree to the corner of the garage, and on to a post that sectioned off the cow pen and chicken yard. A pole raised the lines higher after the clothes were fastened on with wooden clothespins. Eventually blouses, skirts, dresses, underpants, sheets, towels, every washable item in the house flapped in the breeze, and soon dried by the hot sun.

As the soup continued to simmer, Grandma added a handful of rice and a handful of elbow macaroni. While she was in the kitchen she made a pot of starch with boiling water and Argo starch. If the starch grew too thick it was thinned with water and cooled. Grandma then dipped the cotton dresses, shirts, and blouses into the starch pot. She would wring them out, and hang all the clothes on the line to dry. This done, Grandma would come back in and make cornbread and a pitcher of iced tea, with lemon and fresh mint to go with the soup for our noonday meal.

During the summers I spent in Selma, Grandma taught me how to hang small items on the line. Skirts were hung at the waistband, shirts and blouses from the bottom of the side seams, handkerchiefs and panties were hung three together to save line space, because they were thin and dried very quickly. I also learned how to fold the clothes carefully, as I took them from the line, so they would have no extra wrinkles. As if that were not enough work for one day, after we ate Grandma would bring in the clean sheets and pillowcases, set up the ironing board in the kitchen, and press the fresh smelling linens.

Once the starched clothes were dry, they were placed in a basket to be ironed on Tuesday. The tubs were emptied and hung back on their nails. Grandma would take a bath, put on clean clothes, and take a nap. It was my job to wash the dishes and clean up the kitchen. I didn't mind because the serial stories came on the radio at two o'clock. I listened to them as I did my chores. Late in the afternoon she would sit on the front porch and drink a RC Cola that she sent me to buy for her at Roy Rhodes's Cafe. Sometimes Grandma treated herself to a nickel package of salted Planters Peanuts that she poured in the bottle of pop. She drank it as it fizzed and foamed.

Roy Rhodes's Cafe was also a "juke joint," located in the dimly lit room next to the eating area. Beer and wine was sold in that room, where people danced to the music coming from the jukebox. I was told not to go to that door and not to even look in there. That piqued my curiosity so I did look in to see people dancing and sitting around small tables drinking. On Saturday nights, the busiest time at Roy Rhodes's Cafe, they sold freshly cooked Bar-B-Que. Sometimes Grandpa would bring us a sandwich when he came back from having his Saturday night beer.

On Tuesday mornings Grandma sprinkled the starched clothes, rolled them up tightly, and then wrapped them in a towel so the moisture could spread evenly throughout the fabric. Her ironing board was a wide wood board, tapered at one end, and padded and wrapped with old sheets. She set the large end of the board on the kitchen counter, and the narrow end on the back of a kitchen chair. I was taught to iron handkerchiefs, dresser scarves, and play clothes. I enjoyed ironing then, as well as now. I discovered that this was a soothing, peaceful activity—a good time for daydreaming.

Grandma would take a quick break from her ironing to stir pots for dinner, or prepare a quick dish. She always finished the ironing before our midday meal. By two o'clock on summer days the heavy work for the day was completed. It was too hot to tackle anything, except easy tasks that could be done sitting near our small black oscillating Emerson fan. This was the time when I sewed, practiced piano, or did embroidery. Grandma shelled peas, butterbeans, or snapped beans for the next day's dinner.

Supper, after five o'clock, when Grandpa came home from work, was whatever one wanted that was leftover in the refrigerator or from dinner. Looking back, Grandma was an early "women's libber." She would serve Grandpa his breakfast and dinner, but for the evening meal he was on his own to find or fix. I took advantage of this to sit in the kitchen and talk with him as he ate. It was our private time together. Friday afternoon was the exception to the get-your-own supper rule. When Grandpa came from work on Friday he would take me with him to the colored-owned Green Street Fish Market to buy deep sea bass steaks that had been brought in from Mobile earlier in the day. He patronized colored stores whenever he could, even though the prices were sometimes higher. His rationale was we should support our own people in their business ventures so they could prosper. After we got back from the fish market, Grandma would fry the deep sea bass fish steaks to a crisp golden brown, and we all had fish sandwiches and lemonade for supper.

Grandma was also ahead of her time in other ways. Although she never worked outside of her home, she had her private stash of money and taught all of the girls in our family to put away some money of their own. She stored it in a quart tin syrup can that she kept in the bottom of the piano. When I was younger I noticed that sometimes she would go in the living room and close the door for a brief period. When she decided that I was old enough, she showed me how she took the bottom panel from the piano to retrieve her can of cash. I felt grownup to be privy to her secret.

Grandma was born in Selma on December 28, 1891. She lived there all of her life. On the day of her funeral, January 26, 1977 as our family gathered at 1214 Lapsley Street, a policeman came on a motorcycle to serve as escort in the funeral procession to First Baptist Church. He led us slowly on Lapsley, across the railroad tracks, past the Buckeye, and continued left to Jeff Davis Avenue. As we approached Broad Street, Selma's main business street, he sped ahead to the intersection, and with his signals and flashing lights, stopped traffic in all directions. At that point I couldn't hold back the tears. They weren't tears because of the sadness of the day, but because of this white policeman's assignment. In Selma, in 1977, the entire police force in Selma was white. It is a custom in Selma and many Southern towns that on the day of the funeral of a citizen, a policeman is assigned to lead the funeral procession. As the profuse tears continued, my thoughts were of earlier days when the same police department never served or protected Grandma while she lived. I wished that somehow she could know she was being honored. This act of dignity would have pleased her.

I returned to Selma in the spring of 1990 to attend Mama's brother, Uncle Frank's funeral. He had been living alone on Lapsley Street since Grandma's death. While I was in Selma this time, I took a brief two-block walk up the street to Selma University, the school that I had attended the year that my sister was born. Mama and her brother Frank had also attended school there.

Sunday morning, the day after his burial, I felt restless and decided to go for a walk. I asked my niece, Angie, to come along with me. I thought I had no particular destination in mind but my subconscious seemed to have known better. We walked across the railroad tracks, past the rusty tanks of the now defunct Buckeye, and past the house where Grandpa's grandmother, my great-great-grandma, Grandma Edna, had lived before I was born. During my childhood this was the location of the colored-owned Anderson's Funeral home. As we continued our walk I noticed that on the corner of Lapsley and Jeff Davis, the homes had been replaced by a large parking lot and a Big Bear grocery store that was black-owned and operated.

We walked along Jeff Davis Avenue, the street in the '40s and '50s that had been the dividing line between the white and colored neighborhoods. We turned right on to Church Street, a street that in my childhood had been an all-white neighborhood of modest frame homes as well as large, white antebellum style homes with three stories, large Doric columns, long front porches, deep spacious parkways, stately old trees, neatly trimmed hedges, and paved streets and sidewalks. This was the route I had used one evening when I was sixteen returning home from a date with Carol Moore, after seeing the movie "Elmer Gantry," at the Wilby Theater. Grandma asked us which way we had come home. When I told her she almost had a panic attack from fear that we could have been harmed by walking in that white neighborhood at night. In later years this neighborhood fell into disrepair as the original owners died. Eventually, a restoration program was instituted and this area has become Selma's Historic District. One of my classmates from my days at Selma University, Martha Lee Williams, now owns a home in this area.

Angie and I continued our walk through magnificent trees, dogwood, redbud, and beds of narcissus, daffodils, tulips, and pansies. We walked by Parrish High School, the white high school where Grandpa parked his car, and then walked two blocks to work at the Post Office.

We continued our walk past the building that had been the Post Office. I paused to remember how Grandpa kept the sidewalks clean, shrubbery neatly trimmed and the lawn cut and edged. When I was a little girl he showed me the inside lobby of marble floors, glass top tables and brass fixtures that he took great pride in keeping highly polished and sparkling.

From the Post Office we walked one more block to Broad Street. At that point we were a block from Water Street, the last street before the Edmund Pettus Bridge. We wandered into Twice Loved Treasures, a resale and antique store, at the corner of Broad Street and Water Avenue, the same intersection of "Bloody Sunday." As I browsed through the jewelry section I spotted an Australian crystal and gold tennis bracelet that I bought for myself. I asked Angie to select a bracelet as a gift from me.

I still felt unsatisfied and our walk was incomplete. We were at the foot of the bridge. On a whim I said to Angie, "Please walk across the bridge with me." It didn't seem to matter that I had crossed the bridge by car all of my life. Today I wanted to walk across the bridge, something I had never done before.

As we walked on the sidewalk, I paused midway. I stared at the muddy water, the dry russet banks of the Alabama River. I took deep breaths as the tears welled up in my breast but never came to the surface. Angie sensed my mood and kept silent. After we crossed the bridge, we went to the opposite sidewalk and started a brisk pace back to Lapsley Street. I was physically exhausted and emotionally drained by the time we were home again. After a brief lunch it was time for Cousin Mabel to take me to the Montgomery airport for a return trip to Chicago.

During the flight I reflected on the events of the past three days in Selma. I felt that this trip brought some completion to an era in my life. In 1990, I remembered "Bloody Sunday." I had stood in my living room in Chicago in 1965, screamed in horror, and doubled over with sharp stomach spasms, as I watched on TV, the cruelty of the jeering crowds of people with Confederate flags—white men who had the approval of Sheriff Jim Clark and State Troopers—using tear gas, galloping horses, and nightsticks, to beat the assembled marchers. As horrible and as painful as the scene was, with bloody, wounded people lying in the streets like on a battlefield, I couldn't turn away and not watch. I was horrified, but not surprised, that this hateful, bloody scene—this kind of violence, could erupt in Selma. All of my life I had lived in fear of white people in Selma, especially policemen, being careful to avoid unnecessary contact or conversation and to not do anything wrong, according to the Jim Crow laws enforced there.

A year after I felt the eerie compulsion to walk across the bridge, one of my cousins who still lives in Selma told me about our family's participation in the march. I had not known of their involvement in the march so I never had the opportunity to thank them.

· MR. TOM'S FAMILY ·

I RETURNED TO Fitzgerald for a brief visit on Mother's Day, 1998. As I made plans for the trip I decided this time I must go inside the house—the Tom Parks's house. For more than forty years, whenever I returned home, I would wave and say hello to Mr. and Mrs. Rodwell, the new residents, as I stood in Mama's yard. Occasionally I crossed the street and had brief conversations with them on their walkway or front porch, but I always avoided going inside. This time I called Mrs. Rodwell on Sunday afternoon and asked her for permission to visit on Monday morning; she suggested nine-thirty. Sunday night I slept fitfully, tossing and turning, in dread of the next day's visit.

By nine o'clock I was dressed, had eaten breakfast and braced myself for my secret mission. As I crossed the now paved street, I recalled jumping the ditch and running barefooted across the hot dirt street of my childhood. The half-circle, concrete steps were still there. The side wrap-around and second floor porches of my youth had been torn down, as had the magnolia and oak trees. The house was still surrounded by nine large pecan trees. As I glanced to my left, toward the corner, I remembered the shallow, sandy ditch where I'd spent many happy hours in my personal sand pile. I brought water from our back yard spigot in my syrup bucket to make frog houses by molding damp sand around my foot, then gently pulling it out, leaving a tiny igloo-shaped mound. I smoothed out the surrounding sand to create the yard. I formed a low fence by banking the sand with my hands. I planted lantana, buttercup, and verbena blossoms that I picked from our yard and poked them into the sand of the frog's yard. Some days I took jar tops of different sizes to my sand pile and made pies and cakes. This sandy spot had been my private haven.

After greeting the Rodwells on their front porch, I asked Mrs. Rodwell to please walk with me through each room of her house so I could see the changes made since I was last in there. She said, "Sure. Come right in." As I entered the house, memories of earlier years flooded my mind in contrast to the sights before my eyes. The small fireplace and mantle piece with the large Seth Thomas clock in the living room was gone. The living room has been enlarged, using part of the space that had been a large bedroom.

A sleek touch-tone phone had replaced the black rotary phone at the front door that had served the entire neighborhood. The front door had never been locked so that anyone could use the phone located near the door whenever there was a need. Mr. Tom Parks, the owner of the house, was a fireman on the Atlantic Coast Line Railroad during the days when trains were pulled by steam engines. A phone was a necessary part of Mr. Tom's job because he needed to be available on short notice to go out on a run. Accurate time was also important to his job so the dependable clock on the mantle was essential. He also wore a long gold chain attached to a large pocket watch that he kept in his blue, denim overalls.

Whenever there was a disturbance or a neighbor needed to call the police, someone came to the Parks's house and called loudly, "Beedy, call de law!" Tom's wife would call Sheriff Grinner, the town's only policeman, who was a tall, thin, white man. After a while Miz Beedy stopped "calling de law" or allowing neighbors to use their phone to call the police. She had become a businesswoman and didn't want the police anywhere near her. She was selling bootleg whiskey that we called "white lightening" that she kept in the chifforobe in the large bedroom.

The narrow bedroom to the right of the living room in earlier years had been dimly lit with a single bulb hanging from the ceiling cord. I told Mrs. Rodwell that this was Mr. Tom's daughter's room. We called her "Sister." She came back to Fitzgerald from "up North" when she was thirteen years old, with her newborn son. "Rip," as we called him.

Mrs. Rodwell and I then walked straight ahead to the kitchen and dining area. The kitchen of my childhood had a wooden floor, a black iron wood burning stove, a small narrow sink, table and single storage cabinet. Mrs. Rodwell's kitchen was sleek and modern. The large room that had led to the back yard was Mrs. Rodwell's dining room. When the Parks family lived here, this room had bare wooden floors, one large round pedestal table, high-back wooden chairs, and a mahogany buffet. In my childhood, the bathroom, with a footed bathtub, small face-bowl and toilet seat, was next to this room. A modern bathroom was the only room addition to the house.

As we continued to talk, Mrs. Rodwell and I went to the back door and walked outside. As we stood in the yard, I pointed to the area where the rows of pomegranate trees, plum trees, and scuppernong arbor had been. I told her that Miz Beedy let me help her sweep her yard with her brush broom, made from long branches taken from the hedges on the back alley. The thick parts of the branches were tied together to make a handle, with the leafy parts becoming the broom. When I was a little girl, I enjoyed using the broom to make swirls in the sand.

When Mrs. Rodwell and I came back into the house, she listened patiently as I described Miz Beedy and our relationship. I told her that Miz Beedy was a tall medium brown-skinned woman, with a raucous voice. She was coarse and rude to many people, but she was kind and generous to me. She said she liked me because I always acted like a "little lady." When she cooked things that she knew I liked, she called me from across the street to come and eat. She made round hoecake corn bread in a black iron skillet on top of the stove. A broken off piece with a large part of the crusty edge on it was my special treat.

Miz Beedy's teen-age daughter, Marion, who was Mr. Tom's stepdaughter, also lived in this house. She had a small bedroom upstairs. Every time Marion went out alone, with girlfriends or boyfriends Miz Beedy always said, "Keep your dress down and your drawers up." I was puzzled by that until the eleventh grade when my classmate and friend, Betty Ruth, had a baby boy. Only then did I realize Miz Beedy was giving advice on a form of birth control. Marion must have followed her mother's admonitions because she didn't get pregnant.

One of Mr. Tom's compensations for working on the railroad was a free pass for his family to ride in the colored coaches on the Atlantic Coast Line Railroad. I was seven years old when Miz Beedy took me to Atlanta for the first time. We went to see Theron, Mr. Tom's son, who was in Grady Hospital. It was an exciting day for me. We left on the noon train and Miz Beedy let me sit by the window. I pressed my nose against the glass and watched large groves of tall pine trees and fields of corn and cotton go by. As we traveled north I noticed that the hills were red clay and white clay. Miz Beedy told me that she liked to eat white clay. Mr. Tom brought it to her from the mountains of north Georgia. She gave me some once. I ate it but didn't like it. I told Mama I had eaten the clay and she told me that I shouldn't eat clay again.

Mama told me that we would pass through Warm Springs, the summer home of President Roosevelt. As we reached farther north in the mountains of Georgia, near Manchester, there was a sudden lurch and jerking. The train had derailed. Our coach tilted to the side and was caught in this mountainous passage. I bumped my head on the seat in front of me and bruised my leg on the footrest. We sat in this dark hot coach for what seemed to me hours before the rescue workers came in with large flashlights and led us out in single file through a narrow aisle. We walked a long distance before we were directed to get on another train. By the time we got to Warm Springs it was too dark to see the town from my seat in the railroad car. Nevertheless I was still filled with excitement about my trip.

We finally arrived in Atlanta late that night and got a taxi to the house where we were to spend the night. It was very dark because the house on this dimly lit street had no porch light. When we got out of the taxi, I noticed a strong, sweet, pungent aroma in the hot summer air. As we walked through the dark yard, I stepped into something soft and squishy that made the aroma stronger. I had stepped on soft, orange-red, ripe persimmons. When I got on the porch Miz Beedy helped me take off my shoes and clean up the mess. I'm told that ripe persimmons are delicious. I've never wanted to taste one after that unpleasant experience.

The next morning we went to visit Theron at Grady Hospital, the colored hospital in Atlanta. I don't remember the return trip home. It must have been uneventful.

The next time I went to Atlanta, Mama went with Miz Beedy and me. This time we were going to Theron's funeral. He had died of tuberculosis. His wife and children lived in a two-story, brick house, connected by a common wall to other houses. I had never seen this type of housing before and learned later it was called "the projects." Years later when I went to Spelman College I saw similar buildings near the campus and wondered if this was the neighborhood where Theron had lived.

Mr. Tom and Miz Beedy divorced before I was in eighth grade. Miz Beedy and Marion moved away and I never saw them again. As we continued talking, Mrs. Rodwell asked, "Did Mr. Tom ever marry again?"

I said, "Yes. Before I finished high school Mr. Tom married Miss Annie Mae, who lived in Perry, Georgia, about fifty miles from Fitzgerald. She had a daughter named Ruth, who was about four years younger than me. When they moved to Fitzgerald, Ruth lived upstairs in the narrow bedroom that had been Marion's room."

In both appearances and mannerisms, Miss Annie Mae was quite different from Miz Beedy. Miss Annie Mae was soft-spoken and honey-colored, with long soft hair. Mr. Tom boasted of her "fine qualities" and her "sweetness." She worked as a domestic for white families. As part of her work, she went with her white families on vacations to St. Simon Island and Jekyll Island resort areas on the coast of Georgia. Miss Annie Mae lived in the maids' housing on these islands while she did baby sitting, laundry, and other work for her employer. When she came home from these vacations she described the beautiful beaches and parks where she had worked. I didn't know there were such places in Georgia until she told me about these islands. She provided me with more daydreams for "when I grow up I want to be, go, and see." Times and laws have changed. Now I can visit the coastal resort areas of Georgia as a tourist, but I have not gone yet. Mama and some of her friends have been on vacation on Jekyll Island. I have a picture of Mama in a bathing suit, smiling, barefooted, on the beach at Jekyll Island. It is still on my list of places I want to see.

When I finished telling Mrs. Rodwell about Miss Annie Mae, she said, "Tell me about the other people who lived in this house. I heard there was an old sick lady who used to live here." I was glad that Mrs. Rodwell asked me to tell her about the old sick lady. One of the reasons I had never wanted to go in this house again was I didn't want to face the memories of the times I spent taking care of Miss Lula. Today I was relieved when Mrs. Rodwell gave me the opportunity to relive those memories in the presence of her warm support.

I breathed a sigh of relief. "Yes, that was Miss Lula, Mr. Tom's sister. She lived in the large room on the first floor, the room that you redesigned to make a part of your living room." I could still see in my mind's eye the room with the three double beds, a chifforobe, and a large coal-burning fireplace. Mr. Tom's sons, "Buddy" and Cleveland, and his grandson, Rip, also slept in that room. Miss Lula's bed was by the double windows facing the street. Our back yard was across the street facing their front porch.

At Mrs. Rodwell's encouragement I continued my story.

When I was a little girl, Mama told me that Miss Lula, Mr. Tom's sister, came to live here when his first wife, his children's mother, died. My first memory of Miss Lula was when I was four years old. I remember Miss Lula saying as she held Sister's baby, "What a fine baby boy! She done 'rat well by herself."

By the time I was eight years old Mr. Tom and Miz Beedy were married. I don't remember when Sister went back "up North," leaving Rip with Mr. Tom, Miz Beedy, Miss Lula, and his two uncles, Cleveland and Buddy. Mr. Tom and Miz Beedy divorced when I was about eleven years old. After Miz Beedy left there were no more regular mealtimes. Rip ate with our family whenever he wanted to.

Miss Lula was tall, heavy, pecan-colored, with snowy white hair. When she walked, her high, soft, fleshy hips jiggled under her long, cotton dress that was gathered at the waist. She dipped snuff and often had a snuff mop, a small twig from the oak tree, in her mouth, which she asked me to break from the oak tree and bring to her. She used a small coffee can as her spit cup, which she kept on the floor at her side.

Miss Lula had her first stroke when I was about eight years old. She continued to have strokes, each one leaving her a bit more disabled. At the time Sister left, Miss Lula's left arm was paralyzed. She dragged one leg and used a cane when she walked.

By the time I was twelve years old Miss Lula was completely bed-ridden. During the times I was not in school, she called me whenever she needed water, food, or wanted to use the slop jar. If I was in the front part of our house and didn't hear her call me, Mama would say, "Erin, Lula's calling you," or "Erin, go see what Lula wants." I went running barefooted across the dirt street to help her. When she wanted water I propped her head higher on the pillow to help her sip water from the glass with the curved glass straw. On days when the still, fetid air hung heavy in the room, I put cold water in a shallow wash pan and wiped her arms, puffy, scaly feet and legs with a washrag.

Some days when she called, I helped her use the slop jar. Although I weighed less than ninety pounds, I pulled her legs off the bed, angled them toward the floor, and held her paralyzed arm as she pushed the mattress with her stronger arm until she was in a sitting position. After she was sitting on the side of the bed, I pulled on her paralyzed side causing her to rock back and forth. We gained enough momentum until she was able to achieve a standing position. I then pulled her paralyzed leg out far enough to put the slop jar between her legs so she could urinate. When I took the top off the slop jar the strong smell of urine hit me in a pungent wave. When she finished, I put the top back on and moved it away. I then reversed the process of getting her back into the bed. I sat her down first, put her head back on the pillow, picked up her legs and put them back on the bed. I was off duty until the next time she called.

When Mama cooked dinner, she fixed Miss Lula's plate and sent me to feed her. I wiped her hands and face with a small damp towel before she ate. Sometimes I helped her sit on the side of the bed to eat. When she didn't feel as strong, I propped her up in bed and fed her. When she finished eating I wiped her hands and mouth again, took the plate and spoon and ran home until she called again.

I also wanted to go upstairs on this visit. When I was a little girl I enjoyed standing on the second floor porch looking from and getting a different view of our house and yard. As we began walking upstairs to Mr. Tom's and Miz Beedy's bedroom and Marion's small bedroom, I was quiet while reflecting on my reasons for not wanting to come inside this house for nearly fifty years. I was sixteen years old when I had left home in September of 1951 to attend Spelman College in Atlanta. Mr. Tom died during my freshman year. Miss Lula was sent to the state hospital at Milledgeville. I never saw her again. She died while I was in college. After Mr. Tom's death Miss Annie Mae and Ruth moved to the other side of town.

Cleveland and Buddy, her nephews, were not dependable caregivers. Cleveland was more helpful and would empty the slop jar when he came home. Occasionally Cleveland or Buddy scrubbed the wooden floor in the large bedroom. They used Lysol disinfectant in the water. When they emptied the slop jar, they always left water and a little Lysol in it. Even though Lysol doesn't smell as strong as it did in earlier years, I never buy it. The sight of the container or a whiff of it makes me hold back a gag.

During those years that I took care of Miss Lula I never gagged, told anyone, or complained about that room. My conversation with Mrs. Rodwell on this day was the first time I had ever talked about these experiences in such detail. When I finished, I paused, took a deep breath and asked Mrs. Rodwell to lie down on the side of her bed and allow me to demonstrate how I helped Miss Lula sit and stand up. She didn't hesitate. By the time I finished the demonstration of taking Miss Lula's feet off the bed, pulling and rocking until she was standing, I was in tears. Mrs. Rodwell hugged me and said that my job as caregiver for Miss Lula must have been my mission, and God gave me the strength to help this large, heavy, paralyzed woman.

Mrs. Rodwell said she had often wondered why I never came inside her house. After our time together on this visit she understood why I never came inside before. She also said that my story explained the stench of stale urine that permeated the entire house when she first moved to it. The only way she was able to get rid of the stench was by covering all of the walls with fiberboard and painting them. She had all of the floors covered with tile, and had some of the rooms carpeted.

The tears continued to flow as Mrs. Rodwell and I walked out of the front door. She gave me a big warm hug, or as southerners say, "she hugged my neck," and told me what a strong, good, little girl I had been. She also said that I had been "God's gift to Miss Lula." When my tears stopped flowing, I thanked Mrs. Rodwell for allowing me to walk through this house again and for listening to my story, my secret I had never shared. When I regained my composure I crossed the street and joined my family for lunch before the three-hour drive back to the Atlanta airport for my return to Chicago.

My sister was the driver on our return trip so I had the opportunity to reflect on my visit to the house across the street. I had accomplished my secret mission. I had finally faced the memories of taking care of Miss Lula that I had kept locked in the deepest recesses of my mind. After about an hour of driving we stopped for gas and snacks. At that point I was able to change my train of thought and began to look forward to my return to Chicago.

· LIFE IN A GOLDFISH BOWL ·

KEEPING DOORS CLOSED was important to Daddy. In summer the front and back screen doors needed to be kept closed to keep out gnats, flies, and mosquitoes. In winter our house was heated by a wood-burning stove in the kitchen and coal burning heaters or fireplaces in the bedrooms and living room. Most of the time the only rooms that were heated were the kitchen and Mama's and Daddy's bedroom, so closed doors were important to help keep the heat in.

He said, "Close the door."

"You weren't born in a barn."

"Don't slam that door! Open it. Close it again. Open it. Close it again. Now, isn't that better?"

There were many times when the rules were not as clearly defined as they were with the rules of the closed doors.

She said, "You should know better than that!"

"I told you about that one time!"

"Go to the store."

"What took you so long?"

He said, "Tie your shoes."

"Put your shoulders back."

"Stand tall. Walk straight."

She said, "Take off your school clothes."

"Hurry up."

"Wash the dishes."

"Practice your music lessons."

"Get your homework."

They said, "Be back before the street lights come on."

I said, "How come I can't? The other children can do it (buy it, wear it, go there)."

They said, "But you're our little girl and we do and tell you what we think is best for you."

When all else failed, and I whined and asked "Why?" too many times, she said, "Because I said so, and I'm the Mama."

She said, "Go to bed, it's eight o'clock." I said, "But I'm not sleepy." She said, "Just turn off the light. You don't have to go to sleep."

They said, "Do unto others as you would have them do unto you."

This was also posted around the schoolroom walls or written on the blackboards.

For sixteen years I lived in what I felt was a "fish-bowl existence," with every move I made under the ever-watchful eyes and supervision of my parents and adults in our community. These rules were reinforced in Sunday School. I had to memorize the Bible verse, "Honor thy father and mother, so that thy days may be longer upon the land which the Lord Thy God giveth thee." If that wasn't enough to keep me obedient, every adult in our community, family, friend, teacher or neighbor felt they had the right and obligation to scold me and report to my parents any breach of these rules. This was something like double jeopardy. When I did break a rule and got caught, the worst part of it was to have to listen to Daddy's long slow questioning and lectures.

He said," Why did you do it? Didn't you know better? Can you think of a better way it could have been done? I hope you won't do that again. Use your brain!"

When he finished I wished he had just whacked me, beaten me, or given some other punishment, rather than all of that talk. I smile now as I recall those days. As a teacher I used Daddy's method with my students and it was effective. My students squirmed, just as I had. They were bolder than I though, and said, "Why don't you just go on and punish me rather than all of that yang, yang." I only smiled and said, "Oh, no! That would be too easy. I want you to think about what you did and change your behavior next time." I think that was what Daddy was trying to teach me.

Mama's justice was swift and to the point. She gave me a whack on the bottom or a switch on my legs and a loud, fast, high- pitched, all in one breath scolding that sounded like:

"ITOLDYOUNOTTODOTHAT,YOUKNOWBETTER,WHYDIDYOUDOIT?"

The most memorable punishment for an infraction of rules was neither the long slow conversations with Daddy or Mama's swift justice. Every Sunday morning Mama gave me a nickel to put in the offering plate at Sunday School. One Sunday I decided to keep it for myself. By the time I got home she knew that I hadn't put the nickel in the offering plate. I never knew how she found out. We didn't have a telephone. She didn't scold or spank me that day. Instead of going to visit my friends on Sunday afternoons, an important part of my routine, I had to go back to church for the afternoon program, stand up and say that I hadn't given my offering that morning, walk up and give it to the adult in charge. I had never felt so humiliated in all my life. Mama didn't take me or go to church that afternoon but she knew that I had carried out her orders.

In September 1951, three months after my sixteenth birthday, I entered Spelman College in Atlanta, Georgia. There were new rules to learn and follow. These were explained to us during Freshman Orientation Week. After sixteen years of strict rules and close supervision, college rules were liberating. The freedom I felt was like swimming in a large pond rather than a small gold fish bowl.

My housemother said, "You may use the public phones in Rockefeller Hall until seven o'clock in the evening."

I said to myself, "I don't need to use the phone. Mama told me when I left home that I was not to call home except in an extreme emergency. There was no money for unnecessary bills. She promised to write me every week and told me I must write every week. My ten dollar allowance was in the mail the first week of every month and I had to make it last until the next month."

My housemother said, "You will have a "duty work" assignment of a small housekeeping chore, dusting, sweeping or cleaning a part of the bathrooms. These duties will rotate and will only take about ten minutes each day. They must be done by ten o'clock each morning. I will check daily. Three misses or sloppy work and you'll get a note of reprimand."

Some dorm-mates said," I don't see why we have to help clean the dorm. They should hire someone to do that."

I said to myself, "Gee, is that all I have to do! No more bringing in stove wood or coal, washing dishes, getting vegetables from outside or going to the store for something Mama needed for dinner."

My housemother said, "You may have gentlemen callers from Morehouse on Tuesdays and Fridays from four-thirty until five-thirty and on Sundays from four o'clock until five-thirty. You may sit in the dormitory lounge or visit on campus. They must leave promptly at five-thirty, when the bell on Packard Hall rings.

I said, "Boys visiting three times a week, that's great! I never had a date at home. The only time I had a chance to talk to boys was at lunch time at school and the walk home from school."

My housemother said, "Breakfast will be served between six -forty-five and seven- fifteen, lunch from twelve to twelve-thirty, and dinner from six to six-thirty. You must be properly dressed for meals. No hair rollers, hats, scarves, or pants are allowed. You must wear socks or hose, no bare legs allowed."

I said to myself, "Good! I don't have to help cook, or wash dishes. All I have to do is walk through the cafeteria line, get my food, eat and put my tray back."

My housemother said, "Lights out at ten o'clock. The bell on Packard Hall will ring to remind you."

Some classmates said, "That rule is absolutely ridiculous! Do they think we're babies? I was busy all day. I need to stay up late to study."

I said to myself, "I get a chance to stay up until ten p.m. No more lights out at eight o'clock and putting my radio or flashlight under the covers or pretending to be asleep."

The housemother said, "When you leave the campus to go to the Atlanta University Library, West End Shopping Center, or downtown on Saturdays, you must sign out in the dormitory, stating where you're going and with whom you're going. Any other trips away from campus require parental consent."

Some dorm mates said, "This place is like a prison. They're crazy if they think I'm going to be locked up and locked into all of these rules."

I said, "Now I'm able to go out at times other than Saturday or Sunday afternoons. That's Freedom!"

Looking back and thinking of rules, what was prison and restrictions for some of my classmates at Spelman was total joy and freedom for me, after having grown up with my parents in the small southern town of Fitzgerald, Georgia between 1940 and 1951. Enough time has passed for me to be able to rethink feelings of a "gold-fish existence." I feel now that I, as well as the other children of our community, were not like goldfish, but more like precious gold metal, to be refined, molded, polished, protected, and treasured.

Even now, almost a half century since I was a child growing up in

Fitzgerald, when I do something wrong, I hear Mama, Mrs. Dorothy Gibson, Rev. and Mrs. Pettigrew, in Daddy's style saying:

"Why did you do that?"

"You know better."

"No matter how old you are, you're still our little girl."

· SPECIAL FEELINGS OF LOVE ·

GIFTS OF CANDY have always had the capability of making me feel special and loved. The first person that I remember giving me candy was Mr. Lewis Bell. Beginning when I was six years old, every Sunday morning after Sunday School he waited on his front porch, with a tiny bag of assorted, unwrapped, hard candies to give to me. He always said that he was happy that I had gone to Sunday School. He also asked me about school, questions like, "What are you studying, and are you doing good work?" He gave me this bag of candy along with words of encouragement. He told me that the candy was just for me and I didn't have to share it. When he passed my house during the week he reminded me to come by to get my candy after Sunday School. How could I forget this special treat! I kept my special stash in my top dresser drawer and ate only one or two pieces a day so that it would last all week. Mr. Bell continued to have candy for me each week until I finished third grade. At the end of that school term I went to Selma to spend the summer and the following school year in Selma, Alabama with my grandparents.

For as long as I can remember, I always spent summer vacations with my grandparents. Whenever Grandma went downtown she bought assorted unwrapped hard candies from Woolworth's. She gave me a few pieces and hid the rest of it. It took me several summers to find the clear glass, gallon candy jar that she kept in the bottom of the dining room buffet. It was pushed to the back and covered with a dishtowel. After I found the hiding place I would take a few pieces out when she was in the back yard or on the front porch. I was careful not to take so much that she would miss it. By Christmas the jar was full. Then she brought it out of its hiding place and all who came by could have as much as they wanted. Looking back I realize that the candy in my Christmas stocking also came from this jar, and not from Santa Claus. Grandma made it seem to be special candy. It didn't taste nearly as good to me as the pieces I had taken during the summer. I ate only a few pieces of it during the holidays. There were so many other Christmas treats. The candy was no longer important. Mama made a gallon jar of ambrosia with fresh oranges, fruit cocktail and coconut. We had homemade coconut layer cake, caramel cake with pecans, as well as my favorite, yellow cake with crushed pineapple between the layers and covered with white, seven-minute frosting.

Grandma gave me my first box of grown-up candy. It was a half-pound box of assorted, pastel colored, crunchy, sugary candy in the shape of small flowers. She brought it to me on one of her summer visits. I was eleven years old that summer. I remember it so well because it was a bittersweet memory. At the time she came I was away at Cordele, Georgia attending a summer retreat for a week of Bible study at Holsey Institute, sponsored by the Colored Methodist Episcopal Church. During the winter months Holsey was a boarding school serving students who had completed grade school in their respective farming communities, where no pubic high school was provided. When Grandma and Grandpa came Mama called the director and asked him to send me home on the train for an overnight visit. Cordele was forty miles away. As happy as I was to see Grandma and Grandpa and the candy, I was upset because I missed the cookout and picnic that had taken place at Holsey the afternoon I was away. I spent the afternoon and night at home and returned to Holsey the next day. Rev. Lucious Pitts, the principal, was my idol. He was a singer and an outstanding storyteller. Each night he led the story-hour and a sing-along. That was such a wonderful way to end the day. The games, stories, and singing that Rev. Pitts planned for us made it a memorable summer. My week at Holsey was also my first time away from home in a dormitory type setting. I enjoyed being with girls my age who came from other towns in South Georgia. My friend, Yvonne Dukes, from Fitzgerald, was one of three roommates. Having roommates and sleeping on a bunk bed were exciting new experiences for me. I would have preferred staying at Holsey instead of the trip home and the gift of candy from Grandma.

I didn't take the box of candy back to Holsey. Instead, I put it in the top drawer of my chest and nibbled off of it for months.

The next memorable candy episode concerned a one pound box of Whitman's Sampler that I won in a raffle. The day of the raffle I had to leave school at noon to keep a dental appointment with Dr. Tuggle. When I returned to school I was told that I had won the candy. It was the first time that I had ever won anything in a raffle. I opened it when I got home and shared some of it with my family. After that it went to my usual candy-hiding place, for me to savor in private for a long time. I liked the map printed on the inside top of the candy box showing the variety of candy in the box. There was special delight deciding which piece to choose. I especially liked the chocolate covered nuts and ate them first. The cherry creams were my least favorite pieces so they were the last to be eaten.

Each Valentine's Day while I was in college, Daddy's brother, Uncle Frank, who lived in Albany, Georgia, sent me a one pound box of chocolates in a red heart-shaped box. A friend, Eugene Vassar, a nephew of Grandma's neighbor, also sent a velvety Valentine's box of candy. These gifts always made me feel special and loved.

When I was grown and a working mother, I took part of the school holiday for myself. I would hire a baby-sitter and when she arrived, I went downtown for a few hours, wandering through the stores, doing more looking than buying. Before taking the train home I always bought a few pieces of candy from Field's or Fannie May, as a treat for myself. I have kept that tradition alive. When I go downtown now, I drive instead of taking the train. I don't spend much time in the stores. I go for specific items, purchase them, and return home, but I still buy Fannie May candy. I don't feel the need to hide or hoard the candy anymore. I enjoy eating it, sharing it with the cashier at the parking lot, and friends and family. Still, even now, no candy that I buy for myself makes me as happy as the candy from Mr. Bell, Grandma's candy jar, or the gift from Uncle Frank and Eugene Vassar. I still get a warm glow when I remember these kind, loving people and the feeling of being loved and special that they gave me.

· HELEN ·

EVERY SUMMER WHEN school was out in Fitzgerald, Georgia, Mama took my brother and me to spend two months with her parents in Selma, Alabama. After a few days she'd leave us there and return home for a much-needed rest. She had spent the school term teaching second grade, taking care of two children, cooking and sewing in addition to helping Daddy with his monthly reports at school.

The summer that I turned twelve, new neighbors moved to Lapsley Street, two doors from my grandparents. Mr. Warner Reid, Mrs. Helen Reid their daughter Paulette, and her baby brother, Warner Jr. were welcome additions to the Lapsley Street family. They were no strangers to the old-timers on the block. Mr. Reid's uncle and aunt, Houston and Essie Reid lived directly across the street from the newcomers. My grandparents had known Mr. Reid's mother for many years.

I was excited about playing with the new children on the block, even though Paulette was three years old and the baby, whom we called "Brother," was six months old. I had no playmates near my house in Fitzgerald. It didn't take long for me to feel comfortable enough to trust Mrs. Reid with personal and intimate concerns that I had as a young adolescent. Mr. Reid spent long hours as owner of a drugstore on Broad Street. He came home for dinner mid-afternoon, then went back to work and didn't come home again until the drugstore closed at ten o'clock. I began to spend about two hours with Mrs. Reid each afternoon after he returned to work.

I was fascinated by all of the things that Mrs. Reid knew how to do. She painted walls, refinished and upholstered furniture, created murals and sand-cast plaques. She even built a goldfish pond in her back yard. She was a creative and artistic person who saw possibilities in "junk" and turned it into something beautiful. Once she found a forked branch, removed the bark, polished it, shellacked the wood and created a piece of sculpture for her living room table. She collected interesting rocks and embedded them in wet concrete that became a tabletop for her patio. Even though she enjoyed these "unladylike" activities, she had a gentle feminine air. She was about five feet, five inches tall and never weighed over one hundred thirty-pounds. She cut and styled her own straight, light brown hair, which framed her "peaches and cream" complexion. When she got dressed up she wore eye make-up to enhance her expressive brown eyes. Because of her fair completion, hair texture and facial features she was often mistaken for a white lady when she went places where she wasn't known. Although I admired her physical beauty I admired her integrity even more. She could have passed for white, but she was proud of her heritage and would say with dignity that she was "colored" if anyone mistook her heritage.

I had taken my first course in sewing by the time I returned to Selma the second summer after I met Mrs. Reid. She readily accepted my teaching her what I had learned from Mama and my eighth grade sewing teacher. We spent our visits together working on dressmaking projects. Mrs. Reid soon learned all I could teach her. She eventually taught herself tailoring, making her suits and coats and even learned to make fine silk lingerie. This was certainly an example of the student surpassing the teacher.

Mr. Reid became ill during the 1970s and had to close the drugstore, causing them financial hardship. Mrs. Reid's creative genius and survival skills became even more apparent. She started designing and making "teddy bears" from remnants she purchased at the Mill Ends Store. She sold them on consignment in one of the exclusive gift shops in downtown Selma. Each bear had different facial features and hair, created with appliquéd fabrics, yarn, buttons, and embroidery floss. She designed clothes for them so that each bear could have several outfits with matching hats. The bears came in different sizes and colors and were often grouped as a family. She also taught herself French hand-sewing and made exquisite dresses for little girls. Her clients were among the wealthiest people in Selma.

During all of these years she continued to be a loving and nurturing mother. Paulette and Brother finished high school and went away to college. After college Paulette returned to Selma for her wedding. Paulette's wedding dress was another exquisite example of her mother's creativity and skill. The dress was made of ivory peau de soie with a fitted bodice, long sleeves, and a low-cut round neckline. The long full skirt was constructed of individually cut rose-shaped petals. She sculpted each petal by using a pencil and Elmer's glue thinned with water. When the petals were dry she arranged them in overlapping circular rows that were sewn on a lighter weight silk lining. The wedding ceremony was held at the Reformed Presbyterian Church, a mission established for colored people in Selma by Northern whites just after the Civil War. The wedding guests were invited to the Reid's home for a reception immediately after the wedding. I didn't attend the wedding because Mrs. Reid asked me to stay at her house to do the last minute preparations for the reception. I considered her request an honor and privilege and I worked during the reception serving, replenishing trays, and keeping things neat. After all of the guests had gone home, I stayed on with the family laughing, talking and drinking champagne late into the night.

Mrs. Reid had never attended college, but when Federal Government Programs were started in Selma during the 1960s, her skills were so outstanding that she was hired as a sewing teacher. Easily proving herself a capable and dependable person, she was quickly promoted to positions with more responsibilities. She eventually became a director of the Dallas County Community Action Program traveling to neighboring communities to teach and supervise sewing classes. Cooperative sewing centers were formed where quilts, maternity clothes, lingerie were made. Vanity Fair Lingerie was one of the buyers. Army fatigues were also made under government contract. Mrs. Reid supervised the quality of work insuring it was always superior. The training and work at these sewing centers provided income for women in the area enabling them to discontinue receiving welfare assistance. She was also instrumental in helping three black women open a business called the "Baby Boutique" on Water Street near the Edmund Pettus Bridge. This shop sold hand-made gowns and dresses for infants and children. The inventory included baby bed bumpers, pillows, sheets, quilts and accessories using pastel gingham. Mrs. Reid made exquisite dresses for little girls and then taught one of the partners in the venture how to make these dresses to be sold in the boutique. Many wealthy white people from

Helen Reid with Chanelle, daughter of Warner Reid, Jr. (Brother),
and one of Helen's teddy bear creations, 1980.

Selma and surrounding areas were their customers.

In the 1980s when Mr. Reid became seriously ill, Mrs. Reid took over the management of the rental properties that he had inherited from his mother. She proved herself capable as a manager as well and assured financial security for the family. In the mid-80s when Brown's Chicken Franchise expressed an interest in leasing some of their property on Broad Street, she worked along with Mr. Reid, their lawyers and representatives from Brown's Chicken for an amicable lease. In 1987, after her experiences in managing property, I accepted a challenge of restoring and managing some rental property. I had learned from Mrs. Reid that "ladies can do it."

Although I only saw her at Christmas and summer vacations, we continued to share our secrets and dreams. Whatever stage I was in, she always had a kind, understanding ear. It was a relationship of mutual trust, respect, and honesty.

Even though her formal schooling ended after high school, Helen read a lot and had a wealth of knowledge, with an especially strong interest in philosophy. Mr. Earl Patterson, her next-door neighbor, was a handsome pecan-colored man with soft, snow-white hair. He was an eloquent speaker and had a vast home library. He had grown up in Selma and gone away to college at Harvard graduating in the same class as Franklin Delano Roosevelt II. After graduation he returned to Selma to run a grocery store that he inherited from his parents. He was happy to share his college experiences with Helen as well as his extensive library, and they both enjoyed many intellectually stimulating evening discussions.

I don't remember when Mrs. Reid became "Helen" to me. We did not see each other for several months but whenever we were back together it was as though we had never been apart. She was a strong, positive role model for me, with her flair for stylish dressing; beautifully decorated home, love of antiques, her survival with grace, and her life-long quest for knowledge.

I was grown and had a daughter before I found out that Helen was only thirteen years older than me. It was startling to realize that she'd been twenty-five when we first met. When I became an adult, my visits to Selma were always occasions of a reunion, when Grandma's house was crowded with other visiting family members. At Helen's invitation, I always spent the night at her house. I slept in the guest bedroom with the four-poster mahogany bed, large soft pillows, antique lamps, and ruffled, sheer, white Priscilla curtains. We sat up half the night talking. After my bath the next morning, using her fragrant bath additives and lotion, we had conversation and coffee before I went back to Grandma's for breakfast.

It was "déjà vu" when I got married and moved to Rhodes Avenue in Chicago. One afternoon a teen-age girl from two doors down the street came to visit me. I welcomed her with open arms. We had such a good visit that I asked her to come often. With the frequent visits and sharing, we became friends. She asked many questions as she watched me cook, sew, and do other household chores. Her mother was not living in the house with her so she turned to me for emotional support as well. I smiled whenever she visited because I remembered my visits with Helen. My relationship has continued with this young lady through her college, marriage and child-rearing years. When she got married, I planned, prepared, and served at her reception. She became a principal at an elementary school in Chicago. On one of my visits to her school she introduced me to some of the staff as her "big sister-mama-aunt-mentor-friend." She told them how our relationship had evolved from our early years on Rhodes Avenue. I told her staff what a joy it is to have her in my life. I was able to pass on the love, nurturing and knowledge that I received from Helen. I smile now as I remember Helen and think of my younger friend. It seems fitting that I'm ten years her senior.

Her husband, Warner, died during the summer of 1987, a few weeks before my husband's death. When we were together at the end of the summer we shared our feeling and experiences of widowhood.

In 1991, four years after her husband's death, Helen became ill and decided to move to Altamonte Springs, Florida, where her children, Paulette and Brother, now lived. At the time Paulette was a claims manager for CNA Insurance Company and Brother was an electrical engineer. I spent my spring vacation with Helen shortly after she moved. We sat by the pool, went for walks and talked a lot about our "growing up" together times in Selma. That was our last visit. She died less than a year later.

In March 1992, when "Miss Emma," Mrs. Vassar, one of our Lapsley Street neighbors, heard that Helen had died, she asked, "When is Erin coming?" She didn't ask, "Is Erin coming?" There was no doubt in her mind that I would have to be there to pay my respects to Helen. She was not only a good neighbor but also my mentor and dear friend for forty years.

· TRAILBLAZERS ·

It is the responsibility of a writer to excavate
the experience of the people who produced him.

James Baldwin

FROM THE MOMENT we approached the fork in the highway at Montgomery and I saw the sign "Selma-50 miles," I could hardly sit still in my seat. Some of my fondest memories are of the anticipation, preparation and travel to Selma to visit my grandparents at 1214 Lapsley Street. I knew that Grandma would be sitting on the front porch waiting for us. As we turned into the driveway she rushed through the house and met us in the back yard. When I got out of the car, I would smell the delicious dinner she had prepared for us.

My grandparent's house was in the middle of the block. According to my earliest memories, when I was four years old, my brother, "Sonny," the children next door and I were the only children living on the block. I was allowed to go next door to play in their back yard. They liked to play church, with one child as preacher and the other children as the singers, listeners, and shouters. When preaching was over, baptizing took place in an old car tire that became the imaginary pool of water. I didn't like the shouting or baptizing so I only stayed to play for brief periods. One winter, when I was back home in Fitzgerald, their house was totally destroyed by fire, leaving only the chimney, ornamental iron front gate and fence. The family moved away and I never saw those children again. A new white wooden house was built on that lot, leaving the original gate and fence in place, where it still remains.

When I was eight years old Rev. and Mrs. Upshaw and their daughter Mary Ann moved into the new house. We were the same age and became good friends. During our earliest years together, we played hopscotch, hide and seek, rock school and paper dolls. We also created our own games and activities. When it rained and the sun was shining, we ran to get small safety pins from Grandma's sewing basket to stick in the large roots of the large oak tree in the front yard. We put our ear near the pin to listen to the Devil beating his wife. We swore that we heard sounds of their fight. Mary Ann and I helped each other catch June bugs in the fig tree in the back yard. She would catch a bug and hold it by pressing the wings in, while I tied a thread around its leg. When we finished tying her bug, she helped me get mine tied with the thread. We then let the bugs fly away but controlled the distance by the length of the thread. We had made our own remote control toy. When we grew tired of playing with the June bugs we would shorten the thread, untie it, and let the bugs fly away.

We also amused ourselves by making dolls from pop bottles, using the string we collected from the blocks of ice delivered by the iceman. We stuffed the string into the opening of the bottle until it completely filled the opening and flowed over. That became the doll's hair, which we braided, or we wrapped the string around a pencil to make Shirley Temple curls. If we had enough string we made more than one doll and did different hairstyles. As we out-grew these games, we began sewing together, making our own clothes. Both Mary Ann and I took piano lessons. Many days we enjoyed practicing our lessons and playing piano duets together. We also giggled together as we shared our secrets about the boys that we liked.

One time, late on a typical beautiful summer afternoon, as the adults sat on the front porch and the children played in the yard, a parade of Ku Klux Klan drove down Lapsley Street. About ten cars passed, blowing their horns. The first car was a convertible, with a driver, a passenger in the front seat, and one person sitting high on the back seat. The people in the cars that followed stuck their heads and arms out of the car windows, waving their hands that were made into fists.

If their intent was to terrorize us, they achieved their goal. After they passed Grandma called us into the house, locked all of the doors, and kept the lights off. She told me that these were people who did "bad things," like castrating colored men, or hanging them in trees with ropes around their necks, or beating them with whips and leaving them in the woods to die. It was not until several years later that I learned the meaning of the word "castrate," or understood what lynching was. The time of that memorable parade was the summer of 1943. I was eight years old.

My little sister, Alice Rose Goseer, age 6. 1950.
I often took her for rides in a towel-lined basket on the front of my bicycle.

The other neighbors in the block were old-time residents who had lived there, raised their children, and remained there after the children moved away. "Miss Emma" and Mr. Howard Vassar were the exception. They were a young couple who had no children until they had lived on the block for almost ten years. Mr. Vassar was a civilian carpenter at Craig Air Force Base, on highway 80, four miles across the Edmund Pettus Bridge. Miss Emma was a teacher in the county although she did not have a college degree, which was not a requirement in the early forties. After the fire next door and until Mary Ann moved in about four years later, I was the only girl on the block. I visited Miss Emma often and followed her around while she did her work. When she finished her cooking she would give me a jelly biscuit, then I would be ready to go home. I had been taught not to ask for food at anyone's house, so before I left I reminded her that I had not asked her for it. She always assured me that I certainly had not asked her for it.

Miss Emma taught in Dallas County during the winter and began attending summer school, driving the ninety-six miles round-trip each day to classes at Alabama State College for colored people in Montgomery. During these ten years I had finished high school and her daughters had been born by the time she received her Master's degree.

After his work at Craig Field, and on Saturdays, Mr. Vassar repaired and managed their rental property. On Sundays he dressed up in a suit and tie and went to West Trinity Baptist Church around the corner on Small Avenue. He loved his church and the work that he did there as a deacon. When I was nine years old their first daughter, Imogene, was the first child born on the block since my birth. That same year, August 1944, my sister, Alice Rose was born. Four years later Imogene's sister, Carol, was born.

The summer before Imogene was born, Aunt Ilsie came to live with the Vassars. She was a tall, slim, mahogany-colored lady with long black braids. One day she washed her hair and hung her long braids on the line to dry. That was my introduction to wigs. I was an adult before I knew that Aunt Ilsie was not a member of the Vassar family, but a lady who came to their home needing a place to live. They took her in and she lived with them for many years.

In 1992 when the Vassars moved from Lapsley Street they were the last of people who had been living there from my childhood. Imogene and Carol had finished college and moved to Chicago. Grandma, Grandpa and all of the other neighbors had died. Mr. Vassar insisted that he and Mrs. Vassar move to a new housing development of beautiful, spacious homes in a sub-division near highway 80 West. Mr. Vassar died in 1993, within a year after they moved to their new home.

During the summer of 1995 when I visited Miss Emma she treated me as an adult. Having known her all of my life, during this visit I felt bold enough to ask her if she was a millionaire. This had been neighborhood rumor. She laughed and said, "Maybe not now since we paid cash for this house, but we did hit that milestone while we lived on Lapsley." They had acquired their wealth by owning rental properties, hard work and prudent investments. Miss Emma was always secretive about her age, but she continues to live alone, comfortably, in her new home.

Across the street, directly in front of the Warner Reid family, was an older couple, Houston and Essie Reid, uncle and aunt of the younger Reid's. They lived in the largest house on the block and the neatest lawn. It was a white wooden house with a wrap-around front and side porch, a large side yard and driveway. Mr. Reid worked at the post office downtown as a postal clerk. He was also a deacon at First Baptist Church, where Grandma and Grandpa were members.

Mrs. Essie Reid was the fussiest and most meticulous housewife I have ever known. She was a member at Brown Chapel A.M.E. Church, a half block from First Baptist. Mary Ann and I liked to ride our bicycles on her sidewalk where we could have fun coasting down the steep driveway. One day we rode our bicycles on her sidewalk after a rain shower and made tracks. She scolded us as she gave us two brooms to sweep the tracks away. We never rode on her sidewalk again. When Grandma sent me to bring them their milk, butter or eggs, I always went to the back door and into her kitchen. It was always spotless with everything in place. When I was in college, Grandma always sent me to visit Mrs. Reid to "pay my respects." I went to the front door and she invited me to sit in her equally spotless living room. Her house was a great contrast to Grandma's, where people were in and out all day and everything was not always in its proper place. We only dusted once a week. That was one of my Saturday jobs. However, Grandma insisted that I sweep the front porch, steps, sidewalk, driveway, and curb every morning, whether I felt it needed it or not. The Reid's children, Mama's contemporaries, finished college and moved away. Their daughter, Essie Bea, married and moved to Oklahoma. Their son, Robert Daniel, became a professor at Tuskegee Institute.

The Boyntons lived in the house on the corner, next door to the Houston Reids. Mr. Samuel Boynton was a prominent leader in Selma. He had a real estate and insurance company on Franklin Street and was also an agent for the United States Department of Agriculture—teaching farming techniques to colored farmers. As a member of the Dallas County Voters' League, he helped colored people through the ordeal of registering to vote. Mrs. Marie Foster, a young friend of my grandparents, who was a dental hygienist, struggled for eight years before she was allowed to register and vote. Mr. Boynton kept an honor roll of people who finally became registered voters.

On Saturday, September 13, 2003, at the funeral services for Mrs. Marie Foster, she was lauded as a legendary pioneer, an unsung heroine, in the voting rights movement. She was praised for having laid the groundwork, together with Mr. and Mrs. Boynton, that resulted in the Voting Rights Act of 1965. I feel a deep sense of gratitude that Mrs. Foster and the Boyntons were a part of my "village" experience.

Mrs. Amelia Boynton was the colored home economics extension agent. Mr. and Mrs. Boynton, who were early civil rights activists in the 1930s, had helped secure a WPA Grant for Selma's Community Center. Their house became a safe house and a civil rights hotel in the 1960s. Their son, Bruce, now an attorney in Selma, was my classmate during the term I attended school in Selma.

The Pattersons lived across the street directly in front of the Boyntons. Mr. Patterson owned a grocery store that he inherited from his parents. It was located at the corner of Small Avenue and Church Street, four blocks from his home. He was a college graduate, who finished Harvard in the class of 1903 and was a classmate of Franklin Delano Roosevelt. It was a mystery to me why he returned to Selma to run a grocery store. Was it his love for Selma and his family that made him return home to do whatever work he could to live peacefully there? Was he ahead of his time with his training from Harvard and Selma wasn't ready for his talents and skills? We'll never know.

The Pattersons added a large room to the back of their house, which became a classroom for Mrs. Patterson's typing and shorthand classes. Sometimes, when I walked around the corner to watch their backyard water fountain and goldfish pond, I heard the clicking sounds from the typing class.

On Small Avenue, directly behind the Boynton's, was a large two-story, gray stone house where "Ma and Pa Mac," Mr. and Mrs. McIwain lived with their daughter, "Ma 'Berta," a son, Dougie, and eight great-grand children. Ma Mac was the head cook at Perrins Cafe, a restaurant for whites only, located downtown on Broad Street. She went to work every morning in her horse-drawn buggy, taking one of her great-grandsons with her to bring the horse and buggy back home. In the evening, when it was time for her to come home, one of her great-grandsons took the buggy to her for her ride home. When they passed our house she always waved. Sometimes she called out to us that she had goodies for us. She sent a neatly wrapped package to us by her great-grandson, Thomas, Jr., who was my age. These goodies were leftover salads or foods that could not be re-heated or served again at Perrins Cafe. One food that she introduced to me was carrot-raisin salad. It became one of my favorites. Another salad that she brought us was a tangy, wilted, lettuce salad. Looking back I realize that the lettuce was tangy and wilted because the salad dressing had been put on it several hours before we got it. Ma Mac's specialty was chicken potpie. Occasionally, we got a chance to taste this delicacy.

Mr. Jefferies, Grandpa's best buddy, lived across the street from us.

He was the janitor at Parrish High School, the white high school downtown near the post office. He rode back and forth to work with Grandpa. His wife had died as a young woman leaving him to raise their three young children alone. By the time I was aware of Mr. Jefferies, his children were away at college. I only saw them when they came home at Christmas or vacation time. "Aunt Fannie," his daughter, was my first idol. She was a beautiful, soft-spoken, gracious, lady. She finished college at Talladega College, an academically renowned, liberal arts college for colored students, financed by the Congregational Church.

One summer when I was in college, Aunt Fannie, who was now living in San Diego, came home for a visit and asked me to make kitchen curtains for her father. She bought unbleached muslin and green and white medium check gingham. She helped me measure the windows, paid me and left me to make, press, and hang the curtains. I said to her, "You are paying me and leaving town. How do you know that I will finish and hang them properly?" She very graciously said, "You will finish them. They will be well made, pressed and properly hung." She was absolutely right. With that kind of faith in me I had to do my best.

Summer evenings Grandpa and Mr. Jefferies often sat on the front porch in the glider swing smoking their pipes and talking. One evening I heard Mr. Jefferies tell Grandpa about the many sweaters and jackets he found in the students' lockers at Parrish High School, for white children only, when he cleaned out those lockers over the summer. I remember thinking, "How could students leave such a precious item like a sweater or jacket at school?" These were precious to me because I never had more than one at a time. If I ever forgot and left my sweater at school I would not have had another one to wear.

Mr. Jefferies' son, George, who was a contractor by trade, moved back to live with Mr. Jefferies and brought his wife, "Miss Ruth," with him. She was a nurse at the Good Samaritan Hospital, the hospital for colored people, run by the Catholic Church. She walked to the hospital near Broad Street wearing her spotless white uniform, starched cap, white stockings and shoes. They had three sons while they lived in Selma. She continued to work and hired a baby-sitter during her working hours. By the time their first son was born, my sister, Alice Rose, was old enough to go across the street and play with George, Jr.

and help bathe and dress him. Miss Ruth and Alice Rose became great friends as I did with our neighbor, Helen Reid. Mr. and Mrs. Jefferies moved to California before the boys became teenagers.

Our neighborhood had a secret. I learned that a secret is something that is whispered and told to only one person at a time. "Miss Lovie" and Mr. Roy Rhodes lived across the street. Their house had the most beautiful flowers on the block that bloomed profusely all summer in pots and planters on the porch and in flowerbeds lining their walkway. Mr. and Mrs. Rhodes were the owners of Roy Rhodes Cafe down the street by the bus stop and the railroad tracks. Mr. Roy was tall, dark, and slim. Miss Lovie was about five feet tall, plump, and milk-chocolate-colored. She smoked! That was not something that ladies did, at least not in public. She had a hoarse voice and a cough that sometimes comes with being a heavy smoker. Miss Lovie frequently had white ladies, or sometimes a white man and lady visit her. They always came in pairs, parked their car in her side driveway and came to the front door. The neighborhood secret was that she performed abortions. That was the only house on the block that I never went in. If Grandma sent me to take her something I went to the cafe or only to her front door.

I had finished college and no longer spent summers in Selma when Miss Lovie became terminally ill. Grandma told me that when she visited her during her final months Miss Lovie cried a lot and kept saying, "The babies—all the babies—I hear them crying."

On the day that I visited Miss Emma in 1995, she told me, "You're grown now, so we can talk about things I couldn't tell you earlier." I asked her about Miss Lovie and her frequent visitors. Miss Emma said she felt that the police never questioned Miss Lovie's work at home because she did a valuable service for white people. She also told me that for many months after Miss Lovie's death, white couples continued to come looking for her. Miss Emma told me of one person who stood out in her memory, a white man who came across the street and rang her doorbell and inquired about Lovie. When she told him that she had died three months earlier, he wrung his hands, and kept repeating, "What am I going to do? I need her." Finally he asked Miss Emma if she knew anyone else who could help him. She told him no and he went away crying, and muttering, "What am I going to do?"

Mrs. Pope, and her grandson Edgar, lived up the street in the next block. Edgar was two years older than me and was an accomplished pianist. They had a grand piano in their living room, the first one I had ever seen. I was impressed by this large mahogany piano with a top that could be let up to show all of the strings. Edgar was the first boy that Grandma allowed to date me. These dates consisted of him stopping by late afternoons or early evenings. We played the piano for each other. Edgar was more advanced than I so he did most of the playing. Mrs. Pope was pleased with our friendship because she said I was a "nice girl." One day she asked me if I straightened my hair. When I said that I did, she was not as interested in my being Edgar's girlfriend. I suppose she was trying to insure the fact that if we got married and had children, her great-grandchildren would have "good hair," an important class issue for some colored people in the 1950s before "Black Is Beautiful" became a slogan. Mrs. Pope had not faced the fact that Edgar would never have any romantic interest in me, because I was a girl. I think Grandma knew that and therefore was willing for him to visit me.

After Edgar finished college at Alabama State in Montgomery, he returned to Selma to teach music in the colored high school. During the summers, when he was on summer vacation from teaching, he studied music at the University of Iowa School of Music, where he earned his Master's degree. Edgar and I remained friends until his death in 1986, when he was fifty-three years old. He never married or left home.

The Carters—Dorothy, Harold and Nathan—were my other highly talented musician friends. We spent many summer evenings and holidays playing the piano and singing together. Nathan finished college at Hampton Institute. He later graduated from Julliard School of Music and earned a doctorate from Peabody Conservatory of Music. He became head of the Music Department at Morgan State University and conductor of their world-renowned choir. Harold is a graduate of Alabama State College in Montgomery. During his college years, he was associate minister under Dr. Martin Luther King, Jr. and worked with him during the early years of the Civil Rights Movement. Dr. King influenced Harold to attend Crozer Theological Seminary, his alma mater. Harold is currently the pastor of New Shiloh Baptist Church in Baltimore, Maryland. After college, Dorothy returned to Selma and became a teacher. She continues to share her gift of music as a soloist. These friends from my childhood have become life-long friends.

I spent a part of my Christmas and summer vacations in Selma through grade school, high school, and my junior year in college. By the time I was a senior in high school, I began to realize how much family and neighbors supervised my activities, which consisted mainly of my walking or riding my bicycle in the neighborhood, or walking downtown occasionally. I didn't attribute their attention to anything other than the usual adult scrutiny.

I was sixteen years old in 1951, the summer that I finished high school and was allowed to have boys visit me late afternoons and early evenings. We sat on the front porch or on the concrete bench under the chinaberry tree in the front yard, or sang and played the piano in the living room.

The summer after my freshman year in college I returned to Selma. A boyfriend, Carol Moore, asked me to the movies with him to see "Elmer Gantry." I asked Grandma if I could go. She passed the buck and told me to ask Grandpa. He decided I was old enough and gave me permission. Grandma hoped he would say that I couldn't go out at night with a boy. She insisted that Grandpa drive us downtown to the Wilby Theater, one of the three theaters in Selma. Grandpa took us and waited until Carol paid our admission and went to the side entrance and stairs that led to the balcony section where the colored people were allowed to sit.

It was a beautiful, balmy, summer evening with gentle breezes. The sky was clear as we left the theater. The streetlights were not bright enough to block our view of the stars and moon. We began our walk home, leaving Broad Street, to walk along Church Street on the concrete sidewalks, along this paved, tree-lined street, with beautiful shrubbery and fragrant flowers. The walk home with my friend Carol turned out to be a memorable evening.

Grandma was almost hysterical when we got home. She said, "Why didn't you wait for your Grandpa? He went to get you." She hadn't told us before we left home that he would come back and we should wait for him to pick us up. She asked us which way we walked home. She was even more upset when we told her we had come down Church Street. She told us that walking there was dangerous because white boys might have "picked at us" or white people might have called the police if they had seen us walking on their street at night. Carol and I had no idea that our walk home could have caused any trouble. After that evening I never asked my grandparents to let me go anywhere out of the neighborhood after dark. I began to realize that evening how much my grandparents lived in fear for my safety and why I was so closely supervised by family, friends and neighbors.

Later the same summer that I had gone to the movies with Carol, my cousin Cecil came home on furlough from the army. He had an errand to do downtown and asked me to ride with him. We went to Broad Street and pulled into a diagonal parking space near the Prince Albert Hotel. Built by former slaves, it was an ornate replica of a palace in Venice, Italy. A tall, slim, white policeman, armed with his "billy club," and pistol was standing near the parking space. When Cecil got out of the car, dressed in his full army uniform with the two silver bars indicating his rank as Captain, the policeman walked over to the car, inspected the front and sides and said, "Boy, ya parked on duh yeller line. Move it!" Cecil politely replied, "Yes, Sir!" as he got back in the car, backed out, parked again, got out, came around to the passenger side, opened the door for me, helped me out of the car, closed the door and put a nickel in the meter.

When we were out of earshot of the policeman, I asked him what that was all about. Cecil said, "That redneck policeman just wanted to show his authority. I was not parked on the yellow line so I backed the car out and drove back in exactly where it was before." We laughed about this, as we walked along, knowing that when we returned to the car, before the meter expired, the policeman would be nowhere in sight. Cecil had played the role of an "uppity nigger," according to white folk's descriptions. It never occurred to us at that time to fume or resent a behavior and attitude that seemed as regularly unstable as the weather.

The Christmas of my freshman year in college, something good happened that allowed me to have fun after dark away from the neighborhood. Cecil was at home again on furlough. He asked Grandma if he could take me dancing at the Officers' Club at Craig Field Air Force Base, about four miles from Selma, across the Edmund Pettus Bridge. She allowed me to go with him because he had his own car and we wouldn't have to use a taxi or public bus. Cecil was tall, chocolate brown, and handsome, as well as an officer and a gentleman. We were great dancing partners as well as good friends. He continued taking me dancing at Craig Field whenever we were in Selma.

Since I wasn't allowed to go far from Lapsley Street and didn't go to high school in Selma, my circle of friends was small. I spent a lot of time with my friends Mary Ann, Carol Moore, Edgar, Mrs. Helen Reid, and my cousin Geneva. Geneva lived directly behind "Ma Mac" and was married to Fred Martin, Ma Mac's grandson. Geneva lived with Grandma while Fred was in the navy. Their first child, Mabel, who was named for Grandma, was also born at Grandma's house. "Lil Mabel," as she was called is the third generation of my family to live in our family home on Lapsley Street. Mabel moved to her own home in February 2000. At that point Mama decided to sell the family home. Her decision caused days of emotional turmoil. I didn't feel that I wanted to take over the responsibility of managing the house or would ever live there again. But it had been such an important part of my life that I didn't want to let it go.

It is only in retrospect that I began to understand what Lapsley Street, my Selma family, and friends had meant to me. First of all, the adults taught by example. Lessons of a strong work ethic, sharing, caring, and neighborhood pride were daily lessons. Everyone in the neighborhood worked, whether on a job or at home. Our neighborhood was free of any trash on the street, lawns, curbs or sidewalks. If anyone saw trash, it was removed immediately.

At Christmas I could look forward to family and friends visiting our house and my visits to friends in the neighborhood. There were homemade layer cakes at everyone's home—chocolate, caramel, coconut, pineapple, and fruitcakes. We always had a large jar of ambrosia. Family members always came by on Christmas Eve and Mama served oyster stew. I wouldn't eat any, so I suppose my supper was all different kinds of cake.

I always looked forward to my summer vacations in Selma, with a steady stream of aunts, uncles, cousins, and friends visiting from "up North." I also spent a week on the farm with Grandma's sister, Aunt Jennie, and her children and grandchildren.

All of the people I've written about were my family or extended family. They set good examples, supervised, nurtured and protected me. They also provided to the best of their abilities, a safe, peaceful oasis in the midst of racial strife that was ever present in the racially segregated, highly prejudiced town of Selma, Alabama.

• SUMMER SUNDAYS IN SELMA •

GRANDMA AND GRANDPA got up as early on Sunday mornings as they did the other days of the week, so as usual I was awakened by the odors of breakfast cooking. This was worth the early wake-up because our Sunday breakfast consisted of rice, biscuits, and pork chops or steak with gravy. Also, as a special treat on Sundays, I was allowed a cup of coffee, which was more hot milk than coffee, now known as café au lait in the fancy coffee shops. Grandma's favorite brands of coffee were Eight O'Clock, from A&P, or Maxwell House, which she brewed on the stove in her aluminum coffee pot. During the week we ate breakfast in the kitchen at the red and white enamel table with the stainless steel tubular legs. On Sunday mornings the small rectangular table was enlarged into a square by pulling a leaf from under the tabletop. The four matching red chairs also had shiny tubular frames.

After breakfast Grandma started dinner by searing a large pot roast in her big black iron skillet. When it had browned on both sides she put it in the navy-blue and white roasting pan, added chopped white potatoes, onions, carrots, and fresh tomatoes, sprinkled salt and pepper on top, covered it with the roaster top, and put it in the oven at 300 degrees. She was always careful to tell me the oven temperature, but I didn't realize then she was teaching me to cook.

Once the pot roast was in the oven, it was my time to get dressed for Sunday School. My Sunday shoes were black patent leather with a narrow buckled strap across the top. She braided my hair in three "plaits," and she tied a three-inch wide ribbon bow on the top braid. The other two hung down my back. Then I put on my soft, cotton, homemade slip, and my starched organdy, or dotted swiss dress that had a full gathered skirt with a sash that tied in the back. Grandma liked me in pale blue so most of my summer dresses were blue. My socks and ribbons always matched my dress. Just before I was ready to leave for Sunday School Grandma put a dab of her cologne behind my ears, and a tiny bit of her lipstick on my cheeks and lips. She said that I was too pale and needed a little color. I was given a nickel, tied in the corner of a handkerchief, to put in the collection plate at Sunday School and then considered ready to walk the one and a half blocks to West Trinity Baptist Church on Small Avenue for the nine o'clock opening exercises. By the time I was ten years old I was playing the piano for Sunday School and Vacation Bible School.

Sunday School was over by ten-thirty and I hurried home to be ready for our family's drive. We headed up Lapsley Street to Jeff Davis Avenue, crossed Broad Street where the paved part of Jeff Davis ended, driving in the colored neighborhood along the railroad tracks, on the way to Sylvan Street, our destination.

When I was a child, First Baptist Church had a fifty-foot steeple— at that time the tallest in town. In 1978 a tornado ripped part of the steeple from the main body and it has been only partially rebuilt. I always enjoyed walking up the concrete steps of this magnificent structure. This flight of ten stairs was the first tall stairs I had ever climbed. The churches and my school in Fitzgerald all had fewer than five steps. The dark wooden pews were arranged in a rainbow-like arch, where the pews were highest in back and got progressively lower as we walked toward the front. The pulpit, in the center of the sanctuary, had as a powerful and beautiful background the large brass pipes of the organ and stained glass windows. We always sat on the left center aisle about midway. The pews were adorned with a carved round piece of wood on the back of each pew and large carved scrolls on the end of each row that looked like a medallion. Wooden brackets spaced along the back of the pew held the blue *American Baptist Hymnals*. The pews were widely spaced so that any seated person could pass without others having to stand or turn their knees to the side. I have never seen this convenient spacing in any other auditorium.

The organ at First Baptist Church was my first and only experience of hearing a pipe organ until I entered Spelman College. Mrs. Pritchett was the organist at First Baptist and I fell in love with the rich sounds she made on this powerful instrument. That was the beginning for my love of the pipe organ, which continues to this day.

At the close of the worship the choir and congregation always sang this hymn:

> *BLEST BE THE TIE THAT BINDS*
> 1. *"Blest be the tie that binds*
>   *Our hearts in Christian love!*
>   *The fellowship of kindred minds*
>   *Is like to that above.*
> 2. *Before our Father's throne*
>   *We pour our ardent prayers;*
>   *Our fears, our hopes, our aims are one,*
>   *Our comforts and our cares.*
> 3. *We share our mutual woes*
>   *Our mutual burdens bear;*
>   *And often for each other flows*
>   *The sympathizing tear.*
> 4. *When we asunder part*
>   *It gives us inward pain;*
>   *But we shall still be joined in heart,*
>   *And hope to meet again."*

I memorized all of the words to this hymn by singing them so often. When I was older and understood the meaning of the words I began to feel that this hymn exemplified the essence of our community spirit. After the final "A-men" and the organ postlude, the greetings and visiting lasted for about fifteen minutes before we headed home for our family dinner.

First Baptist Church, now on the National Registry of Historic Places, is located on the corner of Jeff Davis Avenue and Sylvan Street, which was renamed Martin Luther King, Jr. Street in 1976. First Baptist Church and Brown Chapel A.M.E. Church, one block from First Baptist Church, were the principal meeting places for the Civil Rights Meetings and where the 1965 Selma to Montgomery March had its origins and send-off point. First Baptist has a long history of being dedicated to community efforts. Our neighbors, "Ma Berta," who at the time of her death was the oldest member, and Mrs. Essie Reid were active members of Brown Chapel A.M.E. Church that became the Civil Rights Movement Headquarters. When Sylvan Street was filled with

Mabel Tate Blevins (1891–1977), my maternal grandmother,
sitting on her porch in front of the window
of the bedroom where I was born.

the troopers on Bloody Sunday, police fired tear gas into the church and one student was thrown through the stained glass windows near the organ of First Baptist Church.

Soon after we returned home from church, about one o'clock, the pot roast was done—juicy, tender, and flavorful. First we took off our Sunday clothes and put on more comfortable ones. If we didn't have company, we fixed our plates in the kitchen and took them to the dining room table that was covered with a lace tablecloth. If we had guests for dinner, we set the table and served the food from large serving bowls. Grandma always told me to be extra careful with the serving pieces. It is only now that I realize that she was giving me, the dishwasher, a break, on non-company meals. After Grandma's death, Mama gave me one of the platters I handled so carefully as a child. I use it for special occasions, and smile as I gently hand-wash it.

Sunday afternoon we visited our relatives in the country. Usually, we went to the farm where Grandma's parents had lived, about five miles from Selma. Her brothers, Uncle Stanley and Uncle Arthur, and their families were still farmers on the family's land. Aunt Willie,

Grandma's sister, taught grades one through eight at the one room school in that community called El Bethel. I was frightened of the deep, dark well where water was drawn using a rope and a large bucket. About once a month we took a twenty-two mile trip to Marion Junction where Aunt Jennie, Grandma's sister, and Uncle Clarence, Grandpa's half-brother, lived. They had nine children. By the time I began spending Sunday afternoons with them four of their older children had gone away to college. One son, "Boe," had remained and was a farmer. Uncle Clarence and Aunt Jennie had four daughters and two grandchildren who still lived on the farm. I always looked forward to an afternoon of fun with my cousins.

Our route to Marion Junction went from Lapsley Street to Seventh Avenue where we made a left turn on to highway 80 West. After traveling about ten miles we passed Camp Selma, the prison for members of the chain gang. As we passed by on those Sunday afternoons I always saw colored men in two-piece suits with three-inch-wide, black-and-white stripes, and matching skullcaps. They had iron chains locked on their ankles and at the end of the chain was a black, heavy ball, a little smaller than a bowling ball. The men stood behind a tall wire fence with barbed wire on top. The white guards walked around the yard holding rifles with the barrels pointed toward the sky.

I also saw the chain gang men on weekdays when we drove in and out of Selma along the highway to Montgomery. They cut weeds and picked up trash along the highway, dressed the same as they were on Sundays. White armed guards supervised them. I saw them again as they dug or worked in the deep, watery holes on Small Avenue, building or repairing water and sewer lines. Even as a very young child I wondered if it was just colored men who did bad things and had to go on a chain gang.

Soon after we passed Camp Selma, we took the narrow gravel road and traveled about five more miles to Aunt Jennie and Uncle Clarence's farm. My excitement grew as we passed Pernel Church and the one room school next door that my cousins attended, both set back from the road in a thick pine grove. We had only about a mile to go before I saw their RFD mailbox and the narrow two-path road with cotton and cornfields on either side. They could hear us coming. I remember Aunt Jennie wiping her hands on her apron as she came out to meet us. That always meant the great afternoon of family fun would begin.

Although we had eaten dinner at home, Aunt Jennie insisted we eat again. She always cooked large pots of fresh vegetables picked from her garden near the kitchen door. Sometimes she caught chickens from the yard and wrung their necks. After dipping the chickens in boiling water she picked the feathers off. She prepared them for frying by pulling out the entrails, washing the fryers, and cutting them up. I didn't like to see the catching and cleaning process, but the fried chicken tasted so good that I managed to forget the earlier procedures. Sometimes Aunt Jennie made ice cream using the fresh eggs and milk from the farm. Every Saturday during the summer Uncle Clarence brought a large block of ice back from his shopping trip to Selma. His stop at the icehouse was his last purchase before returning to Marion Junction. He wrapped it in burlap bags and put it in a washtub in his trailer. My cousins, Jean, Jewel, and I turned the crank on the ice cream freezer while Aunt Jennie whipped up what she called sweet bread, a plain cake, to serve with the ice cream.

Late in the afternoon, as the sun began to go down, we said our "good-byes" and got lots of hugs before starting our trip back to town. Grandpa kept his scythe in the trunk of the car. On our way home he stopped by the side of the highway to cut fresh grass, filling up the car trunk, for Grandma's cow, Alice.

It was dusk by the time we returned home. We hurried in to open the doors and windows so the evening breezes could cool the house before bedtime. Grandma always wanted me to comb her thin, soft, straight hair—soft and white—as she sat at the dining room table nodding. If I stopped playing with her hair she would wake up and say, "You haven't finished yet." I continued combing her hair in different styles until her nap was over and it was my bedtime.

· SUMMER VACATIONS
IN THE COUNTRY ·

SATURDAY WAS MARKET day in Selma. Every Saturday, Uncle Clarence attached his two-wheeled trailer to the car and drove twenty-two miles to Selma from his farm in Marion Junction to purchase supplies. He bought feed for his animals, staples for his family, and a variety of items to sell at his small store at the farm, including kerosene in a five gallon can for his family and neighbors for the lamps used at night. The store house in the backyard between the house and barn was stocked with rice, sugar, salt, coffee, tea, cheese in a large wooden container, a two foot stick of bologna in the red casing, canned oil sausage, cans of snuff, cigars, and plugs of chewing tobacco. The large bags of animal feed were packaged in brightly printed floral cotton sacks. Most everything would be sold by Sunday afternoon, including a full stem of bananas. By mid-afternoon, when Uncle Clarence had finished shopping, he stopped by our house on Lapsley Street to rest and get a bite to eat.

One week each summer, I was allowed to go to Marion Junction with him to spend a week in the country. The trailer, trunk, and back seat of the car were so heavy with his purchases that the car sank down in the back. I sat in the front with Uncle Clarence and held the large brown bag I had packed early in the day with my clothes in eager anticipation of my week on the farm.

Uncle Clarence's last shopping stop for the day was a trip to the icehouse. After he wrapped the large block of ice in the "croaker sack" (a burlap bag) he then put it in an old tin washtub in the trailer. After the icehouse we took highway 80 west on our way to Marion Junction. The two-wheeled trailer bounced and swayed and the car motor labored as it carried this heavy load.

My landmark for our turn-off to the gravel road was the tall metal fence topped with barbed wire and the white barrack-like houses of Camp Selma. This was the prison facility where the men of the chain gang lived. As soon as we passed Camp Selma the next right exit took us to the bumpy, red-clay road that we traveled on for the next ten miles to the farm. Luckily, we didn't lose supplies as we bounced along. We soon crossed the "ku-lunk-a-lunk" bridge, as I called it, because that was the sound I heard as the car and trailer rolled over the large, loose metal plates that were on top of the wooden boards of the bridge. Once across the bridge, cotton fields stretched on both sides of the road for as far as we could see. Small motley-gray clapboard cabins dotted the landscape. Uncle Clarence made stops along the road where his neighbors were waiting to greet him, get news from town and receive the supplies they had asked him to purchase.

As we continued our slow, bumpy ride I knew that as soon as I saw Pernel Church and the one-room schoolhouse, my cousins' school, in the pine grove, I would soon see the large oak tree and the RFD mailbox. At that point we made a right turn on to a narrow car path through the cotton fields to their house.

Uncle Clarence unloaded the trailer—ice first, and put it in the wooden icebox on the back porch. The remainder of the supplies was put in the store. The people from the community knew the time he was due back and began arriving, some walking, others on horseback or by mule and wagon, to get supplies.

Grandma had given me a few nickels and pennies to buy candy during the week. My favorite candy was the thin pink, white and brown coconut flavored candy coated with granulated sugar. I also liked the assorted penny candy in a large glass jar but Grandma told me that I must only ask to buy these items when the store was opened for other customers. The wooden door was always kept locked with a small padlock until a customer came.

Mealtime with Aunt Jennie and Uncle Clarence was always fun for me. Our meals were served on the long oval table that stretched the entire length of the dining room. I remember that there were always a lot of people gathered to eat there, their children and grandchildren, as well as those who had come to work on the farm for the day. At dinnertime, in the middle of the day, the table was loaded with large dishes of fresh vegetables from the backyard garden, peas, butter beans, okra, green beans, corn, cucumbers, and tomatoes. Aunt Jennie used the largest bread pan that I had ever seen to make cornbread and biscuits.

Uncle Clarence was Grandpa's half-brother, fathered by the same white plantation owner. Aunt Jennie was Grandma's younger sister. We were all happy to be what we called "double kin." Aunt Jennie and Uncle Clarence had nine children who ranged in age from my mother's age to my cousin Jean, who was a year older than me. Willie Clarence, Cecil, Edward and Eryn, went away to college and never came back to live on the farm. During the years of my vacations on the farm, Frank (Boe), Geneva, Jewel, Mabel, and Jean still lived at home. Their son, Boe, and his wife, Sadalia, and their three children lived in a small house down a narrow path through the cotton fields. Their children were also my playmates. When Mabel and Jean finished the eighth grade at the one-room school at Pernel Church, they came to Selma for high school and later graduated from college at Tuskegee. Jewel never married and continued to live on the farm with her parents. After high school in Selma, Geneva married and is still living in Selma. Mable became a registered nurse. Jean later earned a Master of Art degree from Georgia State and an Educational Specialist degree from Auburn University.

One day I was allowed to go to the fields to pick cotton, the main crop on their one hundred twenty acre farm. I pulled just the soft part of the cotton off the top of the boll instead of going deep into the boll to take out the seeds as well. I didn't want to go deep because the sharp points of the boll pierced my fingers. Instead, after my first morning in the fields, Aunt Jennie decided that the tiny bit of cotton I picked was not worth the trouble of taking me to the fields and giving me a sack. I never went to the cotton fields again. Jean and I were left "to watch the house."

We played outside in the sandy front yard, and then went to pick wild plums and blackberries. We ate as we picked and were full by the time we got back home. The fruit that we picked and didn't eat was put in our syrup cans and brought back to Aunt Jennie for her to make pies, jellies, and jams.

Jean knew the areas around the farm and took me on many adventures. On one of our walks through the woods I was frightened when a snake crossed our path. Jean said that it was just a little garter snake and wouldn't hurt us. She also showed me snakeskins that had been shed when the snakes had outgrown them.

Jean was more athletic than I and was very comfortable swimming in the swimming hole on Mr. Pink's farm, adjacent to theirs. A tree had fallen across the swimming hole and formed a bridge. Jean used the bridge as a diving board to jump into the creek. I was afraid to jump off the log and would slide down the bank into the shallow part of the creek. We did skinny-dipping so our clothes wouldn't get wet. I don't know if Aunt Jennie ever knew that we went swimming. There were five of us all together but no one ever told of our swimming adventures. It must be true that God takes care of babies and fools. We had double protection because we were both babies and fools.

The farm was far away from city lights so we could see the stars clearly and identify them by their position in the sky. One night we were walking back from summer revival at Pernel Church when all of a sudden we saw a streak of light cross the sky. Aunt Jennie told us that was a falling star. After I became an adult, whenever I hear the song "Stars Fell On Alabama," I remember that night in the country when I saw a star fall.

With no electricity on the farm, our source of light came from glass kerosene lamps with chimneys. The larger children were allowed to carry the lamp from one room to the other to light the way as the younger ones walked behind. By the time I was eight years old, Jean showed me how to trim the wick and clean the thin, glass chimney. We used crumpled up newspaper that we rubbed together in our hands to make it as soft as fabric. We polished the chimney until there was no trace of the residue from the previous night's smoke.

At bedtime, all the children slept in "the children's room." It had two full sized beds with homemade mattresses made of unginned cotton. The mattress with its blue and white striped ticking looked like a giant's pillow. The mattress wasn't tufted so we sank deep into the soft cotton. In the mornings, when we made up the bed we had to shake the mattress and smooth it out before we put the sheets and spread back on. Our pillows were also homemade and stuffed with the soft feathers from the chickens on the farm. Four of us small children slept crosswise in one bed. The challenge for me was to be the first one in bed in order to claim a spot on the outer edge, a more desirable place than between two people.

When Boe's son, Sonny, spent the night we made a game of

listening and trying to guess what we heard. Sonny was the authority and told us if we had guessed right, as we identified the crickets, frogs, night hawks, and other sounds. Sonny could also name the cars and trucks of the neighbors that passed along the dirt road. I remember him saying, "That's Mr. Pink coming home in his 'T model' Ford." It took me a couple of years playing this game before I was able to pinpoint all of the sounds accurately. I still enjoy playing this game by closing my eyes and trying to identify various sounds around my home. When I was a music teacher, I often had my students close their eyes as I played different instruments for them to identify.

The source of water for the entire farm came from the black iron pump that was just outside the kitchen door. We pumped water for drinking, cooking, bathing, washing, watering the garden, as well as water for the animals. Aunt Jennie told me to always leave a can full of water by the pump to prime it the next time someone needed to pump water.

When Jean and I were small, it took both of us at the pump to get water; one to pour the water to prime and then rush to the handle to help the other pump by pulling the handle down, pushing it up and starting again. Jean and I learned to cooperate to get the water to flow into the galvanized bucket. I was such a lightweight that I had to lift my feet off the ground so that all of my weight was used to make the handle go down. When the bucket was full, we put it on the small table on the back porch, replacing the blue enameled dipper.

The only unpleasant part of my time on the farm was having to use the "out-house," the toilet down the path past the barn, chicken house, and pig pen. The out-house was a small wooden structure with a door made of broad boards. The inside had a bench-like seat with a circle cut in it that was placed over a deep hole dug in the ground. The seat could be covered with another wide board with hinges. I suppose that was the forerunner of the modern toilet seat cover. That was one stinky place! Although lime was poured down the hole to help sanitize it, it still had a strong unpleasant odor. We used crumpled up newspaper for toilet paper, rubbing it together with our hands to make it softer. The trip to the out-house just before bedtime was always frightening because I imagined snakes crossing the path at night. Apparently, I didn't take Jean's reassurance to heart.

I didn't need to go back to Selma on Saturday mornings with Uncle Clarence because Sunday afternoon Grandma and Grandpa came to get me. Grandma was always pleased to see me looking well from my "country living." I was pleased with my beautiful suntan from having been outside in the sun so much.

The summer weeks I spent on the farm are some of the most pleasant memories of my childhood. I loved the freedom of doing nothing that I considered work. Feeding the animals, gathering eggs, picking vegetables, fruits and wild berries, "toting water," going for long walks, and sneaking to the swimming hole, I considered all part of the great fun of my unforgettable weeks in the country.

· SELMA BUS BOYCOTT ·

DURING THE LATE 1940s and early 1950s Selma had a public transportation system with a weekday route that left Wilby Theater downtown on the hour. It went through the colored neighborhoods on the north side of town, and then to the white neighborhoods in East Selma. Over the years Grandma had taken me downtown many times. When we left home early in the day, before the sun was hot, we made the walk to town in twenty minutes and rode the bus back, if we had heavy packages.

In June of 1948, when I turned thirteen, Grandma gave me fifteen dollars for my birthday and suggested that I buy two dresses for myself. That was a special treat because most of my clothes were homemade. She decided that I was old enough to go downtown alone to do my shopping. I dressed carefully, all excited about my personal shopping spree. I wore white sandals and my crisply starched light blue, dotted-swiss dress that I had made. I brushed my hair up in a pony tail and tied it with a blue satin ribbon. Grandma watched me as I left the house and called out, "Be careful," as she always did whenever anyone left her house. I walked a half block to the corner bus stop in front of Mr. Roy Rhodes's Cafe.

I boarded the bus, gave my fare to the driver, and made my way to a seat. The front two-thirds of the bus was empty. The back one-third was filled with colored people. I didn't see a "white only" marker so I sat on the right side of the bus, four seats behind the white driver. He immediately turned around and said, "Git outta that seat, girl, you can't sit there."

"Why not?" I said, "The seats are empty."

He shook his finger at me. "Git up and move to the back! Niggers

My maternal grandfather, Frank Herman Blevins (1891–1963)
often sat in the living room with me while I practiced piano.

cain't sit up front. Move to duh back. Them seats is for white folks
that's gonna git on in East Selma."

After I had said, "Why not?", and before he finished his second
comment, a chorus of responses came from the back of the bus.
"Come on, baby, come on back here with us, come on and sit here." A
tall, stout, pecan-colored lady patted a seat indicating that I should sit
with her. When I sat down I felt her soft, warm body touching me. The
bus was perfectly quiet for the remainder of the trip. We crossed the
railroad tracks and soon we were at Jeff Davis Avenue. Two blocks
later the neighborhood became white. By the time the bus driver
completed his route and got back downtown to the Wilby Theater,
only two white people had boarded the bus and were sitting up front.

I got off the bus and went shopping for my dresses. Grandma had
suggested that I shop at Three Sisters or Lerners because she knew
that I had enough money to buy two dresses at those stores. I looked
at both stores but didn't see anything I wanted to purchase. I wore a
junior size five dress and Three Sisters and Lerners only had floral
prints in my size. I thought they looked too "babyish" for me. I walked
further west to Rothschilds Department Store, Selma's most exclusive
department store. I looked in the windows but didn't go in because I

knew that all of their clothes were much too expensive. I left Broad Street and went around the corner to the Boston Bargain Store. A white man in the shoe department said hello and asked me wasn't I Frank's granddaughter. When I said, "Yes, Sir," he went over to another man and told him, "That's Frank's granddaughter." I didn't find a dress there either, so I crossed the street and went to Eagles' Department Store. After looking through all the dresses in the girls and junior departments, I finally found the perfect one for my birthday. It was a pink cotton two-piece Jonathan Logan dress with an A-line skirt, three-fourths quilted, and a plain flounce at the bottom. The short-sleeved top curved into a round low cut neckline from its quilted collar. I smiled as I tried it on. Unfortunately, this one dress would take all of the money Grandma had given me. I was afraid she'd be upset if I spent all of the money on one dress. I kept looking in the mirror and finally decided to buy the dress I truly loved, hoping Grandma would understand and approve. When I showed the dress to her, she was happy that it was a perfect fit, and that I liked it so much.

I told Grandma about the man in the Boston Bargain store telling another clerk that I was Frank's grand-daughter. I asked her how he knew me. She answered, rather matter-of-factly, "He's your Granddaddy's cousin. He has a lot of white cousins in Selma. Some of his half-brothers are doctors. They're all Chisoms."

The part of my trip that I didn't tell Grandma about was the incident on the bus. By the time I crossed the railroad tracks and was back on Lapsley Street, I had regained my good common sense. I knew better than to sit near the front of the bus even though no "colored" sign was posted. I also knew better than to have any confrontation with the white bus driver. Either one of these acts could have put my family and community in jeopardy. This was Klan country and I knew it. If I had told Grandma about the incident on the bus she would not have let me out of her sight for the remainder of the summer. She also would have told Mama and I would have gotten the worst tongue lashing ever. I never rode the Selma bus again. After that day, I always left home about nine o'clock in order to return before the sun was blazing hot on my head and back. I never told my parents or grandparents about my private Selma Bus Boycott.

My never riding the bus again had advantages. On the way to town I took a short cut to Jeff Davis Avenue by walking along the side of the railroad tracks until Mabry Street and passed Don Bosco Boys' Club.

When I passed there I smiled and spoke to the cute boys who were playing outside. After passing Don Bosco I was soon at Jeff Davis Avenue, where I walked up to Church Street into the white neighborhood. There were large trees and concrete sidewalks on both sides of the street so the remaining walk downtown was pleasant. On my way home I treated myself to a pistachio double-dip ice cream cone from Lloyd's Dairy Store with the money I saved by not riding the bus. I also smiled each time I wore my beautiful birthday dress. I continued to wear it until it was faded and thread-bare.

All of my life, I had been taught to have no more conversations or encounters with white folks than were absolutely necessary. When the bus driver told me to move to the back of the bus I got up and went to the back, even though I thought it was a stupid request.

I was teaching in Groton, Connecticut on December 1, 1955 when Mrs. Rosa Parks was arrested for refusing to give up her seat to a white passenger on a city bus in Montgomery, Alabama. Her act of courage sparked a nonviolent protest that ended when the U.S. Supreme Court declared bus segregation illegal. Whenever I see a picture of Mrs. Parks or read about her, I feel a sense of gratitude for the sacrifices she and the people of Montgomery made. I also feel a secret bond with her for my private bus boycott.

· SUMMER OF '44 ·

IN MAY, WHEN school was out, Daddy drove Mama, Stanley Jr. ("Sonny"), and me to Selma to spend the summer. He returned to Fitzgerald and hired himself out as a house painter to supplement his income as principal of the colored school. I turned nine years old that June. Mama was pregnant with her third child, due in August.

It was a southern custom in the 1940s that the daughter returns to her parents' home for confinement and birthing, and stays an additional month for recovery. My brother, sister, and I were all born in the same large bedroom and mahogany bed on Lapsley Street in Selma.

This summer was the first time I was aware of gender bias, even though I didn't know the name of it. Sonny got involved with boyfriends in the neighborhood, joined an art class that did soapstone carving, began coronet lessons, and got a paper route delivering *The Selma Times-Journal*. One of his friends, William Anderson ("W.J.") also lived on Lapsley Street. They often played together in musical ensembles. My brother continued his music and became a band director. "W.J." began to focus more on art and is an artist of great renown. Currently, he is a Professor of Art at Morehouse College.

I became Mama's personal maid. My duties included bringing her ice water, food, when she didn't feel like coming to the table, combing her hair, and doing anything else that she asked me to do. The thing that I remember the most was propping her feet up on a stool and taking them down. Her feet and legs were swollen and had to be elevated often. What she did during the latter part of her pregnancy was the next step up from complete bed rest.

Grandma bought a blue, used bicycle for herself that summer and made the mistake of telling me that when I learned to ride it she would give it to me. She had no idea the extent of my determination and motivation. During Mama's naps and my time off from my duties, I practiced riding from the backyard to the front side walk, to the corner and back. The bicycle had no training wheels so I took quite a few falls and suffered skinned knees, ankles, and legs, but by the end of the day that Grandma made that promise, I had learned to ride her bicycle. By dusk I proudly showed off my new skill. Grandma continued to ride the bicycle when she needed it for her errands. After that summer the bicycle was all mine.

On the evening of August 10, Grandma told me to go around the corner to Grandma Tucker's house to tell her, "It's almost time." Grandma Tucker, Amelia Ann Tucker, better known around Selma as "Miz 'Melia Ann," was Grandpa's mama. She was a midwife, delivering white as well as colored babies. She worked for white families who could afford to pay her. She delivered their babies and stayed at their homes for three weeks to take care of the personal needs of the mother and the newborn. It was the custom in the '40s that after childbirth the mother was instructed to stay in bed or indoors for a month, with no responsibilities other than holding and feeding her baby. Grandma, family members and neighbors did the cooking and washing for Mama. What a sharp contrast to present day attitudes and practices towards maternity care, with their brief hospital stays and return to work policies.

Grandma Tucker came to Mama immediately and preparations for "birthing" began. Sonny and I were told to go to bed early. That night we slept in the adjoining room to Mama's. The three doors to our bedroom were closed. I heard the constant walking back and forth from the front room, through the hallway, dining room, back porch, and bathroom. I heard conversations about heating water and getting clean rags. As the night went on I heard all of the screams, moans, and groans of "birthing a baby." During the early morning hours of August 4, after all was still and quiet again, Grandma came to wake Sonny and me. "Come and see your little baby sister." She said it as though I should have been surprised. I hadn't slept at all that night and never understood how Sonny slept through all of that noise and activity. I was completely exhausted and ready to sleep.

I'll never forget that morning when I first saw my baby sister. She was dressed in a diaper, diaper shirt, and was wrapped in a white flannel blanket that Mama had made with white embroidery blanket stitches around the edges. Grandma unwrapped my baby sister so I could see her hands, feet, and legs. I had never seen such tiny, delicate hands and fingers. Her feet were long and narrow and her soft, rosy legs were as smooth and velvety as rose petals. I was allowed to stroke her legs and curly black hair. Mama told me that her name was Alice Rose. She was named Alice after Daddy's Mama, and Rose after Daddy's grandma, Ma Rose. We never knew these grandparents because they died when Daddy was a teenager. After that introduction and brief visit I was allowed to go back to bed and sleep late that day.

The following week I was allowed to take a week's vacation. Grandma's sister, Aunt Willie, lived in the Fairfield section of Birmingham during the summer. During the school year she lived in a two-story log cabin house that was on her family's ninety-six acre farm. She taught in the one-room colored school in the El Bethel community about eight miles west of Selma. On holidays and some weekends she went to Birmingham to visit her husband.

Aunt Willie, Grandma's older sister, was her only sibling of five children to go to college. Their father, my Grandpa Will Tate attended Johnson C. Smith College in Charlotte, North Carolina, before he moved to Alabama. When Mama was a girl, Aunt Willie lived in Selma and was married to her first husband, Uncle "Ned" Tate. Aunt Willie's maiden name was Tate, so I liked to say all of her name, like a chant, "Miz Wil-lie Earl Tate Tate Cole-man." Uncle Ned's father was white and the owner of the Selma Stock Yards. Uncle Ned started working with the cattle there when he was a young boy, learned the business and became a cattle broker. I remember Uncle Ned as ginger-colored, with hair as soft, white, and fluffy as clouds on a clear summer's day. By the time I knew him, he and Aunt Willie were no longer married. He came by to visit Grandma and Grandpa often, for brief visits, especially when Aunt Willie was in town. I always knew him as Uncle Ned and it took me a many time of sitting quietly and listening to "grown folks talk" to realize that Aunt Willie and Uncle Ned had been married to each other and divorced. When Aunt Willie was married to him she owned her own car and did the driving when they traveled. One of their trips was to the Black Hills of South Dakota.

When I was seven years old, Mama gave me a ring made of pink, green and yellow gold that Aunt Willie had given her when she came home from that trip. Some of the other family gossip that I learned while sitting quietly as the grown folks talked was that Uncle Ned had lots of money, was a big time gambler, drinker, and had lots of girlfriends. Uncle Ned's mother, Aunt Ciely, owned her home and worked as housekeeper for a rich white lady. By the time I knew her she had beautiful antiques and jewelry that her employer had given her. Aunt Ciely gave Aunt Willie all of this jewelry and Aunt Willie passed it on while she could see us enjoy it. Aunt Willie gave me a gold ring with an emerald-cut pink stone, and gave Mama and some of her other nieces jewelry from Aunt Ciely's collection. Mama gave me a pair of coral cameo earrings and a tan cameo brooch that belonged to Aunt Ciely. We always called Aunt Willie "our fine aunt." She liked knit suits, lots of dressy clothes, hats, shoes, fancy tablecloths, and pretty dishes. She was generous with Grandma and her sister Jenny and bought pretty dishes and tablecloths for them.

During Christmas vacation, and when school was out for the summer, Aunt Willie lived in Fairfield with her second husband, Lewis Coleman. On the Saturday afternoon after Alice Rose was born Grandma allowed me to go with my older cousin, Geneva, on the ninety mile, three and a half hour bus trip from Selma to Birmingham. Aunt Willie met us at the bus in Fairfield. Geneva spent the week with her Grandmother, "Ma Mary," who lived in another section of Birmingham. The next day, Sunday morning, we walked up and down the many hills that are characteristic of Birmingham's terrain, on our way to church with Uncle Lewis. This was a new experience for me because Selma and Fitzgerald are flat.

Uncle Lewis was tall, dark chocolate brown, and the most muscular man I had ever seen. He wore a black suit and tie and a white shirt to church and talked a lot in his role as Deacon in his Baptist church. During the week he wore blue denim overalls to work at the steel mill. He carried his lunch of lunch meat and white bread, store bought cake or cookies and a large thermos of milk to work each morning in his large metal lunch bucket.

Even at nine years old, I thought the way they lived with each other seemed strange. When Uncle Lewis came home from work on Monday his manner was quite different. Instead of being the outgoing, talkative Deacon, he was a man of few words and many grunts. He sat on the front porch and read the newspaper and had almost no conversation with Aunt Willie or me. When he did speak it was in short sentences with a voice of authority. There was one room in the house that I was not allowed to go in. Monday morning, after Uncle Lewis had left for work, Aunt Willie opened the door to show me newspapers stacked from floor to ceiling occupying more than two thirds of the room. There was no furniture. Aunt Willie's only comment was that Uncle Lewis liked saving old newspapers and we shouldn't bother them.

One end of their front porch had stacks of chain-link fencing that Uncle Lewis said he was going to use as a fence across the front yard. Aunt Willie told me that it had been on the porch for several years. The back yard was littered with old boards and odd lengths of old lumber. Some of the pieces had rusty nails in them. There was a large Elberta peach tree in the back yard loaded with sweet, delicious fruit. Some of the branches hung over into the alley. The inside door that led to the outside back door was kept locked and Uncle Lewis had the only key. There was no access to the back yard from the front or sides of the house. Many of the peaches fell to the ground and rotted. Uncle Lewis gave us peaches when he wanted us to have them, saying that he didn't want us in the yard to get stung by the bees. I felt that there were enough peaches for the bees and me. I'd never gotten stung by the bees in Grandma's peach, plum, or fig trees, or our fig tree in Fitzgerald. The neighborhood boys picked and enjoyed peaches from the branches that hung over the fence in the alley, and never got stung either.

One of Aunt Willie's friends who lived up the hill had a bicycle and she let me ride it every day. I was able to practice my newly acquired skill. Each morning I went up the hill on 53rd Street to get the bicycle and returned it before dark. I spent most of my vacation days in Birmingham alone, riding the bike.

Near the end of my week in Fairfield, Aunt Willie took me shopping in downtown Birmingham. We walked three blocks to the trolley line. For the first time in my life I saw the movable "colored" and "white" signs to designate seating on public transportation. In Selma the unwritten law was that colored people boarded the front of the bus, filling it from back to front, many times causing a large vacant space in the middle. Before we left home that day, Aunt Willie told me not to drink a lot of water because we would be away from home longer than the times we went shopping in downtown Selma. There were no stores or places where we could use a toilet in downtown Birmingham. I already knew that there would be "colored" and "white" drinking fountains because I'd seen them in Woolworth's in Selma. When we were to make a purchase we watched to see that there were no white customers nearby because they would get waited on first, even if we were next in line. That saved us from the humiliation of being passed over while the clerk waited on a white customer.

That trip downtown was also the day that I rode an escalator for the first time. We were in Lovemans, one of Birmingham's largest and finest department stores. I was fascinated by what I called rolling stairs. Aunt Willie told me that it was called an escalator. She held my hand and told me to watch and step when I saw a full step, and to hold on and step off when the step started to disappear. She held my hand until I was no longer frightened. We rode up and down several times. When we left there, we went window shopping at Pizitz, another large department store. I don't remember what we bought that day but I never forgot the trolley and escalator rides.

The summer of 1944 was memorable another way. It was the only time in my life that I was ever hungry for hours and days at a time. Aunt Willie didn't like to cook. There were stale, bought cakes, cookies, and potato chips on her dining room buffet. She told me to help myself to these "goodies." Whenever the ice-cream man came around ringing the bells on his bike with three wheels, Aunt Willie gave me a nickel to buy a Popsicle. The sweet ice killed my hunger for a short time. After that summer I didn't eat another Popsicle for more than thirty years. I was not used to eating "goodies," so I ate very little of them at Aunt Willie's.

During my summers in Selma, I was used to eating breakfast and Grandma's noonday meal of fresh vegetables, meat, cornbread, and sweetened iced tea with fresh lemon juice and mint. On Friday afternoon of my vacation week I asked Aunt Willie if I could please have some "plain old food like Grandma cooked," because I was tired of goodies. She went to the store and bought pork chops, potatoes, and a cabbage and cooked dinner, the only one I had all week. Uncle Lewis ate the stale cake, cookies, and potato chips for snacks at night. I don't know what or where Uncle Lewis ate dinner after his day at the steel mills. He kept lots of milk in the refrigerator but somehow I knew that I was not to drink his milk. It seemed cruel to me that I couldn't even get to the backyard to get peaches to eat. I lost several pounds the week I was there. I was already small and thin so the weight loss was quite noticeable to my family when I returned to

Selma. Grandma asked me what did I have to eat at Aunt Willie's. I told her about the Popsicles and the peaches in the back yard that I couldn't get. I also told her about the goodies on Aunt Willie's buffet. I didn't visit Birmingham again until the summer of 1952, just after completing my sophomore year at Spelman College. Before I left Selma for this visit Grandma gave me enough money to buy food. One day during that visit, the course of my life was changed forever.

· SPELMAN COLLEGE ·

FROM THE EARLIEST time I heard about college the comments to me were always, "When you go to college," never, "If you go to college." Aunt Willie, Grandma's sister, was the only one of five siblings to attend college. She told me of Tuskegee Institute, located sixty miles from Selma. "Big Eryn," Mama's cousin, attended Tuskegee and left after her sophomore year to marry Malvin Moore. Aunt Willie said that I could go to Tuskegee and find a husband, too. I was about six years old and certainly not interested in finding a husband. Aunt Willie also taught me of Booker T. Washington, the founder of Tuskegee and George Washington Carver, the scientist who conducted experiments and developed over three hundred products from peanuts and sweet potatoes. Aunt Willie turned her conversations into history lessons long before black history was a course of study.

I learned more about college life as I browsed through Daddy's black leather yearbooks and purple felt photo albums embossed with the black initials PC, from his days at Paine College in Augusta, Georgia. When Aunt Willie said I should go to Tuskegee, Daddy said I should go to Paine. Mama spoke quietly saying, "She's going to Spelman." These conversations took place before I was ten years old.

Daddy did persuade my brother, Sonny, to go to Paine and Mama didn't object. He was unhappy at Paine because he loved playing wind instruments and wanted to be able to practice freely. With no practice rooms at Paine, he was forced to practice on the football field after complaints of the noise he made when he practiced indoors. Sonny stayed to complete his freshman year. The next term he transferred to

Clark College in Atlanta, a co-ed school across the street from Spelman. Clark had a strong music department and encouraged his involvement in music. One day I visited him for open house and he had his highly polished alto saxophone out of the case, on his bed, propped up on his pillow.

During my senior year in high school, Mama requested an application form from Spelman, the only college application that I submitted. The spring of my senior year Mama began coaching me on taking tests. She knew I would be required to take placement tests so she taught me how to read graphs, see relationships in similar shapes, and to look for the best answers. She told me if I didn't know the answer to a question or could not work a puzzle, move on and come back to it later, if time permitted, to work it out or take a guess. During Freshman Week, as I was taking placement tests, I recognized them as different versions of the tests with which Mama had helped me. I felt quite comfortable taking the tests. I don't know where she got her copy and I never asked. I was accepted at Spelman and entered as a freshman in September, 1951.

My childhood friend, Agatha Jones, graduated from Spelman in 1950, and returned home to Fitzgerald to teach at Monitor High School. She was my teacher for English and Literature my senior year and gave me reading and writing assignments that she didn't give to my classmates. When I complained about the extra work, she turned a deaf ear.

Agatha also told me about the dress code at Spelman, no pants could be worn on campus except on Saturdays. Hose or socks were always required, except in the dorm. Hats, gloves, and hose were mandatory whenever we went downtown shopping. During my first month at Spelman, I became aware that juniors and seniors broke this rule by not using the sign out sheets in the dorm, only signing out to the Atlanta University Library, or leaving the campus without telling anyone they were going downtown. I was afraid to break any rules for fear of being "campus bound" or the worst possible thing, being sent home. Agatha told me that "calling hours," the time when fellows from Morehouse could visit freshmen, were on Tuesdays and Fridays. The hours were limited to four thirty until five thirty, and on Sundays, after vespers, from four o'clock until five thirty. This sounded great to me! I was sixteen my freshman year and had not had "callers" at home in Fitzgerald. I looked forward to meeting fellows from Morehouse.

When my acceptance letter arrived, a list of "What to bring" was included—two sets of sheets for a twin bed, a spread, blanket, and towels. A white dress was required for special occasions such as Founder's Day and the Christmas Carol Concert.

September and the long awaited day finally arrived. Mama's brother, my uncle Frank, had for my graduation gift, given me two pieces of royal blue with ivory trim Samsonite luggage. I packed them with items that I needed the first few days on campus. The other items were packed in Mama's old black wardrobe trunk. I checked it on my train ticket. Spelman workers picked it up at the train station. Among the items packed in the trunk were my winter clothes, many that Mama had made, including a tan, swing back coat. As a part-time job, Daddy measured and placed orders for tailored suits. Each time five customers placed orders for suits he was allowed one free suit for himself or a family member. From his part time job I had three custom-made tailored suits to take to college. My spread was blue chenille made for a full sized bed. It had deep hems on both sides to make it fit the twin size dormitory bed. I was unhappy with this spread, even though it was new. Mama wouldn't let me buy a twin size spread because we had no twin beds at home and she said the spread would have to last for more than four years.

Although I had spent most of my life in Fitzgerald, and had finished high school there, my Selma connections continued to influence my life. I always spent summers and Christmases in Selma. During the summer of 1951, shortly after I finished high school, I returned to Selma for a brief visit. While I was there, Mrs. Thedora Fisher James came to visit her mother, Mrs. Rose Fisher, a neighbor who lived in the next block on Lapsley Street. When Grandma heard that Mrs. Fisher's daughter, Mrs. James, was in town she sent me to meet her. Mrs. James was a Spelman graduate, the mother of Minnie Rose, a junior at Spelman, and the wife of Mr. Willis Lawrence James, music teacher and director of the Spelman Glee Club. Mrs. James was a gracious lady and asked me to contact her in September, when I arrived at Spelman.

These introductions were the beginning of life-long relationships. Minnie Rose became my "big sister," a tradition at Spelman where incoming freshmen, during Freshman Week, are chosen by a junior to serve as a role model, mentor, and friend. I not only gained a friend, but a family away from home. Mrs. James invited me to their home for

Saturday dinners several times during my college years. I spent every Thanksgiving Day while at Spelman with the James' family. I met her sister, Mrs. Gertrude Fisher Anderson, also a Spelman graduate, who owned a candy factory in Birmingham. Their sister, Mrs. Mildred Fisher Doty, another Spelman alumna, also came for Thanksgiving dinners. The Thanksgiving Day gathering of aunts, uncles, nephews, and cousins became a part of my extended family.

When Mrs. Fisher became ill, she moved away from Selma and came to Atlanta to live with Mr. & Mrs. James. Mrs. Fisher died in 1952, during my sophomore year. Her body was returned to Selma for burial. On July 10, 1968 the day of Daddy's burial in Selma, I wandered to nearby family plots and discovered that Mrs. Fisher was buried near my Grandma, Grandpa, Daddy, and Edgar Zeigler, my friend from high school days.

What an exciting day it was as I boarded the train and was greeted by other freshmen students on their way to Morehouse and Spelman. We happily shared our lunches as we anticipated college life. There were some upperclassmen on board who were going back early to help with Freshman Week. They told me of the special relationship between Morehouse and Spelman. "Miss Maroon and White," the Morehouse homecoming queen was chosen from Spelman's junior or senior class. Many of the fraternity queens and attendants were Spelmanites. I was told about the Morehouse football and basketball games. Saturday night dances and basketball games were held at Morehouse's gym, affectionately called "the barn." These activities were an important part of the social life on our campuses. Before my college days I had only seen one football game in my life. When I was a junior in high school, Daddy took me to a homecoming game at Paine College. The only dances I had attended before college were my junior and senior prom and the ones held after our high school basketball games.

The basketball games and dances are some of my happiest memories of my college days. I cheered at the games until I was hoarse. I never missed a Saturday night dance. The fellows knew that I loved to dance and as soon as one dance was over another fellow was waiting to ask me for the next dance. The "jitter-bug" and "swing" were my favorite dances. I was always happy when the band played a waltz and I had partners who liked to dance from one end of the gym to the other. My friends, Colin Cromwell, from British Guiana S.A.,

Finley Campbell, from Detroit, and Otis Hammonds from Birmingham were my favorite partners. By eleven o'clock and the final dance, my feet and legs were aching, but I was ecstatic. Holding hands with my date and slowly strolling through the quadrangle on the brick sidewalks back to Spelman was the perfect end of an evening of fun.

My arrival at Spelman and Freshman Week were even more exciting than I had anticipated. At home my little radio with no knobs had been my window to the world. From my very first day at Spelman, I felt that it was the door to a whole new, exciting world. Although all of the students were colored and female, there was diversity. Students came from small southern towns, farms, as well as metropolitan areas across the country. There were daughters of cooks, teachers, college professors, farmers, laborers, land owners, lawyers, waiters, porters, maids, undertakers and ministers. We were all "colored," with the full range of skin tones and hair textures. There were the "haves" and the "have nots,"—students with unlimited allowances and charge accounts at Atlanta's finest stores, and students with no allowances. Some students were on the "Five/Four" plan, where they remained at college for five years, while taking a reduced class load and working on campus. My allowance was ten dollars a month, with instructions from Mama to make it last all month, because she had no more to send me. During my freshman and sophomore years my brother, Sonny, was in school at Clark College. With two children in college and the small incomes from teaching, my parents struggled to make ends meet.

During Freshman Week, the first week in September, I officially became a Spelmanite. A reception committee met me at the train station. These were upperclassmen who had returned a week early to help freshmen get adjusted to school and to acquaint us with the Spelman traditions. They took us on tours of Spelman and Morehouse, our brother school across the street. During that week we were given medical exams and tests to determine our reading and comprehension levels. The results of these tests determined where we would be placed for our academic work. Since I had read every thing I could get my hands on and Mama had coached me on taking tests, my scores were high enough not to be placed in a remedial group as some of my classmates were.

During Freshman Week Orientation we were also introduced to the campus organizations, such as the Glee Club, YMCA,

Granddaughter's Club, University Players, and the academic clubs. I auditioned for Glee Club and Atlanta-Morehouse-Spelman Chorus. I was fortunate that Mr. James and Mr. Harreld, the directors, were more interested in teaching than having students with great voices— I didn't have a great voice. Participating in these organizations provided some of the most enlightening and memorable moments of my college years. Although I had participated in drama in high school I didn't audition for the University Players. With piano and flute practice, Glee Club, chorus and orchestra, classes, work, and calling hours, my days were quite full. Mandatory study hours were from seven until nine o'clock each evening.

During the first semester of freshman year, roommates were assigned alternating weeks to go to the library to study, while the other one stayed in the room. Between nine and ten o'clock we sat around visiting, laughing, talking, and eating a bedtime snack. By the time the bell on Packard Hall rang at ten o'clock for "lights out" I was always ready to end the day. The ten o'clock "lights out" rule never annoyed me. I was awakened every morning at six when the large brass bell rang. I went non-stop all day and by ten o'clock I was exhausted. Mr. James, the director of the Glee Club, and my flute teacher, often said to me, "Little Goseer, (his name for me) slow down! Every time I see you walking across the campus you are in a hurry." He was right. I was always in a hurry. I felt I had so much to learn and so many things to do.

During Freshman Week we were also taught the Spelman Hymn, and lectured on Spelman traditions and rules. Agatha Jones had prepared me for much of this during my senior year in high school, such as the large bell in the tower of Packard Hall, the sophomore dormitory that rang at six o'clock a.m. for wake up and several tines during the day calling us to meals, daily chapel, and special activities such as convocations and concerts. By the end of Freshman Week, placement tests were completed and we were allowed to register for classes before the rest of the upper class students arrived on campus. On Saturday night the long awaited party to meet fellows from Morehouse was held in our dining hall on the first floor of Morgan Hall, the freshman dormitory.

There are two incidents that stand out in my memories of that week. Miss Florence Read, our president, walked up to me, with a warm smile and twinkling eyes, and said "Hello, Miss Goseer. You're from Fitzgerald, Georgia. Welcome to Spelman." I was almost shocked speechless. First of all, I had never been greeted by a white person as "Miss Goseer," nor had I ever shaken hands with a white person. I wondered how she knew my name. I remembered later that I had submitted the required snapshot with my college application. Miss Read had cared enough to memorize the names, faces and home town of each incoming freshman. My next two years at Spelman, with Miss Read as president, changed immensely the way I perceived the world. More later about Miss Read and the impact she had on my life.

The second memorable event of Freshman Week was my piano audition with Mr. Kemper Harreld, the head of the music department. After hearing me play the piano and assigning Mrs. Ella Bowman Clark as my teacher, he asked me to show him my teeth. I felt puzzled at this request, but I complied. He said that my teeth were good and straight and I should learn to play the flute. He loaned me a flute and told me my teacher would be Mr. James, Mrs. Thedora James' husband. The lessons were offered to me free of charge and he told me that I must practice every day and play in the University Orchestra during the spring concert, while sitting next to my big sister, Minnie Rose. At the beginning of my junior year, after Minnie Rose graduated and entered Radcliffe to study for her Master's degree, Yvonne Jackson became my flute partner. During my junior year spring concert, Yvonne and I played the flute duet for "Sheep May Safely Graze" by Bach. I felt proud of my accomplishments.

Mr. Harreld and Mr. James also opened new doors to my world of music. No longer was I limited to listening to music on my little radio. During Freshman Week Mr. Harreld told me that music majors were required to subscribe to the symphony series in downtown Atlanta. Miss Read had a rule that Spelman students must not go to any segregated facility. This concert series was the one exception to the rule. Her reason for this exception was the benefits outweighed the indignity of going around to the back side of the Municipal Auditorium and walking up to "Buzzards' Roost," the top balcony, where the colored concert goers were allowed to sit. For four years I attended these concerts with a faculty chaperon. The music was always thrilling.

The culminating activity of Freshman Week was the Sunday morning church service at Friendship Baptist Church. In preparation for our one and a half mile walk to Friendship, we were told that the

My freshman year at Spelman College, September, 1951.
It was the beginning of new horizons in my life.

proper dress for this church service were dressy shoes, hose, hat, purse, and white gloves. The upperclassmen who were helping with Freshman Week activities added a practical note, "Wear comfortable shoes for this long walk." We assembled in the quadrangle and walked in twos up and down hills to the corner of Mitchell and Lee Streets to Friendship Baptist Church.

It was here, in the low, dark basement of Friendship Church, in 1881, that Spelman had its humble beginning. Eleven students and two white women from New England, Miss Sophia B. Packard and Miss Harriet B. Giles, under the sponsorship of the Women's Baptist Home Mission Society, began classes. John D. Rockefeller and his wife, Laura Spelman Rockefeller, had become interested in Miss Packard and Miss Giles and the school early on. The Rockefeller's first gift to Spelman was made in 1883. They continued their financial support and several campus buildings bear their names.

The following week, "duty work," housekeeping chores in our dormitory that took about ten minutes each morning, were assigned. The rotating assignments of dusting a corridor or a flight of stairs, or cleaning face bowls, showers, tubs, and toilets were a part of our daily ritual. By ten o'clock our "house mother" checked our rooms and "duty work" each day. If the cleaning was not to her satisfaction we received a note of reprimand. I had "duty work" for my four years at Spelman. When my daughters entered Spelman, Audrey in 1974, and Greta in 1984, these rules and many others had changed. I had told them of the strict rules and duties that were a part of my life at Spelman. They were pleased that those rules were no longer in effect.

Classes began with the required courses of biology, literature, social studies, physical education, one elective, and a required one-credit hour class called "Personality Development." For the latter, the entire freshman class met once a week in the large lecture hall in Giles Hall. Mrs. Freddye Henderson, our teacher, an elegant and gracious lady, demonstrated and lectured on grooming, make-up, hair styles, appropriate dress, and behavior. This large room had a stage we walked across to receive tips on good posture, while holding our shoulders and head erect and feet straight. She suggested that I should walk with my feet pointed straight, instead of my natural and comfortable "slew-footed" position. She finally gave up trying to get me to walk "the correct" way. I had no trouble with my head and shoulders being erect because that had always been comfortable.

The second semester of my freshman year, our one-credit hour required class was Speech 101, where our teacher, Mr. Baldwin Burroughs, working with small classes, helped us to improve our diction, pronunciation, and breathing. This was not an easy class for me, because, in part, he was trying to help me eliminate my southern accent and drawl that were as much a part of me as my arms. More than forty years later, I have not completely lost my drawl, although I no longer live in the South.

After classes began and I had learned my way around campus, I began to explore the surrounding areas. Morehouse College, Clark College, and Atlanta University were a short walk from Spelman's front gate. Morris Brown College was about a mile away, down Chestnut Street and up the hill on Ashby Street, now Martin Luther King, Jr. Drive. I saw Morris Brown College when football season began, because Morehouse used their stadium for their home games. Morehouse now has its own stadium. I loved going to the football games even though I didn't know the rules. I enjoyed the warm autumn afternoons outside, sitting behind the band, clapping and cheering with the crowd. I could relate quite well to Andy Griffith's humorous monologue "What It Was, Was Football," a popular recording on the radio in the 1950s.

Many Saturday evenings, after the football games, Spelmanites were invited to dances at the Morehouse gym, a wooden frame building not much larger than the basketball court. The bleachers surrounding the court were ten rows high. After football season, basketball games were played at the barn some Saturday nights. I enjoyed basketball and never missed a game. I knew the rules because I had been the official score keeper for my high school basketball teams. I didn't have to wait for the crowd to cheer before I joined in, as I did at the football games. A larger, brick gym replaced the barn after I left college. Whenever I return to Atlanta and pass the corner where it stood, I smile as I recall the fun that I had there at dances and basketball games.

In preparation for the 1996 Olympics in Atlanta, the Olympic Committee built a new gym on Morehouse's campus and included an Olympic size pool. It was the latest in technology and design. When the Olympics were over the gym became the property of Morehouse.

West End Shopping Center was a mile from Spelman's back gate. Freshmen had permission to go shopping and return to campus by five-thirty. Sears was the largest store, with two floors and escalator. As a child, I had shopped at Sears through their catalog. It was a great feeling for me to walk the aisles, and see and touch the items for sale. Woolworth's Ten Cents Store, also located in West End, was much larger than McCellans Ten Cents Store that I was accustomed to in Fitzgerald. I enjoyed browsing there. The West End Shopping Center was larger than all of downtown Fitzgerald. The Spelman rule was that freshmen, during the first semester, could only go downtown with an upperclassman as chaperone. We also had to wear hose, gloves, and hats. The upperclassmen didn't like this rule so it was difficult to get a chaperone for a Saturday afternoon trip downtown. They avoided following this rule by leaving the campus and not signing out on the sign-out sheet in their dorm. When I became a sophomore I broke that rule too, and left the campus without signing out, so I didn't dress up.

When we left the campus to go downtown we were not subjected to the segregated public transportation system that was the law in Georgia. We boarded the bus at Fair and Chestnut Streets, one block from Spelman, at the far corner of the Morehouse campus. The Fair

Street bus to downtown Atlanta didn't have a "colored" sign on the seats. The bus was always filled with students and a few adults who had boarded the bus in the colored neighborhood of southwest Atlanta for the brief ride to downtown Atlanta. The end of the Fair Street line was at Rich's Department Store. Rich's soon became my favorite store, with its escalators, elevators, and displays of crystal, china, jewelry, clothing, and house wares. I enjoyed the Saturday afternoons I spent browsing, daydreaming about what I would buy when I had enough money. It never took long for me to purchase the few items I could afford—stockings and other small items of clothing.

Once I felt comfortable shopping at Rich's, I ventured farther downtown to Davison's Department Store on Peachtree Street near Five Points, window-shopping at the smaller stores along the way. One Saturday afternoon, as my roommate, Lillie, and I walked from Rich's Department Store to Davison's, I saw a pair of shoes that I really liked in the window of a small shoe store. Lillie and I walked in the store and looked at the shoes on display. Lillie stood by silently as I pointed to a pair of shoes and told the clerk that I wanted to try on in a size six and a half. The shoes on display in the front were my correct size. The salesman took them from the display rack and invited me to the back of the store to have a seat and try them on. I smiled and said, "I would like to try them on here, up front where they were displayed." He continued to walk to the back, holding the shoes, and again invited me to the back of the store to try them on. I continued to smile and stand in the front saying, "I will try them on up here."

Finally he said, in exasperation, "Y'all from Spelman, ain't you?"

I smiled and said, "Yes," as I sat in a seat in the front. Lillie was quiet during my conversation but sat up front with me. He walked back to the front, bringing the shoes with him. They were black patent leather and mesh with three inch heels. They were perfect, except for the fact that I was wobbly as I walked in them because I had never worn high heel shoes before. This was also my first time standing up to a white man for fair and just treatment. I left the store light-hearted and happy. When I wore the shoes the next day I felt proud and even taller than the extra three inches.

When we walked out of the shoe store Lillie smiled and commented that I was determined that I was not going to sit in the back of the store to try on the shoes. She told me that she was proud of me. We walked back towards Rich's to get the Fair Street bus to campus. Planters Peanut Company's "Mr. Peanut" was standing on the corner near the bus stop, wearing a monocle, dressed in a high-top hat, a tan peanut-shaped suit, black shoes, white spats, and holding a walking cane. He did fancy dance steps as he passed out samples of nuts. With the tantalizing aroma of the roasting nuts and the taste of the sample, we made our final purchase of a small bag of nuts before boarding the bus back to campus.

In 1951, when I entered Spelman, the total student enrollment was less than five hundred. The campus setting was a traditional picture of neatly manicured lawns, ivy covered red brick buildings, stately oaks, and towering evergreens. In winter the grounds and buildings were decorated with glossy green holly and its bright red berries. In spring, delicate pink and white dogwood trees, pink, white, and red azaleas bloomed for our April 11 Founder's Day Celebration. In May, during Commencement Festivities, large white magnolia blossoms filled the air with their sweet aroma.

Mr. Bullock, one of our faculty members, liked to grow and arrange flowers as a hobby. He decorated Sisters Chapel for the Christmas Carol Concert, using holly and evergreen from our campus. He also created unique arrangements of magnolia blossoms and leaves and placed them on the stage of the chapel for Baccalaureate and Graduation Days. I first met Mr. Bullock at my home in Fitzgerald, my junior year in high school. He came to speak at our graduation program. Daddy had met him at Atlanta University when he was a student in one of Mr. Bullock's summer courses. I enjoyed visits with Mr. Bullock some afternoons as he worked in the rose garden. It was a pleasant reminder of the days at home when I followed Daddy around the yard or helped him with yard work. I have always preferred working outside rather than doing indoor housework. Mr. Bullock always cut three roses and gave them to me whenever I visited him in his garden. He showed me how to cut a rose at a slant just above the top five-leaflet, to insure continuous blooms. I always felt so special and loved to have a gift of his fragrant roses to take to my room. In 1983 Bill Cosby, through a generous donation, made it possible to build The Cosby Center on Spelman's campus—formerly the site of the rose garden.

Mr. Bullock lived five blocks away from campus in a house on Ashby Street. He arrived on campus early in the mornings and stayed until late afternoons. He also came on Sunday mornings to teach a nine o'clock Sunday School class. Because I had known Mr. Bullock before I came to Spelman, I joined his class. One spring Saturday afternoon he took us to the Atlanta Cyclorama in Grant Park. We saw the oil painting and multi-media presentation of the Battle of Atlanta. All of the action of that terrible day is captured in a three dimensional, 358 foot painting in the round, with sound effects and narration to highlight each facet of the battle. My feelings on seeing this display were akin to putting one's hands over one's eyes but leaving the fingers spread open for a peek. This realistic presentation, for me, was both gruesome and fascinating. Mr. Bullock also planned and selected the site for our annual Sunday School picnic, away from campus, in a peaceful, wooded, lakeside area so that our day would be a complete change of pace.

As I became more in tune to the rhythm of the campus, I began to feel that Sisters Chapel was the heart of the campus. This magnificent structure, with its simple elegance of six Doric columns at the front entrance, was a gift from the Rockefeller family. The plaque in the front entrance reads:

> *The Sisters Chapel was built with funds from*
> *the estates of Laura Spelman Rockefeller and*
> *Lucy Maria Spelman for many years loyal friends*
> *of Spelman College and daughters of Lucy Henry*
> *Spelman after whom the College was named.*
> *May the beautiful Christian spirit of these sisters*
> *and their lives of unselfish service ever be*
> *an inspiration to those who cross this threshold.*
> Anno domini *1926*

During my four years at Spelman, as a student and on all of the occasions that I've returned to Spelman and Sisters Chapel, I've always felt like a thirsty plant that's getting its roots watered.

While a student there, from 1951 to 1955, daily eight o'clock chapel and three o'clock Sunday vespers were compulsory. We had assigned seats and a staff member who sat in the balcony and checked vacant seats took attendance. It was here that I heard commanding speakers, world leaders, outstanding theologians, world renowned musicians, and famous poets. This is also where I heard and performed some of the world's greatest music.

Half-way into my first semester I began to realize that Atlanta University, Morehouse, Clark, Morris Brown, and the International Theological Seminary, combined to create an island of freedom in the midst of an ocean of Jim Crow laws and segregation in Georgia. Sisters Chapel was a strong focal point because it had the largest seating capacity for convocations and concerts. Nationally and internationally known guests of Spelman, Morehouse and Atlanta University, as well as faculty members and local ministers were speakers there.

Early in September of my freshman year, Dr. Benjamin E. Mays, president of Morehouse, delivered a message at Sunday vespers that I never forgot. The sentence that made me almost jump out of my seat was, "It doesn't matter where you're from, it's where you're going that counts, even if you're from Fitzgerald, Georgia." I thought to myself, "How can this tall, dark, handsome, articulate, intelligent man, president of a college, even know about this small town in south Georgia?" Many of my classmates and teachers had never heard of Fitzgerald. As Dr. Mays continued his speech, he shared the story of his humble beginnings as the son of former slaves and sharecroppers in Epworth, South Carolina, a rural community surrounded by poverty, racism, and overpowered by the Ku Klux Klan. He finished college at Bates College in Maine and earned Masters and Ph.D. degrees from The University of Chicago. Dr. Mays concluded his speech with a paragraph that I was able to remember and paraphrase. Years later I read it in the book, *Quotable Quotes of Benjamin E. Mays*, published by Vantage Press, New York, N.Y. I remembered the first time I heard it.

> *It must be borne in mind that the tragedy of life*
> *doesn't lie in not reaching your goal. The tragedy*
> *lies in having no goal to reach. It isn't a calamity to*
> *die with dreams unfulfilled, but it is a calamity not*
> *to dream. It is not a disaster to be unable to capture*
> *your ideal, but it is a disaster to have no ideal to*
> *capture. It is not a disgrace not to reach the stars,*
> *but it is a disgrace to have no stars to reach for.*
> *Not failure, but low aim is sin.*

I was too shy to introduce myself to Dr. Mays after vespers to tell him I was from Fitzgerald, and how much I appreciated his message. After that day I took advantage of every opportunity I could to hear him speak, and I hung on to his every word. He helped me to believe that even a little girl from Fitzgerald, Georgia could "reach the stars." In the spring of my senior year, I did meet Dr. and Mrs. Mays and told them how his speech at the beginning of my freshman year had inspired me. Mrs. Mays asked me my daddy's name. When I told her his name was Stanley Goseer, she said, "I knew your Daddy when he was at Paine College." I was thrilled to know that this beautiful, gracious lady knew Daddy.

The first weekend in December I experienced one of the most important events on campus, The Christmas Carol Concert. The Glee Club, under the direction of Mr. James, and the one hundred-voice Atlanta-Morehouse-Spelman Chorus, under the direction of Mr. Harreld, with accompanists and music teachers from Morehouse and Spelman, were responsible for the long hours of rehearsals that prepared us for this weekend. In Glee Club and Chorus rehearsals, during my four years of participation, I learned German, French, Sicilian, English, Swedish, Spanish, Italian, and Haitian carols as well as our own Negro Spirituals. Each year students from the creative dance class joined us on stage for one carol. They wore long, soft, flowing skirts over leotards and accompanied their interpretive dance movements with finger cymbals and castanets, adding a bit of spice and change of pace to the concert. "The Feast Of The Holy King," was one of the outstanding dance/choral renditions. The syncopated rhythm of the words "Viva, viva, viva" with the accompanying finger cymbals, castanets, tambourines and claves were an entirely new musical experience for me. I had quivers in my stomach as we sang this carol. In addition to carols from many lands, our repertoire included works by outstanding composers.

In 1953 one of the selections on the Christmas Carol concert was the Bach chorale, "Oh Jesu Sweet, O Jesu Mild." Our Registrar, Miss Gladys Weber was ill. The men of Buildings and Grounds did an electric hook-up to her room on campus so she could hear the live Saturday night program. She sent word to us that we sounded "like angels, singing in a heavenly choir." Her praise was reward enough for our long hours of rehearsals. Miss Weber died the following Monday. On Thursday, Glee Club members assembled in Sisters Chapel again to sing "Oh Jesu Sweet," this time for Miss Weber's funeral. She was quiet, dignified, warm and friendly and took personal interest in all of the students while supervising their course of study.

On the two evenings we performed, Glee Club and Chorus members were required to meet at the chapel at seven o'clock for warm-ups and a final rehearsal before the eight o'clock performance. The attire for young ladies was white dresses. I wore, for the first time, the white, waffle-pique dress that Mama had made. Before the day of the concert, appointments were made to have our dresses measured so that each dress was the same length from the floor. The young men wore dark suits, white shirts and dark, solid ties.

The chapel was thoroughly cleaned and the decorating began. The tall, stately, cedar that stood in front of the chapel was aglow with blue and white lights, welcoming everyone to the concert. Inside, Sisters Chapel was bedecked with huge green Christmas wreaths, decorated with red ribbon that the art students had made. Mr. Bullock, Mr. Smith, and the men of Buildings and Grounds cut holly, pyracantha and magnolia leaves for decorations. A cross of red pyracantha berries against a background of magnolia leaves blanketed the central door of the stage. Two large wooden candelabra, covered with greenery, each holding fourteen white candles were a part of the imposing background on stage, in front of the brass pipes of the organ. The stained glass windows in shades of gold were banked with evergreen and holly, out of which pure white candles rose. I had never seen such beautiful Christmas decorations in all my life and was thrilled to be a participant in the concert.

The candle-lighting ceremony signaled to the audience the beginning of the concert. The chapel was filled long before the actual beginning of the concert. On each of the two evenings all seats were filled in this one thousand seat auditorium. Crowds lined the walls, filled the vestibule and overflowed into the cold night. Race and creed were forgotten as hundreds of guests sat or crowded together in the chapel. Hundreds more were turned away for lack of space.

The program opened with an organ prelude as we lined up at the front entrance for our processional, "Hail to the Lord's Anointed." I was five feet, two inches tall, and always third or fourth in line on the alto side. My roommate, Lillie, was four feet eleven, and always first in line. Because I was one of the first to get on stage, I had time to experience the beauty of the processional, as well as the sea of all colors of people in the audience, before my attention had to be focused on our director. My participation in the Christmas Carol Concert in 1951, as a freshman and a sixteen year old, was the first time I had been a part of an integrated audience. It was the policy at Spelman that all people were welcomed on our campus, but there were no reserved sections for our white guests.

About midway through the program the audience was invited to stand and join us in singing "Joy to the World." Later in the program, "Silent Night" was sung while everyone was seated, with only the golden flames of the candles to light the auditorium. The electric lights were turned off one other time during the concert, when we sang the spiritual, "Behold the Star." A tin, three-dimensional star illuminated from inside, was suspended high above the center stage door while a part of the chorus went backstage for an antiphonal chorus.

Near the end of the program the audience stood once again and joined us in singing the joyous, booming, Hallelujah Chorus from Handel's Messiah, and remained standing to join us singing the spiritual, "Go Tell It on the Mountain." The full chords of the pipe organ playing "Hark the Herald Angels Sing" signaled the end of the concert, and the recessional began. At the beginning of the evening each guest was given a large, four-page, white program with the words of the carols printed in green ink. The first page had a border of green holly and red berries. At the top of the second page, a request was printed asking that there be no applause during the entire program. The audience honored this request. We did not need applause to know that the audience had enjoyed the program. The air was charged with electricity and we were greeted with enthusiastic nods and warm smiles as we walked toward the front exit doors. I was bursting with pride as I returned the nods and smiles expressing my joy and pride as a participant in this glorious concert.

Our president, Miss Read, instituted the annual event of The Christmas Carol Concert in 1928. I have returned many times since my college years to attend this concert. Since the Martin Luther King, Jr. Chapel was built on Morehouse's campus, with its greater seating capacity, the concerts have been increased to three nights, with two performances at Morehouse's King Chapel and one performance in Sisters Chapel. It continues to be one of the highlights of the Christmas season in Atlanta, maintaining many of the traditions of the earlier years. It is now taped and broadcast over the educational radio station in Atlanta and in recent years it has been video taped and shown on national television.

I stood in awe of Miss Read, our president, from the first time we met, September,1951, when she gave me a firm handshake, called me by name and told me that I was from Fitzgerald, Georgia. She was an enthusiastic, brisk-walking, high-energy woman, with slightly graying hair, a warm smile and twinkling blue eyes.

As Sisters Chapel was the heart of our campus, I began to feel that Miss Read was its soul. She set high standards and encouraged us to develop fundamental virtues of honesty, pride, courage, and thoroughness. She was a constant inspiration through her subtle, tactful, well-chosen chapel talks. As an intellectual, she was strong in her convictions and shared them freely. She blinked her eyes and smiled as she told funny stories. Miss Read, whose name was Florence Matilda, made a joke of the first three letters of her first and middle names, "Flo Mat." She said that although these letters spelled "flo mat" (a play on the southern pronunciation of floor mat) she was not in any way someone to be walked on, and challenged us not to allow anyone to walk on us. She instilled in us her pride and love for Spelman. We would not dare walk on our lawns as a shortcut to a destination, but if we were relaxing and enjoying a stroll around campus, walking on the grass was acceptable.

It is interesting how the mind stores information, and then retrieves it at the most unexpected times. In one of Miss Read's chapel talks she said that what we do, even seemingly insignificant things, defines us. One of her examples was the placement of a postage stamp on an envelope. She said that a person receiving a letter with a stamp on crooked or upside down might get the impression that the sender was not a meticulous person. I developed the habit of carefully placing stamps on letters. Miss Read practiced what she preached. I received a card from her with a New York postmark, the year after she left Spelman. I smiled as I noticed the perfectly placed stamp. I still have the Christmas card from her. I still try to place stamps perfectly straight but it is more difficult now, with the new self-stick stamps that won't slide.

Miss Read enjoyed our hymn singing and encouraged us to sing with conviction. Many times she changed a hymn to fit a particular speech or occasion better. Freshmen were the last to leave chapel and if the singing was weak after the upperclassmen marched out, she had us repeat the hymn and project our voices more. Two of her favorite hymns from our American Student Hymnal were "Be Strong," with lyrics by Maltbie D. Babcock, and "Carry On," with lyrics by Robert W. Service. I want to share these words with my readers because I feel they express some of Miss Read's philosophy.

BE STRONG
1. *We are not here to play, to dream, to drift;*
   We have hard work to do, and loads to lift,
   Shun not the struggle! face it! 'tis God's gift!
   Be strong; O men, be strong!
   Be strong, O men, be strong!
2. *Say not the days are evil, who's to blame?*
   And fold the hands and acquiesce – O shame!
   Stand up, speak out, and bravely in God's name,
   Be strong; O men, be strong!
   Be strong, O men, be strong!
3. *It matters not how deep entrenched the wrong;*
   How hard the battle goes, the day how long;
   Faint not , fight on! tomorrow comes the song:
   Be strong; O men, be strong!
   Be strong, O men, be strong! Amen.

CARRY ON
Carry on! Carry on!
Fight the good fight and true,
Believe in your mission,
Greet life with a cheer,
There's big work to do,
And that's why you are here.
Carry on! Carry on!
Let the world be the better for you
And at last when you die,
Let this be your cry;
Carry on, Carry on,
Carry on, my soul carry on!

With the optimism of youth and a strong yearning for freedom and justice, I sang these songs with deep conviction and full voice.

During the week of final exams, "I Would Be True" was a chapel hymn that was always posted. I refused to part my lips to sing this because I felt it was reminding us to be honest, with the implication that we might not be, during exams. The words are, *"I would be true, for there are those who trust me; I would be pure, for there are those who care; I would be strong, for there is much to suffer; I would be brave, for there is much to dare."* I have read the words to "Be Strong" and "Carry On" many times as an adult and continue to appreciate these messages. Even now, I won't sing or play "I Would Be True."

I worked in the music library my sophomore and junior years. I was hired as a campus postal clerk my senior year. My checks were fifteen dollars a month. In addition to the ten dollars a month from home, I felt rich! With that much money and careful budgeting I could now afford to buy more than basic toiletries. Occasionally I bought shoes, a new scarf or blouse, earrings, chocolate candy, and small gifts for friends.

At the end of my sophomore year, June 1953, Miss Read retired after twenty five years as president of Spelman. Mr. Trevor Arnett, President of the Board of Trustees gave a summary of Miss Read's work before she came to Spelman. The following is an excerpt from *The Spelman Messenger*, August 1953:

> *Before Miss Read came to Spelman she had served*
> *as executive secretary of the International Health*
> *Board of the Rockefeller Foundation. She had also*
> *been alumnae secretary of Mount Holyoke College,*
> *her alma mater, and then secretary of Reed College*
> *in Portland, Oregon. She performed patriotic service*
> *with the medical section, Council of National*
> *Defense, in Washington, D.C., and with the YWCA*
> *in France from 1918-19. She was given the Royal*
> *Medal of Reward in Gold with Crown by Denmark.*

Although I knew Miss Read for only two years, she left lasting impressions. Whenever I think of sincerity, graciousness, faith, perseverance and brilliance, she is one of the women in my life who comes to mind. It was through her invitations and influences that world renowned leaders, speakers and artists were visitors on campus and at our chapel vespers and convocations. I feel fortunate to have spent my first two years at Spelman as part of "The Read Era."

In retrospect, Monday through Friday, eight o'clock compulsory chapel attendance, three o'clock Sunday Vespers, special convocations, commencement and Baccalaureate, were as much a part of my education as the course work. Each weekday morning we were summoned to chapel by the hymns being played on the chimes keyboard located in the back entrance of Sisters Chapel. The same was true of Vespers and other significant events on campus. My roommate, Lillie McKinney, had the honor of playing the chimes our senior year. In chapel and vespers I had the opportunity of listening to organ preludes and learning hymns from the *American Student Hymnal*. I still enjoy playing and singing many of these hymns.

Chapel, vespers, and convocation speakers included faculty members from the Atlanta University Center, leading theologians, both colored and white, from the greater Atlanta area as well as international guests.

Mr. John Wesley Dobbs, grandfather of Maynard Jackson, Jr. who became Atlanta's first black mayor, spoke to us in Sisters Chapel. Rev. Martin Luther King, Sr. was a frequent speaker at Sisters Chapel. Rev. William Holmes Borders, Dr. Benjamin E. Mays, and Dr. Ralph Bunche were among the notable speakers who helped me dream of the great possibilities of my life, despite the obstacles of racism.

In September 1953, after Miss Read retired as president, a new position was created at Spelman. Dr. Wallace T. McAfee, a white man, was appointed college minister. I never knew where he came from or anything about his background. I had become accustomed to Miss Read's sincerity, the tone she set for chapel and the high quality of speakers, world-renowned people, both colored and white, who came to our chapel services. When I read *The Poisonwood Bible*, a novel by Barbara Kingsolver, I was reminded of Dr. McAfee. The preacher in this novel, Nathan Price, was a southern Baptist preacher whose goal was to civilize and convert people he considered "heathen" in the Belgian Congo in 1959. I always had the feeling that that was Dr. McAfee's mission for Spelman students. He spoke to us in condescending tones, never making eye contact. If we responded to him with any firmness or conviction we could see his neck and face turn red. In one of his chapel talks he referred to us as "you people." We were too well-trained and polite to boo him. There was no audible sound when, as though on cue, the entire student body hung their heads and did not raise them again until he sat down. Dr. McAfee didn't return to Spelman for a second term.

In my senior year, Rev. Norman Rates, a young black man, came to Spelman as our college minister. He was warm and friendly, and he and Mrs. Rates soon endeared themselves to the students. He quickly learned our names and addressed us all using the title "Miss." Mrs. Rates was pregnant that year and we admired the happy couple as they went for their afternoon walks around the campus. Their first child was born that spring.

Rev. Rates became a Spelman institution. He retired as college minister in May 2000. He was away during some of the years on sabbatical. He retired at one time but was asked to return. Over the years when I've visited the campus, I still seek out Rev. Rates to get my hug and greeting, "Hello Miss Goseer. How are you? It's so good to see you. How is your friend Miss McKinney?" I'm always amazed that he remembers me and so many other students after all of these years.

In addition to great speakers of the time, notable artists were frequent guests on our campus and gave performances in Sisters Chapel. Virgil Fox, organist at Riverside Church of New York, came to Spelman every other year and gave a recital. His brilliant playing, informal commentaries and explanations preceding the renditions contributed enormously to my appreciation of the music.

I had never heard a live program featuring violin and piano music until my freshman year at Spelman when Irene and Sylvia Rosenberg were presented in concert. The day before the concert Mrs. Boynton, from our music department, explained and demonstrated on the piano the themes from the works they would play the following evening. Mrs. Boynton helped me understand and appreciate the Rosenberg recital. Mrs. Boynton was a large lady with long, thick red hair that she piled high on her head. She spoke with a German accent that was strange to my southern ears. She was not my piano teacher, so I was quite surprised, after I graduated, when she invited me to her home for dinner. I was teaching in Groton, Connecticut at the time and she had returned to her home in Stonington, Connecticut for the summer. She knew that I was in Connecticut and had gotten my address from the Alumnae Office. I remember it as a pleasant visit. She was a vegetarian and served a cheese soufflé and other interesting dishes that I had never eaten. Apparently, my Spelman education was continuing.

Looking back, by the end of my sophomore year at Spelman, May 1953, my behavior was, according to *Webster's Dictionary*, that of a sophomoric person—"a know-it-all, whose thinking is immature or foolish." I had the knowledge and confidence of a two year old who, in his struggle for independence, exclaims, "No, I do it!" or "No, me!" My actions on the train ride home at the end of the term were those of a wise fool, another description of a sophomore.

As I boarded the train in Atlanta on that sunny June morning for the five hour ride to Fitzgerald, the colored porter was standing on the platform near the steps. The white conductor, standing in the doorway, mistook me for white and directed me to the white coach. I didn't bother to tell him I was not white, as I walked into the coach for white people. I choose a window seat on the fifth row, left side. The other passengers were seated in the middle and farther back. This coach was the cleanest one that I had ever seen.

I didn't talk to anyone the entire five hour trip. When the conductor came by for tickets I gave it to him without any comment. I got up to use the toilet once, more out of curiosity than need. I wanted to see what the toilet was like on this coach. I drank water from the water fountain, using a small cone shaped cup. As I drank it I looked back at the white passengers. They were reading or napping and paid no attention to me. I walked back to my seat slowly and for the next few hours looked out the window at the passing landscape of pine trees, young corn, peanut and cotton crops, farm houses and small towns. It was a lonely trip for me. I missed the conversation and camaraderie of the porter and colored passengers that I had always enjoyed on previous train trips. As the train approached Fitzgerald and began to slow down, the conductor shouted "Fitzgerald, next stop Fitzgerald, all out for Fitzgerald!" I stood and walked toward the exit. Since I was only five seats back and there were no white people in front of me I was the first person off the train, with the white passengers following me. I was walking toward Daddy's car as the colored passengers were getting off the train.

Mama and Daddy greeted me with warm hugs. On the drive home they were quiet and I sensed tension. When we got inside the house Mama's first question was, "Didn't you ride down in the white coach?" When I said, "Yes," I got the longest, strongest tongue lashings she had ever given me. I tried to explain that the conductor had directed me to the white coach. She said, "I don't care what he said, you know better and so do the people in Fitzgerald." She explained that if any white people had seen me get off the white coach first, it could cause great trouble for us. She continued by saying that if white people thought I was trying to "pass" they might refuse to sell us what we need, or worse still, cause them to get fired from their teaching jobs. She went on and on in an almost hysterical voice until she finally said, "You're only going to be here for a short time, but we have to live and work here, and your actions today could cause us great harm."

After her expressions of anguish and fear I felt as contrite as a two year old who has been sent to face a corner wall. I never rode in a segregated white coach again. The colored coach was more fun anyway, even if it was older with ragged upholstery. There were always people to laugh and talk with and a porter who came to tell jokes and stories.

At the end of my junior year I stayed after Spelman's Commencement to sing in the chorus for the Atlanta University Commencement and to attend my hometown friend, Ira Wenze's graduation from Morehouse. His mother, two sisters, and I left Atlanta together on the midnight train and arrived in Fitzgerald at five the next morning. Daddy was out of town so I had to get a taxi home. Mrs. Wenze hired one cab for the four of us. We lived only two blocks apart. The white cab driver took Mrs. Wenze, Portia, and Eleanor to their front door, but Mrs. Wenze said, "Take this child home first." The cab driver told her to get out but she would not and insisted that he take me home first. The driver was angry, but when Mrs. Wenze refused to get out, he drove to the front of our house, took my luggage out of the trunk, and put it on the porch. When he was out of earshot of Mrs. Wenze, he asked me who was at home. I told him that Mama was there. He said he would come back and put my luggage inside just as soon as he dropped his other passengers off. When he said that, I felt fearful and nervous. I thanked him, but told him that was not necessary because I could put it inside. As he walked to the cab I dragged my luggage inside, latched the screen door and locked the wooden door.

I told Mama what had happened. She said that my fear and nervousness was for good reason. I was right for not opening the door while he was there or telling him that he should not come back and set the luggage inside. I went to see Mrs. Wenze the next day and told her what the driver had said to me. I thanked her for protecting me.

She told me that she knew that he was up to no good and that is why she insisted on seeing me safe inside my door.

On May 18,1954, the day after the U.S. Supreme Court in the landmark *Brown vs. Board of Education* decision declaring segregation in public school unconstitutional, we woke up to our campus littered with sheets of typing paper. I picked up several pieces. The crudely hand printed message said, "Now I'se gwine to Georgia Tech." There was also a smiling "pic-a-ninny" caricature with many tiny braids standing on ends. A small crop-duster plane must have flown over the campus during the night dropping these flyers on our campus. The entrance gates on campus were locked each night and Mr. "Will Shoot," our campus security person, patrolled the campus at night. A few of us spoke quietly among ourselves about this mean act. By noon the men of Buildings and Grounds had cleaned up all of the litter. This unpleasant incident was never discussed with the student body in chapel or convocation. Fortunately, many years later, students from the Atlanta University Center and students from Georgia Tech work together in exchange and dual degree programs.

I returned to Spelman in September 1954, one of seventy-four seniors. I had the opportunity to be a part of Freshman Orientation Week to greet freshman and acquaint them with Spelman traditions. I also had the honor of serving as hostess at my table for our family-style dinners on Sunday. After we all stood and sang our grace:

> *God is great and God is good,*
> *And we thank him for our food.*
> *By Thy hands must we be fed,*
> *Give us this our daily bread,*
> *Give us this our daily bread.*
> *A-men.*

After we were seated, it was my responsibility to set the tone for conversation and to ask the server for more food if it was needed.

For all of my senior year, chapel continued to be as much a part of my education as classes. Many world leaders came to our campus as guest speakers. His Excellency William U.S. Tubman, President of the Republic of Liberia, John Hope Franklin, noted historian, who in 1955 was professor of history at Howard University, and Chester Bowles, ex-Ambassador to India, were among the notable guests that continued to broaden my world. In a dance recital, The Pearl Primus Dance Company introduced me to songs, rhythms, and dances of Africa as well as the Caribbean. For the first time in my life, I saw and heard homemade marimba-like instruments. During a visit to South Africa, in the summer of 2000, on two occasions I had the opportunity again of sitting close to, watching, and listening to groups using similar instruments. As a part of an interactive drumming session, I was given the opportunity to play drums and later take my turn dancing. The seeds for appreciation of these rhythms were planted at Spelman and were full blown that evening. I surprised my colleagues when I danced with such joy and abandon.

One of my most memorable evenings at Spelman was January 30, 1955, when Dr. Wilbert Snow's good friend, Robert Frost, joined him on stage at Sisters Chapel for an evening of poetry reading. In the opening remarks Dr. Snow, with his fine sense of humor said, "What an unusual evening this is to have snow and frost in May in Atlanta." We laughed at his play on words. I've never forgotten the thrill of hearing Robert Frost read *The Road Not Taken*, *Take Something Like A Star*, and *Stopping By Woods On A Snowy Evening*. When I've come to crossroads in my life, I recall the words of these poems, and they have influenced my decisions.

With my work in the Spelman Post Office, student teaching, and all of the other activities, my senior year seemed to have raced to an end. Prom time came and I made my own dress for the prom—a red and pink strapless, silk floral print. Mama sent me two more of her designer originals for the senior luncheon and tea. One of the dresses was made of deep pink, sheer cotton with narrow bands of white lace. The other dress was light turquoise with narrow bands of tucks on the tightly fitted bodice. My cousin Eryn and I wore the same size shoes so she loaned me two pairs of her pretty high-heeled shoes that matched my new dresses—a pair of pink floral sandals and a pair of bone-colored sling pumps. I felt a little sad when I had to return these beautiful shoes.

The long awaited graduation weekend finally came. Mama, Daddy, Alice Rose, Grandma, Grandpa, and Aunt Willie came to Atlanta for the celebration. The high point of the weekend was not walking across the stage at Sisters Chapel to receive my diploma, as I had anticipated. To my surprise the greatest thrill happened on Saturday afternoon, the day before graduation. I invited my family to Sisters

*A month after my graduation from Spelman in 1955,
my family gathered on our lawn in Fitzgerald. I'm wearing
a blue linen suit that I made for my first job interview.*

Chapel to listen to me play the pipe organ. Their applause and congratulations were worth all of the long hours of practice.

After graduation exercises on Sunday afternoon, I proudly gave my diploma to Mama. She had wanted to attend Spelman when she finished high school and was unable to do so. I had lived out my dream as well as hers.

• BIRMINGHAM REVISITED:
SUMMER OF '52 •

AT THE END of my freshman year at Spelman after returning home to Fitzgerald for two weeks, I left for my regular summer visit to Selma. Aunt Willie had also invited me to spend a week with her in Birmingham. I hadn't been there since the summer of '44, when I was nine years old. This time, my cousin Jean, who had just completed her sophomore year at Tuskegee, traveled with me on the bus from Selma to Birmingham.

This week's visit at Aunt Willie's turned out to be a happy experience, unlike that first visit, partly because it was great having my cousin there with me. The goodies, (cookies, cake, and potato chips) were still kept on the dining room buffet. I didn't eat any of them. Uncle Lewis' milk was still in abundant supply but I didn't drink any of it. Inaccessible peaches were still growing in the back yard. The newspaper room was now completely filled from ceiling to floor so one could barely open the door. The chain-link fence and gate that had been stored on the front porch in 1944, was now installed across the front yard.

Grandma had remembered how thin I was when I returned from my first visit with Aunt Willie so she gave me money for food. With the grocery store a block and a half away, Jean and I were able to buy whatever we wanted to cook.

On Sunday we went to church as we had done on my first visit. It was a pleasant surprise to see a few of my friends from Morehouse. Jean and I were invited to a play that was being presented in the neighborhood on Monday night. The fellows called for us, walked us home after the play and came back on Tuesday afternoon to visit.

On Wednesday, Jean, Aunt Willie, and I went shopping together in downtown Birmingham. The trolley still had the moveable "colored" and "white" signs and the stores still didn't have restrooms for their colored customers. We enjoyed sightseeing and shopping in Lovemans and Pizitz as I had when I was nine. This time I was comfortable using the escalator.

At Spelman, one of the traditions was pairing freshmen with junior "big sisters." Gwen Mitchell, one of my big sisters, lived in Birmingham. Before I left college for summer vacation, I told Gwen of my plans to visit my aunt and she asked me to spend a day with her. When I called her, she arranged to pick me up at about eleven o'clock on Thursday. Jean was away for the day visiting her grandmother, Ma Mary. When Gwen arrived at Aunt Willie's she wasn't alone. She introduced her brother, Aldus, to Aunt Willie and me, explaining that she had asked him to drive her to Fairfield. Gwen told us that her brother had just returned home on Monday after serving two years in the Army. The only time I heard him called Aldus was when Gwen first introduced him to us. I had never heard the name before and didn't remember it afterwards, probably because the rest of the day his family referred to him as "Junior."

Gwen told Aunt Willie that they would bring me back before dark. On the drive to Birmingham we passed United States Steel in Fairfield and drove through the neighborhood of Ensley with its large open blast furnaces and smoke billowing into the sky. The buildings were a dirty dark red color from the smoke and soot of the steel mills. The acrid odor of the iron ore permeated the air. I saw mountains for the first time in my life as they formed the background for the red and orange flames from the furnaces and huge smoke stacks. Gwen's brother was quiet during the drive as she pointed out the sights of Birmingham and chatted about Spelman schoolmates. At some point Gwen told me that before he went to the Army, Junior had attended Morehouse and would return there in September. Although he spent the day with us he didn't initiate any conversation with me. I was shy and said very little to him.

We finally drove up to a large, two-story red brick house with brick and concrete pillars on the long front porch. Urn-shaped stone flower pots on the sides of the steps were filled with red and white petunias and geraniums. This house was the largest and only brick house in this neighborhood of small frame houses. An elementary school was across the street.

When we entered the living room, I thought I had never seen such ornate decorations. There were maroon velvet draperies, two ornately carved wooden love seats and matching chairs with tufted beige-colored backs and plump brocade cushions. The table lamps had silk shades. Large porcelain figurines and a green glass vase graced the white wood mantle over the red brick fireplace. A gleaming walnut-colored baby grand piano dominated a smaller room to the right of the living room. Porcelain figurines were displayed there as well, on the brown metal radiator covers. At the side of the piano there was a floor lamp with a shade that looked like an upside-down bowl. I had seen a lamp like it in the viewing room at Rigg's Funeral Home in Fitzgerald. Gwen told me that this was the music room.

Mrs. Mitchell, Gwen's mother, proudly showed off her guest bedroom. The headboard was tufted with pink taffeta to match the quilted center and deep ruffles of the spread. The wood around the headboard was carved in the shape of roses, a motif that was repeated on the dresser and chests. The dresser supported a mirror divided into three parts, with a stationary center and moveable sides. A pink fabric-covered stool was fitted in the center curve. Matching pink taffeta ruffled draperies were pulled to the side with ruffled tie-backs revealing white sheer curtains. Mrs. Mitchell told me that the furniture was hand-carved in Italy and the fabric headboard, spread and draperies were custom-made. The only comment I dared make was, "Oh, it's so pretty!"

The walls in the hallway leading to the second floor were completely covered with snapshots. Mrs. Mitchell told me that her hobby was taking pictures of family and friends, especially at holidays and special occasions. She arranged and taped the pictures to the wall to form a collage, then covered it with a clear sheet of plastic. As Gwen showed me the pictures she told me about the people. I remember thinking that this was a great way to display photos but I've never done it in my home. The closest thing that I've done in copying this idea was to make a collage for my daughters, Audrey and Greta, using their earliest pictures through college graduation.

After Gwen and Mrs. Mitchell had shown me the bedroom, Mrs. Mitchell continued working in the kitchen and setting the dining room table. When Junior left to pick up Dr. Mitchell from his office for dinner, their mid-day meal, Gwen took me into their back yard with its formal flower beds, lush lawn of St. Augustine grass, round tables, and red and white lawn chairs. A goldfish pond was in the middle of the yard with a fountain in its center. I told Gwen that I'd never seen such large gold fish. She explained that the fish had lived in the pond for many years. They had survived because part of the pond was deep enough for the fish to cluster during the cold weather, yet they came up to be fed year round.

After I was introduced to Dr. Mitchell, he began asking about my experiences during freshman year. It wasn't long before he was teasing me about being so tiny and even commented that my light brown dress was the same color as my eyes. I soon realized that he wasn't going to allow me to sit quietly at dinner and that he was one of those people I had to stand up to. Aware that he welcomed my comments, I relaxed and began to enjoy the conversation. Junior was still not very talkative. During dinner, Dr. Mitchell told me that he was a graduate of Morehouse in the class of 1920, and that Dr. Mays, the current president, was his good friend. Mrs. Mitchell was a graduate of Spelman High School. After dinner Junior took Dr. Mitchell back to his office. Gwen and I played the piano and later sat on the porch swing. Junior drove us back to Fairfield later that afternoon.

That night I had the most vivid and prophetic dream I've ever had in my life. I shared it with Jean the next morning and never told another person of that dream until more than fifteen years later.

· LOVE IN BLOOM ·

I RETURNED TO Spelman in September to begin my sophomore year. After registration was over and classes started, weekly Wednesday night chorus rehearsals in Sisters Chapel resumed. I recalled that Gwen had told me that her brother was returning to Morehouse in the fall. When I saw him again, at the first rehearsal that year of the Atlanta-Morehouse-Spelman Chorus, he was sitting in the tenor section directly in front of me, in the first alto section. I recognized him immediately by the back of his head and neck, the same view I had of him from the back seat of the car on my trip to and from their house the previous summer. I tapped him on the shoulder and said a nervous, "Hi." He smiled at me and my heart did flips. The next day, I asked Gwen his name and she told me it was Aldus. This time I didn't forget it.

The weeks passed and I began to look forward to chorus rehearsals in ways that I never had done the year before. I especially looked forward to my seat in the alto section with Aldus in front of me. He began turning around to smile and say "Hi" to me; my heart raced and my hands got sweaty. I began to have trouble concentrating on my parts in the music. I thought he had the most beautiful smile and the prettiest straight teeth that I had ever seen. I don't remember when he started walking me back to Packard Hall after rehearsals and staying on campus to visit me after Vespers on Sunday afternoons. On those dates we walked around campus or sat on the benches outside and talked. I felt there wasn't anything I couldn't talk about with him. When the weather turned cold he came calling at the dorm and we sat in the lounge and talked. I do recall that I tried to call him "Junior" like Gwen and her friends called him. He asked me to call him Aldus, rather than use his nickname. He invited me to the homecoming dance in October. After that he invited me to all of the other dances at Morehouse. I loved to dance and was always excited to be his guest. By spring he was a full blown "Spelman Willie," the name we gave to Morehouse fellows who came to Spelman as often as the rules allowed. During that time he told me that Gwen and her friends, who were then seniors, admonished him to "leave that little baby girl alone, she is much too young and inexperienced for you." He continued to visit me and I continued to keep secret the dream I had when I first met him.

When summer came I went home to Fitzgerald and then to Selma for my usual visit. Aldus went home to Birmingham and worked as a house painter. We wrote letters to each other almost every day. The high point of my day was to meet Mr. Kimbrough, our mailman, at the corner before he reached our house. Grandma would read my mail if I didn't hide it carefully. I found this out when she quoted things from my letters. I began leaving some letters out for her to read and hiding others. The happiest time during that vacation was when Aldus drove to Selma from Birmingham to visit me. Grandma fixed company dinner with her delicious fried chicken. She even made ice cream for us to freeze outside in her ice cream churn. Although she was polite to him all day, she teased me after he left calling him "that old Yaldus boy," refusing to pronounce his name correctly.

After our summer vacation, we returned to Atlanta for the beginning of my junior year. Aldus continued to visit me that fall. Just before Christmas he told me that he had applied for a transfer and had been accepted at Lincoln University in Jefferson City, Missouri. He explained that he hadn't wanted to tell me earlier because he didn't want me to influence his decision to leave Morehouse. Lincoln operated on the quarter system and he enrolled there for the second quarter. His studies at Morehouse had been in preparation for medical school, but sometime that fall he had decided he wanted to become a lawyer and Lincoln University, in Jefferson City, Missouri, was the place he should go.

When he left I thought I would die from loneliness and a broken heart. My grades at the end of the semester did a dramatic drop. My "B" average dropped to almost all "Cs." I received a letter from Daddy, an unusual event, after my grades were sent home. This time the letter only said, "What's his name? Love, Daddy." Mr. Harreld, my music

*My husband, Aldus S. Mitchell. This photo was taken
for his graduation from the University of Chicago Law School in 1958.
He was one of 86 graduates and the only colored man in the class.*

teacher and director of the chorus, sent for me one day for a conference in his office. His first sentence was, "This is not the end of the world. I know you miss Aldus but you must stop grieving and get your old pep back." I had no idea Mr. Harreld was so observant and so concerned about my well-being. By spring I was bouncy again. Aldus and I wrote to each other almost every day. I never stopped going to the games and dances or talking to fellows when they were on campus. I always told my dates that Aldus was my boyfriend and I wasn't going to get serious with them. They accepted my position and I had many friends. My senior year continued the same way and all the fellows knew that I was "Aldus's girl."

Aldus graduated from Lincoln a few days before my graduation. He was present at my graduation as were my parents and Dr. and Mrs. Mitchell. Mama told me later that she was greatly relieved that we both finished college. She and Daddy, who had been her teacher, had gotten married after her freshman year of college. She told me that the first time she saw me with Aldus she knew that I loved him and hoped that I would finish college before I got married. Mama's cousin Eryn, my namesake, married her college sweetheart before her graduation. Both Mama and Eryn went back to college and finished after their children were teenagers. Mama began teaching many years before she had a college degree, as many teachers in the South were allowed to do. She went back to college during the summers as she continued to teach. She graduated from Albany State College with a Bachelor of Arts Degree in May 1953, a day before my brother was awarded the same degree from Clark College in Atlanta. It had been difficult for her and her cousin and she didn't want me to experience those hardships.

The fall after our graduations from college, Aldus came to Chicago and enrolled as a first year student at The University of Chicago Law School. He had used his G.I. benefits to help with his college expenses. These benefits were exhausted by the time he went to law school. The Alabama State Board of Education, as well as other southern states, had a policy of giving grants to colored students who attended graduate and professional schools in integrated schools in the north. This was to thwart colored students from seeking admission to white universities in the south. This-out-of-state grant was given if the state provided a course of study in a graduate or professional school where a colored student had applied. The state of Alabama had a law school at the University of Alabama at Tuscaloosa, Alabama. In 1957 Governor George Wallace blocked Autherine Lucy from entering the University of Alabama, with his unforgettable statement: "Segregation now. Segregation forever." Aldus applied for and received this special grant from the Alabama State Board of Education, which allowed him to attend The University of Chicago Law School. The irony of it all was that Aldus's first choice of a law school was the University of Chicago, so the state of Alabama did him a favor by giving him a grant to study there.

After graduation, I went to Groton, Connecticut and taught fourth grade at Groton Heights Elementary School. I came home to Fitzgerald for the holidays and my family drove to Selma for our traditional Christmas visit. Aldus also came home to Birmingham for the holidays and visited me the day after Christmas 1955. That was the day he asked me to marry him. He gave me a solitaire diamond engagement ring. During the spring of 1956 we set the date for August 4, 1956.

I continued to keep secret the dream I had the night I first met Aldus, a dream I began to believe would actually come true. The dream had been that I was the bride in an exquisite ankle-length white dress. The setting was the lawn and flower garden on the side of our house in Fitzgerald. In the dream Aldus was the groom. He did not appear in the dream until I had completed the walk down the white cotton fabric aisle that had been laid on the lawn. At the time of the dream, I didn't remember hearing his name and we had said very few words to each other all day. Aldus and I were married on August 4, 1956, in Fitzgerald, four years and one month after the dream. It was an afternoon wedding at home on the side lawn.

After we had been married about ten years and had two daughters, I told Aldus of the dream I had the night after we first met. I thought that after all that time he wouldn't tease me but he did. He laughed and said, "I was trapped from the beginning! I didn't have a chance! I couldn't have escaped if I had wanted to." Then his voice changed to a serious tone and he said, "I remember the day I first saw you. Your hazel eyes were bright and wide open and reminded me of a very young doe. You were so tiny and quiet until Daddy made you talk. I'm so glad that you married me. No one ever had or would have been as kind and good as you have been to me."

· AN EXCITING NEW WORLD ·

WITH MY STUDENT teaching behind me, my college years ending and the energy and enthusiasm of youth, I felt eager and ready to go out and conquer the world.

Dr. Wilbert Snow came to Spelman my senior year, as visiting professor, after retiring form Wesleyan University in Middletown Connecticut. By the second half of spring semester during my senior year at Spelman, my American Literature teacher had also become my mentor and friend. The first and one of the most memorable conversations I had with Dr. Snow was the day he returned one of my written assignments with a grade of B+ and a paragraph of handwritten comments telling me what a fine job I had done in the analysis and writing. I stayed after class to talk with him. My first question was, "Is this a Spelman B+ paper for colored students? Would it also be a B+ paper at Wesleyan?"

"By all means!" He responded, "I don't have double standards for students here and white students at Wesleyan. I said that it was a good paper. I would have graded it B+ at Wesleyan."

"Thanks," I said. "I needed to know that." I felt good after that conversation. I thought about it for many days and decided that if I could write a B+ paper for Dr. Snow, I would try for an A. On the next assignment I was more careful with my sentence structure and punctuation. I received an A- with positive and encouraging comments on the last page. Each time he returned one of my assignments I smiled and said, "That's as good as a white boy's paper at Wesleyan."

One day Dr. Snow asked me what my plans were after graduation. I told him I planned to be a teacher. He gave me the name and address of the superintendent of schools in Groton, Connecticut and suggested that I should apply for a teaching position there. In an earlier conversation I had told Dr. Snow that I had visited New London during the spring of my senior year in high school and loved the area. Groton was one of the adjacent towns. He told me to use his name as a reference when I followed his suggestion and applied to teach in Groton. The response was quick along with a request to see the superintendent for the required interview after graduation.

In the meantime, Mama had talked to the principal of the high school in a town nine miles from Fitzgerald and had secured a job for me as music teacher. All I had to do was sign the contract. Mama tried to entice me with the fact that I could stay at home, drive my brother's car to work while he was away in the Army, and save most of my salary to build a "nest egg." This plan wasn't at all appealing to me. I found the idea of working in Groton far more interesting. Dr. Snow's suggestion of applying to work in Groton excited me. I refused to sign the contract that Mama had secured for me. That choice reminded me of the evening earlier in the spring at Sisters Chapel when I heard Robert Frost read from his poem, *The Road Not Taken*.

> *Two roads diverge in a wood and I—*
> *I took the one less traveled by,*
> *And that has made all the difference.*

I never regretted my decision to try for the job in Groton even though the only person I knew was Mrs. Cook, Mama's friend, who had taken me to Connecticut the spring of my senior year. Mrs. Cook taught in Fitzgerald for several years and drove home to New London each Christmas, spring and summer vacation. Her husband, Hoke and son Roy, lived in New London all year.

After graduation I went home to prepare for my interview in Groton. I made a light blue linen suit with an A-line skirt and a short fitted jacket with three-quarter length sleeves, to wear to the interview. Mama traveled with me by train to New London. This was the first time she had ever traveled beyond Alabama or Georgia. Mrs. Bea Cook picked us up at the train station and took us to her home on Cliff Street.

On the day of the interview, the superintendent's secretary greeted me warmly, and told me that the superintendent was eager to meet me. As I walked into his office he rose from the chair behind his desk, came toward me with a broad smile and extended his hand. His first words to me as we shook hands were, "Welcome to Groton, Miss Goseer. I'm happy to see you. I'm sorry that you had to travel so far for the interview. It is our policy that we interview all of our prospective teachers." With hardly a breath and without waiting for any response from me, he continued, " When I received your application and letter of recommendation from Dr. Snow, I knew that I would hire you. Dr. Snow was also my college professor at Wesleyan. I have just the spot for you, a fourth-grade class at Groton Heights School. I've told the principal, Mrs. Brown, about you, and she is pleased to have you join her faculty. Enjoy your vacation and I'll see you in September."

That was the extent of the interview. We shook hands again. I thanked him and went outside to join Mama and Mrs.Cook who were eager to hear what had happened. We hugged and laughed as I told them about my meeting .

When we arrived back to Mrs.Cook's house she suggested that we take a driving trip to Montreal, Canada. She asked Jacqueline Dell, a former teacher in Fitzgerald, to join us. Mama already knew her. I met Jacqueline as we prepared for our trip. I was away at college when she was teaching in Fitzgerald. The previous year Jacqueline had married John Dell, a former Georgian, moved to Connecticut and began teaching in Groton. Now I knew two people in New London.

Mrs. Cook was the only driver in the car. We left New London early one morning and headed north through Massachusetts, New Hampshire and Vermont and across the Canadian Border to Montreal. I was too excited to sleep during any part of the eight hour drive. I had never seen landscapes as lush and as green as the forests of New Hampshire and Vermont.

We spent the night at a motel away from the downtown area of Montreal. The four of us shared a large room with two beds. This was Mama's first time staying in a motel or having meals served in a restaurant. The white waitresses were kind and gracious and, seeing us take photos, asked to have their pictures taken with us. We spent two days in Montreal. This city, with its metropolitan air, tall buildings and dual languages of French and English was the most exciting place I'd ever been. The people of Montreal were friendly and helpful as we explored this beautiful city. They were also patient as they tried to understand our southern accents. We shopped and took some sightseeing bus tours. Mama bought the two of us a pair of tan, wedge-heel shoes of the softest leather I had ever worn. With these purchases I learned the different number sizing system for European shoes, an added bonus to all of the new experiences of this week.

While we were shopping downtown I was surprised to see a tall, dark, handsome, erect man, wearing a dark suit and tie, coming towards us on the sidewalk. I'm sure my mouth flew open as my heart skipped a beat. I didn't know that colored people lived in Montreal. I learned later that many dark people had traveled from Haiti and made Canada their home.

It was also on this trip that I experienced a ferry ride for the first time. The car was driven on board and stored. We stood on the deck as the ferry crossed the waterway. I loved feeling the motion of sailing, a new sensation for me.

On our return trip we took a wrong turn, got lost and spent half a day driving on roads through the Canadian countryside. We stopped to ask directions but the people in the countryside spoke only French and we spoke only English. The map that we were using didn't have the small country roads printed on it. After many miles of wandering we finally came to the Canadian/American border entry point and continued south, this time traveling through up-state New York, and on to Connecticut for our return to New London.

What a wonderful vacation for us! There were many "firsts" for Mama, too. She had never seen mountains, lakes, ferries, non-English speaking people, or the inside of a motel. She still remembers our trip as her first big traveling experience. Many years later she told me that I made a wise decision by choosing to work in Groton, rather than Georgia. She also said that my choice was the beginning of many new experiences for her. In later years she traveled to many other states and foreign countries, but she still remembers our trip as her first big traveling experience. In 1970 she received a grant to travel and study in India. Since then she has traveled to China and Jerusalem.

We returned home by train. I visited Selma briefly and returned to Fitzgerald to prepare for the new school term in September and the beginning of my teaching career in Groton, Connecticut.

My immediate and extended family was with me at the train station the last week in August as I left for my return trip to New London. This was my first long train ride traveling alone. I was ticketed through to New York City on the Atlantic Coast Line Railway. In 1955 the law was that coaches were segregated below the Mason Dixie line. When the train reached Washington, DC all of the passengers in the "colored coach" were assigned new seats in an integrated coach. The first half of the trip in the segregated coach was fun because I had people to talk to, share lunches, and a porter who came by as often as he could to tell a joke or story and see if we needed anything. When I arrived in New York I had to change to a commuter-type train with hard seats and straps for the standing passengers to hold on to. I was fortunate that the train wasn't crowded and I and was able to sit. My trunk had been checked through to New London and I only had a small carry-on bag with me. The porter told me which track to look for on the New Haven Line. I wasn't frightened as I went in Grand Central Station to look for the New Haven Line because Mama and I had done it earlier in the summer. By the time I arrived at the new track, the train for New London was waiting to depart.

Mrs. Cook met me at the train station. This was her first year teaching in Connecticut after many years of teaching in Georgia. By the time I returned to New London Mrs. Cook had found a furnished apartment for me. Her neighbors, Luigi and Lyda Visco, owned a large wooden house on a corner and had created three small apartments, each with private entrances. My first floor apartment had two rooms— a small bedroom, large kitchen , a closet in the hallway and a bathroom that I shared with Clara Barger, a single colored-lady who was a beautician downtown. My apartment was heated by a large kerosene heater which the Visco's teenage son filled whenever necessary. The Viscos were kind and friendly to me. Whenever Mrs. Visco made her delicious apple coffee cake she gave me a piece. Mr. Visco met his wife in Hawaii while he was in the Coast Guard. When I met Mr. Visco he was a Coast Guard Chief Electronics Technician and was teaching at the Coast Guard Station at Avery Point in Groton. He was of Italian decent and grew up in Connecticut. Mrs. Visco told me that she was a "mongrel—Hawaiian and a little bit of this, that and the other."

On the first day of school Mrs. Cook dropped me off at Pleasant Valley School where the general orientation meeting for teachers new to Groton was being held. The superintendent greeted me personally and again welcomed me to Groton. I was one of three new colored teachers hired for this term. It was not difficult for us to spot each other in this otherwise all white group. When the meeting was over, we gravitated to each other, introduced ourselves and exchanged addresses. Blanch Nelson and James "Jim" Douglass were from Hartford and were assigned to Pleasant Valley School. Blanch was a graduate of Bennett College in Greensboro, North Carolina. After college, Blanch returned to Hartford, lived with her parents and worked in a drapery and upholstery store for several years. This was her first year of teaching. Jim had served in the Armed Forces. After he was discharged he enrolled at The University of Connecticut, using his GI benefits. He had graduated in June and this was also his first teaching assignment. Blanch and Jim lived in Groton at a rooming house owned by Mrs. Perkins, a native of Jamaica. Blanch went home to Hartford every weekend. She invited me home with her several times. Her parents welcomed me and her mother fixed special meals for us including delicious cakes and other special desserts. I was introduced to kale for the first time at their home and enjoyed it. Since then it has become one of my favorite vegetables.

Jim didn't go to Hartford every weekend. The first weekend after school began he invited me to go "crabbing." I had no idea what crabbing was but I accepted his invitation. Jim and I joined a group of friends at the beach. They brought buckets and netting to catch the crabs. When the buckets were full we took them to a friend's house. The crabs were boiled in beer. They showed me how to pull the crabs apart and find the "dead man"—a part of the crab I was told was inedible. I didn't want to eat any part of the crab so I only had salad, bread and beans for dinner. Nevertheless, I loved the experience of "crabbing"—not catching crabs but being on the beach with new friends and enjoying the party afterwards, including not eating the crabs.

I was the only, and found out later the first, colored teacher at Groton Heights School. The red brick, two-story building sat on a hill overlooking the Thames River. The Groton Monument, a tall granite obelisk, commemorating the stand of the colonists in Fort Griswold when the British attacked in 1781, was at the back of the school. I was assigned to the second floor, fourth grade classroom located in the front of the building with a marvelous view of the Thames River. The school was a Kindergarten through 6th grade school with a faculty of eleven teachers. Mrs. Brown, our principal, was also the principal at Col. Ledyard School.

My students were warm and receptive. When all of the fourth-grade students met for their room assignments, I saw names I had never seen or heard before. After a few mistakes in pronouncing their names, Mrs. Pierson, the other fourth-grade teacher, finished reading the names for me. The children were patient as I learned last names like Volpe, Worjacki, Gault, and Pfiel. They were also patient with me as I learned to teach in the "real world," quite different from the "book learning" in education courses. My students and I developed a great love for each other. They thought that I was beautiful, and told their parents so. Many of my students had never seen anyone with skin coloring as dark as mine. Neither had they seen hair the texture of mine. At five-feet two inches and weighing less than a hundred pounds, I was close to their size. They liked to touch me, hug me and feel my hair. I didn't mind at all. I needed the hugs and close contact. Many times at recess I played ball and jumped rope with my students. One day one of my so labeled "slow students," Elsie, asked me how old I was. I told her that I couldn't tell her. Her comment was, "You look like a teenager to me." She was pretty close in her guessing. I would not be twenty one years old until June.

Since the Groton/New London location is a sea coast area, the children and their parents had strong nautical interests. A submarine base, navy base, and the Electric Boat Company were located here. Mrs. Pierson told me that many of the students' dads worked at the Electric Boat Company, where many of our renowned under-water fighting vessels, including the USS Nautilus, the first nuclear-powered submarine, were built. This historic atomic submarine was launched at Groton on January 21, 1954, about a year and a half before I began teaching there.

Mrs. Pierson also told me of the high interest the students had in submarines and ships. She warned me that on the days when students told us that a submarine or large ship was due in, it was better to stop regular classroom work and allow the students to go to the windows and watch their arrival. The students knew the approximate arrival time because the families had been notified. We eagerly watched the clock all morning. As soon as I saw the ship we all went to the windows, squealing and waving with delight. After the ship or submarine had docked, I allowed the children to talk quietly among themselves and draw nautical pictures. After this project the children calmed down and were willing to go back to their regular schedule. I was happy that Mrs. Pierson had told me what to expect and how to handle the excitement. She gave the advice, "Don't fight them, join them." My students became my teachers during these activities.

At the first PTA meeting at the end of September I won an enrollment award and my class won the attendance banner for having the highest number of parents in attendance. Parents told me that their children had insisted they come and meet their new, young, pretty teacher. One of my students, Carol, drew a picture of me, cut it out and put it on our bulletin board. The drawing had a head full of dark curly hair that was a third as large as the pencil-thin body. I regretted later that I hadn't saved this precious drawing.

Many times I followed my students' lead in how best to work with them. It proved to be a successful method. During the first week of school, one of my students, David, a slim, blond boy who wore a hearing aid and had a speech impediment, came and whispered to me that he couldn't read, but he could draw really good. He also told me that on the weekends he went down by the pond near his house and drew frogs and lily pads. I asked him to please bring some of his drawings for me to see. The following Monday he brought the most beautiful drawing of frogs, water lilies, and pond scenes using colored pencils and crayons. I asked him if I could show them to his classmates and display them in our classroom. He shyly agreed. His classmates loved his drawings too. I asked him to write a story about drawing and visits to the pond, saying not to worry about the spelling, just write it like it sounded. He finished his story and came up quietly to my side to show it to me. I asked him if he would read it to me. After he read it to me, I hugged him, told him how well he had done and asked him if he'd like to read it to the class. His classmates were attentive as he read about his drawing. I continued to encourage him to share his drawings with us. After awhile he felt comfortable enough in reading group to read the stories in our texts and supplementary books aloud. For the remainder of the term he continued to share his art with us. Later I regretted that I didn't ask him to give me one of these beautiful pieces.

One of the most rewarding experiences of my entire teaching career happened that year. At the end of the term I received a very touching, sensitive letter from David's mother thanking me for teaching her how to love her son through my loving and accepting him. She admitted that she had not been as understanding as she should have been and had favored her younger child, a beautiful daughter. I was too young and inexperienced to fully appreciate the depth of that letter and didn't save it. David did learn to read that year.

One of the required units of study for the fourth grade was learning about the state of Connecticut. Since I knew very little about Connecticut, I was learning along with my pupils, trying to stay a topic ahead of them in my preparations. I learned to use seven magic words, "I don't know. Let's look it up." These words continued to be helpful throughout my teaching career. One of the projects we did in our study of Connecticut required each child to make a free hand drawing of the state, showing major waterways, towns and cities, indicating something special about each one. There were many drawings of submarines on the map for Groton since many of my students' dads worked on submarines. The children also were required to include somewhere on the map a drawing of the state bird, the robin, and flower, the mountain laurel. To get this project started, I suggested they use crayons, water colors, tempera paints, glue, clay, and the side of a large corrugated box as the base. Without me giving explicit instructions on how "it had to be," their imaginations and creativity soared. As a beginning teacher I had no, "This worked last year" methods of getting the task done. I used such strategies as "Let's try this" or, "What do you think?" these magic words continued to be helpful for my entire teaching career. I was reminded of the words from the song, "Getting To Know You," that says, "by my pupils I'll be taught." When the year was over I wondered who had learned the most, my students or me. It had been a great teaching/learning experience.

After the successful map project, I gained enough confidence to pursue another bright idea. I discussed it with Mrs. Pierson, suggesting that each student make a drum, using a gallon ice cream container or a large, round oatmeal box, rubber from old inner tubes and jute cord. Decorations in bright colors would cover the sides. Holes had to be punched in the rubber before lacing on the tops and bottoms. Mrs. Pierson and I were already working together for music classes. She told me that she had never done anything like this, but she would cooperate if I really wanted to do it. We worked on this project in a large open room in the basement. This was a difficult project but the children thoroughly enjoyed it and were happy to play and take home their own handmade drums. What I learned was to never try that again, unless I had partner/teacher as willing to help. I never had another teaching partner as willing as Mrs. Pierson so my

```
                              GROTON HEIGHTS SCHOOL
                              244 Monument Street
                              Groton, Connecticut


                                             February 13, 1956


        Dear Mr. and Mrs. Goseer:

                Because I have a big girl of my own who is now away from
        me, I have a very strong feeling that you people give a great
        deal of thought  to your girl away from you--wondering what
        she may be doing, how she may be doing, and whether or not she
        is happily adjusted.  It gives me a great deal of pleasure to
        speak for our entire group here at Groton Heights, when I tell
        you that we just love Erin.  She is proving herself very much
        of a lady and to my knowledge has never mishandled any situation
        which may have arisen.

                Like any new teacher, she is living reality and finding
        that textbook versions of how to do the job aren't always those
        that work.  She has come a long way in using just plain good
        judgment with any problems the children might have.  Her teaching
        is most effective and, I am sure, will remain effective simply
        because she is open to suggestion and constantly willing and
        eager to take any form of suggestion or criticism and profit by
        it.

                The children have reacted most pleasantly to her.  As a
        matter of fact, the mother of one of our more difficult little
        fellows talked with me this noontime, stating that for the first
        time he was not only contented in school, but loved his teacher.

                All the nice things that parents like to hear about their
        children can be said about Erin.  Perhaps I can put it even
        stronger by saying that, if away from me or with me my young
        lady is giving as good an account of herself as Erin is, I
        shall be very proud and happy.

                                        Sincerely,


                                        Dorothy Gray Brown,
                                        Supervising Principal


        DGB/m
```

future students never made those kinds of drums.

One morning in late fall, Mrs. Brown brought a student to my class who had recently moved to the area and enrolled at Groton Heights. Dagny McClosky had very long blond hair and was taller and larger than the other girls in the class. She walked with an awkward gait as she carried a large, brown briefcase to the empty desk near the back of the classroom. I heard some snickers as she bumped into desks as she walked by. In a matter-of-fact tone, her mother had told me that Dagny was a genius who needed more challenge than a regular class could provide. She informed me that Dagny would be bringing her briefcase to school every day because she had special projects she worked on that they assigned and reviewed at home. It didn't take a full day for the class to realize that Dagny was the brightest child in the room. She was a math whiz and was the first to solve every problem, waving her hand high whenever I asked the class a question. By recess time the next day, all of the girls wanted to play with her. She wasn't awkward on the playground. Perhaps she had stumbled earlier because of all of the heavy books she carried in her brief case. Dagny was one of the brightest students I ever had in my entire teaching career. I've often wondered if I taught her anything that year.

On my first day of school at Groton Heights, I also met Betty Stuntz, a first grade teacher with the palest skin coloring and brightest red hair I had ever seen. She asked me where I lived. When I told her Cliff Street in New London, she told me that her husband, Steve, had recently begun working at the Electric Boat Company down the hill from my apartment. She asked me how I had gotten to work that morning. I told her that I walked two blocks to Montauk Avenue bus line to downtown New London, transferred to the Groton bus and got off three blocks down the hill from the school. She offered to pick me up at my apartment the next morning. She continued this for the entire term. There were only three days during the year that I had to take the bus. She never accepted any pay for doing this great favor. We stayed late every day after school preparing for the next day, waiting until it was time to pick Steve up. What a great blessing her kindness was. I didn't know the word "synchronistic" at that time—or was it another one of those times my guardian angel was watching over me?

Betty and Steve had two daughters, Anne and Kay. Many years later I teased Betty about being courageous enough to invite me to her home and not being afraid that I would "contaminate" her daughters with my "southern accent." Even in Groton in 1955, it was not a common practice for white people to associate with colored people on a social level. Betty and Steve risked criticism and rejection by reaching out to me. Betty was the first teacher at school to include me in her social activities, and told the Groton Heights teachers what an interesting person I was and how much she enjoyed my company. With that, I felt she planted seeds of acceptance. Some days after school Betty invited me to have dinner with them and spend the night. I had my first glass of wine at dinner in their home. I didn't know that I should sip it, so I drank it quickly like it was juice. By the time dinner was over I was seeing double and could barely sit up. Steve teased me and said he had no idea that I had never had wine before. At dinners after that he reminded me to sip the tiny bit that he poured in my glass.

Betty and Steve lived in Uncasville, a community north of New London. They liked to explore and took me with them on family outings to places of interest in the Groton/New London area. Our friendship deepened over the years. I've visited them wherever they've lived and they've visited me. In 1965 I took my daughter, Audrey, to visit them after they had moved to Sudbury, Massachusetts. Their neighbors saw the colored people in her yard and asked her if we were "Fresh Air" children from New York. The Fresh Air Fund Program was an outreach program to bring inner city children to suburban areas for a vacation in a different setting. Betty shocked her neighbors by telling them that we were her friends visiting from Chicago. Betty and I enjoy laughing about presumptions that people have made about our relationship. In 1965 it was still uncommon to see white and colored people together socially. I suppose, in the strictest sense, we were "fresh air children." Betty and Steve also took us to places of interest in this area. One of my outstanding memories is the day we drove to the fishing port of Gloster, Massachusetts. Artists from all over the country had gathered to paint old wharves, the moors, sand dunes, rocks, surf and sea. I've also remembered the crooked streets, old houses and docks. In 1975 I took my younger daughter, Greta, with me when I visited Steve and Betty at their new home in Palo Alto, California, they took us sightseeing in San Francisco, Napa Valley, Stanford University, the Pacific Ocean at Monterey, red-wood forests, mountains and other places of interest in the area. Betty even took me to her Fiber Arts Group meeting. By 1975 her neighbors were not shocked to see us at her home.

Betty has often visited me at my home in Chicago. One time she told the members of her Fiber Arts Group that she was coming to see me on Chicago's south side. They told her they were concerned and afraid for her safety. Her response was that my friends and neighbors always welcomed her, and I spoiled her by cooking special meals for her and taking her to interesting places in the Chicago area. She told them that I had taken her to the beautiful Chicago Botanic Gardens and the exquisite concrete lace B'hai Temple as well as to a party at a penthouse apartment on Chicago's South Shore. On the days that I went to work she felt comfortable enough to walk to the park and the shopping area near my house. One day she went out alone, by bus, to the Field Museum.

Betty, the rebel, is still fighting stereotypes. In 1997 my daughter Greta and I attended their daughter Kay's wedding in Sandwich, New Hampshire. Even in the late '90s, Betty still felt she had to pave the way for the appearance of her "colored children." By the time the wedding festivities began Betty's closest family members already knew about me and my relationship with Betty, Steve and their daughters. Betty had prepared the others so their mouths wouldn't hang open when they saw us. The family and wedding guests were gracious to us, the only "people of color" present.

I've often teased Betty about adopting me, "this little stray colored child." When I asked her why wasn't she afraid that my "colored, southern accent and idioms" wouldn't rub off on her white children she just laughed and said, "It was great that some of it did rub off on them. They have the greatest admiration and respect for you." Looking back at all of the struggles and strife of the Civil Rights Movement, it seems to me that much of the fear was that if the young people had been allowed to associate with each other, they might have grown to respect each other and want equality for all.

Mrs. Millicent Hewitt, one of the first grade teachers, lived a block away, down the hill from Groton Heights School. Many days she went home for lunch and began inviting me to join her. Her daughter, Carol, who was near my age, was away at college. When Carol came home on brief breaks, Mrs. Hewitt invited me to have dinner with her family. Carol was a music major, with the marimba as her major instrument. She played for me and showed me the fundamentals of holding the mallets and playing the marimba. I was pleasantly surprised that I was able to transfer my musical knowledge and experience to the new instrument. After that experience I became more confident in playing mallet instruments.

Mrs. Roberts, the other first grade teacher, had no children, and began asking me to spend some Saturday or Sunday afternoons with her. She lived in Niantic, but would come to New London to pick me up and bring me back after our visits. Many times she took me sightseeing through the interesting small towns in the area, showing me the historic churches and landmarks including a visit to the historic Marine Museum and Mystic Seaport.

When Dr. Snow returned to his home in Middletown, Connecticut, after his year in Georgia, we became pen pals. He and Mrs. Snow invited me to spend the weekend at their home. When I told Mrs. Roberts about the invitation, she volunteered to take me there, thirty miles away, and to come back for me on Sunday afternoon. After I left New London and moved to Chicago, Mrs. Roberts kept in touch with me. When Dr. and Mrs. Snow were old, and no longer able to write to me, Mrs. Roberts sent me newspaper articles of their activities and the death announcements and tributes. Dr. Snow died in September 1977 at the age of 93.

The year that I taught in Groton I had the great pleasure of spending two weekends with Dr. and Mrs. Snow. I remember those visits as times of great conversation and music. I had an opportunity to attend a concert of the Wesleyan Glee Club and to meet some of Dr. Snow's white students. After the concert Dr. Snow commented that the Morehouse Glee Club sang with more gusto and conviction. Some of the songs were the same that the Morehouse Glee Club sang. I agreed with Dr. Snow's critique and we laughed together about the fact that Morehouse Glee Club did indeed sound better.

Mrs. Ruth Pierson, the other fourth grade teacher, was helpful in sharing ideas, methods and materials. She had a sense of humor that I had to get used to. I think that she meant well but many times her teasing was painful. One day, at lunchtime, I had a nosebleed in the teachers' lounge. Her comment was, "You've got red blood! I thought you were a blue-blood. You're no different from us." She and Mrs. Brown, our principal, also teased me about my southern accent, often repeating and trying to imitate what I had just said. One day, when I was tired of this teasing, I told them that I had learned to speak long before I could read, and their speech sounded funny to me. Mrs. Roberts spoke up and told them to stop the teasing, that their behavior was cruel. They never tried to imitate me again.

Audrey Remmert, the kindergarten teacher, was a kind, soft-spoken lady who accepted me from the first day we met. She never married and, to me, fit the stereotype of an "old maid" with her soft prematurely gray hair, genteel manners and conservative dress. Her influence and my admiration for her led to my decision to become a kindergarten teacher. I named my first daughter Audrey. We wrote to each other for many years after I left Groton.

By the time Mrs. Terani, the sixth grade teacher, decided that "colored" wasn't so bad and it was all right to associate with me, I didn't care at all how she felt about me. In the spring Mrs. Terani invited me to her home for dinner and to meet her daughter who had come home from college. My guess is that she invited me to her home for dinner to show her daughter how "liberal" she was. In any event, that evening at her home was not important enough in my life for me to remember what happened there. I just remember Mrs. Terani as looking like the witch in *Hansel and Gretel*, with her long, crooked nose, strident voice, and phony smile.

Gerald Fitzgerald, the fifth grade teacher in the classroom next door, was an example of the kind of teacher I didn't want to be. He had a loud, raucous voice that disturbed our lessons. He showed, what appeared to me, an unusual number of educational movies that we could also hear in our room. He was the only teacher in the building to whom I never was able to relate. I stayed after school every day to do planning for the next day and to practice piano. "Gerry," as the other teachers called him, complained about me playing the piano after school. I guess we were even. I listened to him scream all day and he had to listen to my piano playing after school. I took piano lessons once a week at Connecticut College. The piano in my classroom was the only one available for my use, so I really didn't care whether my playing after school got on his nerves or not. Needless to say, there was no love lost between the two of us. (The Brahms Rhapsody, op. 79, no. 2 in D minor that I studied that year was one of the pieces I used for my audition in for admission to Chicago Musical College of Roosevelt University in 1977. More than fifteen years had passed between my serious piano study at Connecticut College and the audition at Roosevelt. The chairman of the piano department said that I was a little "rusty" but he could tell that I had performed at a high level. I was enrolled at the graduate level for piano study.)

• • •

On Friday morning before the Christmas holidays, Betty picked me up as usual. I had packed one piece of luggage and carried it to school with me because I was leaving for Georgia immediately after school. Mrs. Brown, my principal, had her husband arrange, through his company, a flight from Groton to New York City, and from New York to Atlanta. Mrs. Brown took me to the airport. In addition to my luggage, I had two large shopping bags someone had given me to carry the Christmas gifts I had received from my students that day. These gifts were a pleasant surprise. This was my first experience at flying but I was more excited about my gifts and the anticipated trip home.

After the brief flight from Groton to New York, I was told that there was no reservation or space available for me to fly to Atlanta. I never felt more distraught and alone in all my life. I was in tears when a kind and caring colored skycap asked me what was wrong. When I told him what had happened he said, "Listen to me and do exactly what I say. I'm going to call a hotel near Grand Central Station and make reservations for you to spend the night there." After he made my reservations he continued his instructions by saying, "I'm going to get a cab to take you to the hotel. When you get to the hotel, go directly to the desk and give them your name and you will be given a room number. A bell boy will take your luggage to your room. After your luggage is in your room, go to the restaurant in the hotel and get a hot meal. After you finish eating go back to your room, and stay there until morning. Get a good night's sleep. Order breakfast to be brought to your room. After breakfast, check out of the hotel, get a cab to Grand Central Station and buy your ticket to Fitzgerald. The train will leave in the afternoon. Keep your luggage with you and stay in the station until time to board your train." He asked me if I had enough money to pay for the cab, hotel, food and train ticket. I told him I did. He hailed a cab, told the driver where to take me and assured me that everything would go well and I would be on the train to Georgia the next afternoon.

I followed his instructions. The next morning, loaded down with my shopping bags of Christmas gifts, and my blue Samsonite luggage with the ivory trim, I went to Grand Central Station and bought my train ticket to Fitzgerald.

Shortly after I went back to the waiting area, I saw Grandma's next door neighbor, Mrs. Upshaw. She had just arrived from Selma to spend the holidays in New York City. What a surprise to see someone I knew in this large crowd of people. We talked for a little while and I told her what had happened to me the day before. After we finished our conversation, Mrs. Upshaw went on her way and I looked around for a place to sit. The station was so crowded that there wasn't a vacant space on the benches. I sat on my luggage, pulled my shopping bags close to me and held my coat in my arms.

After I had been sitting there a few minutes, a neatly dressed, medium height, middle-aged colored man came over to me and started talking. He asked me where I was from, where I was going, and why I was in New York that day. He was curious about my bags filled with gifts so I told him about my fourth grade students. He was a patient and good listener. He told me that he enjoyed coming to Grand Central Station on Saturdays to meet new people. Our conversation continued and after a while he suggested that I allow him to put my things in a locker so he could take me sight-seeing in New York. He would bring me back for my four o'clock departure. He tried to create the persona of "Mr. Friendly," even telling me that his wife knew that he enjoyed coming here on Saturdays to meet new people. None of his friendliness convinced me that I should trust him or leave the station with him. My "gut" feeling was that he was "Mr. Stranger Danger" and I should only talk to him in this open, crowded station. After he realized that I was not going to put my luggage in a locker and leave the station, he continued his conversation for a few more minutes, said good-bye and walked away.

I sat on my luggage again and continued watching the travelers. Many came in from the streets of New York with melting snow dripping from their hats and coats. Others rushed to the center of the station to check the information board for arrival and departure times. I also observed other nervous people like me, just sitting and waiting. I continued watching these interesting people until close to four o'clock, when it was time for me to board the Atlantic Coast Line train that would take me to Fitzgerald. As I boarded the train I was assigned to an integrated coach. I sat quietly in a window seat and looked out at the passing scenery. I don't remember what I saw. I was still feeling overwhelmed from all of the events of the past two days. After we passed Washington, DC, the conductor instructed the colored passengers to move to a coach that had been designated as the segregated colored coach. As the colored coach was formed I saw some of my schoolmates from Atlanta who had gone to graduate school in New York and other Eastern schools. We all sat together, laughed and exchanged stories of our adventures "up North." Time seemed to fly in this happy setting.

When I arrived home Mama and Daddy were eager to hear about my adventures in New York City trying to get home. I opened my gifts and shared the delicious homemade cookies and candies that my students had given me. Both Mama and Daddy were happy that my students were so kind and generous.

I spent a day in Fitzgerald before we all traveled by car to Selma for our usual Christmas visit with Grandma and Grandpa. This Christmas, 1955, was one of the most memorable holidays of my life. That's a story for another time.

• • •

On Sunday afternoon, the last day of Christmas vacation, throngs of people crowded Grand Central Station. After arriving on the Atlantic Coast Line Railroad from Georgia, I elbowed my way through the crowd to get to the information board in order to see the time and gate number for the next train to New London.

When I boarded the train for New London, the coach was as crowded as the petals on a rosebud. I hung on the leather strap but the car was so packed I could have been held up by the crush of people around me. As the train stopped at towns along the northeastern coast, passengers got off and seats became available. By the time we reached Old Saybrook, the last stop before New London, I turned around before I took a seat. My heart leaped as I broke into a big smile when I saw this tall, chocolate-colored, handsome coast guard cadet. He returned my smile as I said, "You're Javis, aren't you?"

He answered, "Yes," and came and sat on the seat with me.

I said, "I'm Erin, and you're the person people have been telling me I should meet."

"I've heard about you, too," he replied. "Some ladies at Shiloh Baptist Church have been trying to arrange for us to meet, but the Sundays I've been there you weren't, and the Sundays you came I wasn't there. I'm happy that we've finally met."

Javis L. Wright Jr., Cadet First Class, entered the United States Coast Guard at New London, Connecticut, September, 1955 the first colored student ever admitted there. This was his first time living away from his family. As we shared experiences, I understood how he felt. I was also living alone for the first time in my life, far away from family and friends, except for the four years of dormitory living I had spent at Spelman College. His experiences as a first year cadet were similar to the strict rules I experienced at Spelman: early morning wake-ups, room inspections, curfew, required clean-up duties in addition to high standards of scholarship.

We continued our conversation as the train pulled into the station at New London. He was returning to school at the Coast Guard Academy after spending the holidays with his family in Philadelphia. After we claimed our baggage, he asked for my address and a date for the following Saturday afternoon. I told him how to get the Montauk Avenue bus from downtown to the stop near my apartment on Cliff Street. That was the beginning of many Saturday or Sunday afternoon visits. Many times I served as a sounding board for Javis as he made the adjustments of missing his family and close friends, and being the only colored student in his new surroundings. I was making similar adjustments at work and living in this new community. He knew that I had just accepted an engagement ring the week before we met, so we kept reminding ourselves that we were "just friends."

As our friendship grew I felt comfortable enough to invite him for dinner. I enjoyed cooking and he was happy to have food away from school. One day he told me that he had written his mother and told her that he had met a little girl in New London who could make cornbread almost as good as hers. He had told me what a good cook his mother was, so I took that as a great compliment. She was originally from South Carolina and our styles of cooking were similar.

Sometimes Javis and I went to the movies at the Garde Theater in downtown New London. We went to the early afternoon shows so he would get back to campus in time to make curfew.

When spring came and the date was set for the Annual Spring Ball at the Academy, Javis invited me and submitted my name and address to his commanding officer. Since most of the guests of the cadets were students at Connecticut College for Women, the next-door neighbor to the Coast Guard Academy, my address attracted attention. Javis was asked by his commanding officer to explain who I was and why he had invited me. When he told the officer that I was a teacher, he was questioned further, "Where did I work and how old was I?" His commanding officer called my principal to verify my age

I made this sequin studded dress for my Junior Prom
at Spelman in 1954 and also wore it to the Coast Guard Academy
Spring Ball in 1956.

and to get a character reference. When Mrs. Brown told him that I was twenty years old, a beginning teacher and a young lady with high standards, he approved the invitation. I was only sixteen months older than Javis.

Mrs. Brown told Mrs. Pierson about the phone call and my invitation to the ball. Word soon spread to the other faculty members. They were excited and asked me what I planned to wear. I told them I'd written Mama immediately about my invitation to the ball and asked her to send the dress I had made and worn to my junior prom at Spelman. It was light blue, strapless, with a tightly fitted ruffled bodice and two layers of fully gathered netting over a matching blue taffeta lining. The hand-sewn sequins at the bust line added a bit of sparkle.

On the Saturday evening of the ball, after I was dressed, Mrs. Cook, Mama's friend who lived next door, and Mrs.Visco, my landlady came to see me and admire my dress. After they left Javis soon arrived by cab to pick me up. I'm sure they were peeking from their windows as we left because the next day when they asked me about the ball each of them said what a cute couple we were.

I was nervous as I entered the ballroom and saw all of the cadets and officers in formal attire and the young ladies from "Conn College"(as it was called around town) in their elegant gowns. I'd often seen these students in downtown New London and on the Conn College campus when I went each week for piano lessons. They were highly visible downtown. Although they didn't wear uniforms, they dressed very much alike in their penny loafers, short kilt-type skirts, sweater sets and navy blue pea jackets. When I saw them on the streets and recognized them as Conn College students I realized how people in Atlanta always knew Spelman students when they saw us. I suppose we had some identifying plumage, too. In the 1950s the catalog of The Connecticut College for Women listed the cost of tuition and fees and stated that families with incomes of less than a stated amount need not apply. I was a special, part-time student, enrolled for piano study only, so an exception was made. I don't remember what my piano lessons cost, but it was a big bite out of my salary.

After Javis and I had danced a few times, his commanding officer sent for him. Javis excused himself. When he came back he told me that his commanding officer had told him to bring me over to meet him. My hands began sweating and I shook my head, no. I told Javis that I was nervous and afraid to go over and meet him. He pleaded with me, explaining that he would be in trouble if I didn't go. I didn't fully understand military protocol and the consequences of refusing to carry out the officer's orders, but I reluctantly went to meet his commanding officer, sweaty palms and all. He said that he was happy to meet me and admitted he had been skeptical about Javis inviting me to this ball. He thought I was an "older woman," since I was already a teacher and Javis was a freshman, and he was simply trying to protect him from trouble. After a few more minutes of conversation he dismissed us and told us to have fun. I was relieved. The meeting was not as bad as I had anticipated.

I don't remember any details of the ballroom, whether there were tables and chairs, or if punch was served. Neither do I remember the band or any special music. I do remember that Javis and I only danced with each other during the entire evening. For all of these many years that Javis and I have been separated, I've had what feels to me like uncanny occurrences. Whenever I play or hear "Autumn Leaves," I think of Javis. Perhaps my subconscious remembers "Autumn

Leaves" as our special song at the ball.

Javis continued to visit me throughout the spring. Since he liked my cooking and I liked to cook, it was always a pleasure for him to have dinner with me, taking a break from eating at the Academy.

I have never forgotten the day in late spring when school was almost over, when I last saw Javis. As he walked to the door of my apartment, he asked for a parting kiss. I refused, explaining that I was getting married to Aldus that summer and I didn't think that it would be right.

He asked again, saying, "just one good-bye kiss."

I hung my head and shook it .

He turned without saying another word. As he walked away I looked up and saw his broad, straight shoulders, erect head and elegant stride. I watched him until he was out of sight, the tears flowing down my face. He never looked back. The tears continued to flow, as I stood glued to the walkway. I regretted then, and have regretted for the rest of my life, that I was so rigid that day. My fear was if I had allowed Javis to kiss me I would have been torn about my decision to marry Aldus. It was "the frumpy fifties" and I had been thoroughly indoctrinated on what was "proper." A vow was a vow, never to be broken.

I never saw Javis again. My pen pals in New London wrote and told me that he didn't return to the Coast Guard Academy in September of 1956. During the summer he went on cruise aboard the U.S. Eagle sailing to Halifax, Nova Scotia, as part of his training. I received one letter from him that summer. While he was on cruise he became seriously ill.

About twenty years from the time we met, I saw an article about Javis in the history section of *JET Magazine*. He was listed as the first African-American to attend The United States Coast Guard Academy at New London, Connecticut. I called the Alumni Office at the academy inquiring about him. No information was available. I looked in the Philadelphia telephone directory to see if his name was listed, again no luck there. That's all I learned about him for more than forty years.

In the spring of 1995 I saw an ad in the *Chicago Tribune* for Old Friends Information Service in Orinda, California, offering, for a fee, to do a search of an old friend if the name, place, date of contacts and any other information was sent to them. They stated that they were not a detective agency and were interested in reuniting old friends, only with the consent of the person being sought. The second half of the fee would be charged only if they found the "old friend" and the person agreed to exchange phone numbers and addresses. It took nine months for me to get the courage to initiate the search. After I mailed the initial application and check I received progress reports. In a letter dated May 20, 1996, I received a message saying they had indeed found Javis " Jay" Wright. He said he was the person I was looking for and agreed to exchange phone numbers and addresses. I responded immediately by mailing my final payment. I was thrilled to know that Javis was alive and well and living in Texas.

A few days later he called and sounded as calm as if we had been talking to each other every week for the past forty years. His voice had the same gentle, warm quality that I remembered.

He said, "Hi, Erin. This is Jay." (I had never called him anything but Javis.) He continued by saying, "I was surprised and happy that you had been trying to find me. I just got your phone number today."

I was so excited it's a wonder I didn't faint. I'm sure I sounded like a babbling brook in my eagerness to learn more about him. I told him that I had always wondered about him—his health, where he was, what his life had been after he left the Academy. I also told him that I feared he wouldn't remember me. He told me that he had not forgotten me and had never known anyone else named Erin. During our conversation he said that he had been hospitalized for ten months after he came off the cruise in 1956. He didn't return to the Coast Guard, but after his hospital stay he went home and finished college in Philadelphia. He had been married, had children and grandchildren, but at the time of our conversation was single. With that information my heart started pounding at the possibility of us being friends again. I had been a widow for nine years. I wrote to him a few times and he called me again, in response to a poem I wrote to him expressing my feeling of regret the last time that I saw him.

At present the friendship has not been renewed. It appears that he is not interested and I respect and accept this fact, regretfully. I am not sorry however, that I made the effort to find him. To know that he is alive, well, and has a satisfying and successful life is helping, in some ways, to bring closure to my years of concern for him.

• • •

On February 3, 1956, United States Marshals were present when Alabama's governor, George Wallace, tried to block the entrance at University of Alabama's Law School, to prevent Autherine Lucy from entering. His shouts were, "Segregation now! Segregation tomorrow! Segregation forever!"

The next day newspaper headlines and front pages were filled with pictures and reports of this incident. I was on recess duty with Mrs. Pierson that morning when she asked me why my parents didn't just move away from the South rather than be subjected to such unjust acts. She continued by saying that she would be happy to have me or my parents live in her neighborhood. I paused and took a deep breath before I responded to her comment. I remember feeling angry with her for even suggesting that Mama and Daddy move away from their home, family and friends. With this long pause, I think she realized that she had stepped over her boundaries and touched an open wound. When I finally spoke I said, "Why should they have to leave Georgia in order to be treated fairly? They were born there and have lived and worked there all of their lives. They have every right to live there in peace and harmony and have all of the rights and opportunities that white people have. This is their home, and they don't want to leave."

Mrs. Pierson's response to my emotional outburst was, "I never thought of it that way. I guess I wouldn't want to leave my home either."

That was the end of that conversation and she never brought up any other racial issues with me. She wasn't through with it, however. In the spring, when she met Mama, she brought up the subject again in a rather roundabout way. More about that, later.

My brother Sonny's wedding was in late spring of 1956, in Newark, New Jersey. Mama came by train from Georgia. Mrs. Cook and I drove down to Newark, leaving New London in the early morning on the day of the wedding. After the wedding, Mama rode back with us and spent almost a week with me.

During the week we made preparations for my wedding that was set for August 4th. We went shopping for invitations and thank you notes. When the clerk wanted to put Mr. and Mrs. Aldus S. Mitchell Jr. on the front of the notes, I objected and said, "My name has to be on there, so put Aldus and Erin Mitchell." She said that was an unusual request and tried to convince me to allow her to print it in what she considered the proper way. I didn't agree so she reluctantly printed it the way that I suggested. She promised to mail the invitations to Fitzgerald.

The next big shopping decision concerned selecting materials and patterns for my wedding dress and veil. Mama wanted to shop in New London because the department stores in Fitzgerald didn't sell bridal lace. We found a store that had a large assortment and we selected white silk organza fabric with a silk embroidered floral design and a scalloped edge. We then bought white satin silk for the separate strapless under dress. Mama also purchased unbleached muslin to make a model first, to insure a perfect fit. After this was finished, and fit perfectly, she planned to rip it apart and use it as a pattern for the satin under dress. She took my measurements before leaving New London so she could begin the sewing before I got home. We also found a bridal hat at the fabric shop and Mama bought veiling to attach to the hat.

Our next stop was the music store to buy records of wedding music. The store had listening booths so we were able to preview some possibilities before making our final selections. I had planned a garden wedding so I thought the records would work well.

One day, during her visit, Mama came to see me at school at lunch time, where she had the opportunity to meet Mrs. Brown and all of my co-workers. She had received a letter from Mrs. Brown earlier in the term—a sort of report card. Mrs. Brown told her that I had made a good adjustment and was receptive to her suggestions of effective ways to relate to the students. She also told Mama that it was a joy to have me working there, that the parents and children loved me. I didn't see this letter until the summer of 1998 when I was at home going through Mama's treasures of letters and photos. When I told Mama I had found the letter, she said that she thought she had told me about it earlier. She gave me the letter that day and I added it to my own collection of treasures.

Mrs. Pierson also told Mama how much she loved working with me and how cooperative I had been. Then she shifted gears and had, as she described it, "a mother-to-mother talk." Her comments to Mama were that, "Erin has been friendly, but a very private person, very young to be so serious, and not very trusting—like someone who has been hurt."

Mama's response to her was, "Yes, I know." Mama can also be a very private person and not very trusting. She certainly was that day with Mrs. Pierson. After she said, "Yes, I know," she changed the conversation, and didn't give her any further information about me.

Mama and I talked about Mrs. Pierson's comments later that night. She said, "Mrs. Pierson had no idea, absolutely no understanding of what it's like to be colored and grow up in the South." That was the beginning of a conversation that Mama and I had never had before. She continued, "Yes, you've been hurt. We've all been hurt by white folks who have treated us like second-class citizens. She has no idea how it feels for a child not to be able to play on swings, slides and see-saws in a park, not to be able to use a public library, to have only dirty, worn, textbooks that are the discards from the white schools. Yes, you learned early to be secretive and not friendly or trusting of white folks."

I told Mama about the comment Mrs. Pierson had made the day I had the nosebleed. Mama thought, as I had, that her sense of humor was not very kind. I also told her what Mrs. Pierson said about her not minding having us as a neighbor. Mama's comment was, "I don't want to live in Connecticut. I don't think it's a lot better than the South. You're one of the first colored teachers hired in Groton, and the first one to teach at your school. Bea Cook was just hired to teach in Connecticut this year, after applying many years ago and having good references. She's an experienced teacher with a Master's degree from New York University."

Mama knew that I had learned to trust some white folks. She knew of the friendships I had with Miss Sara Downer my housemother, Miss Reid our President, as well as the white teachers and staff at Spelman. She also knew how much I loved Dr. and Mrs. Snow. I had told her how good Betty and Steve Stuntz had been to me and what great times we had together.

Friday afternoon after work, and at the end of Mama's visit, Steve and Betty took us to dinner at a Chinese restaurant. Mama had the opportunity to see first hand how well Steve, Betty and I related to each other. Dinner at the Chinese restaurant was another "first" for Mama, an enjoyable experience, as she tried eating with chopsticks. Afterwards she kept them as a souvenir. Saturday morning Mama left New London for her return trip home, to begin the sewing and other details in preparation for my wedding.

As the school term came closer to ending, I had strong feelings of separation from people and places that had become dear to me. At

*My sixth grade teacher gave me this sheer pink blouse
as a back-to-school gift in 1954.*

recess my girls hugged me often and stroked my hair. The boys began
to hold my hands and talk to me.

I began to walk to the beach near my apartment every afternoon. It
was as though I was trying to store up the scents, sights and sounds of
the Thames River to take with me when I left Connecticut. It must
have worked because even now, almost fifty years later, I can sit
quietly, close my eyes and revisit my special spots along the beach.

My time spent in Connecticut had been a year of freedom,
exploration, self-discovery and joy. I had mixed feelings about leaving.
That year couldn't have been any more exciting if I had spent it in a
foreign country. It was a whole new, wonderful world of love and
acceptance. But the strong pull of another kind of love, and the desire
to be married to Aldus, tugged at my heart, and won. When school
was out I returned to Fitzgerald for my August wedding and the move
to Chicago.

· A DREAM COMES TRUE ·

I RETURNED TO Fitzgerald early in June after completing my first year of teaching in Groton. I already had some ideas of what I'd like for my wedding. When I was four years old I was a flower girl in Mama's cousin Eryn's wedding. It was on a summer's day at her home in Marion Junction, Alabama, where I later spent many happy summer vacations. The second large wedding that made a great impression on me was the summer after my freshman year at Spelman. Maude Moore, a cousin of my dear friend and neighbor, Helen, had a beautiful garden wedding at sunset, on a Saturday in August. I felt honored when Maude asked me to be a hostess. She had just graduated from college at Hampton University. I never forgot that beautiful wedding at Helen's mother's house in the large, beautiful yard of their farm home at Sardis, a few miles from Selma. With these two weddings making such strong impressions on me, it was easy for me to make decisions for my wedding. During my first week at home, I went to Hires Jewelry Store on Pine Street, the main shopping area in our town, and selected my silverware pattern, "Old Master" by Towle. The Hires Store window display featured framed 9 x 12 photos of the white brides-to-be, with their gift selections near their pictures. When I made my selections the owner didn't ask or suggest that I bring a picture to be displayed.

I chose my china and stemware from Fletcher's Pottery and Gift Shop on Grant Street, around the corner, one block from the main shopping district. My pattern of dishes was white with tiny pink roses, green leaves, and a thin gold rim. The stemware also had a thin gold border. Mrs. Fletcher, the white shop owner, asked me to bring in a photograph, which she displayed on the counter with my china and stemware choices. Many years later one of Mama's friends told me that the day she went to select a gift for me Mrs. Fletcher commented, "She is such a pretty little girl. I hope that she is not marrying a darker boy." This was before "Black Is Beautiful" was popular and we were still called "colored people." Mrs. Fletcher's point was that the darker the skin tone, the uglier the person was considered to be.

With the wedding date of August 4th less then a month away, Mama and I were busy attending to the many details in preparation for the big day. Mama continued to work on my dress and had me try it on often to insure a perfect fit for my twenty-one inch waist and thirty-one inch bust. After finishing my dress, she made my sister, Alice Rose's dress. She was twelve years old and my junior bridesmaid. Her dress was pink cotton with a fitted bodice, cap sleeves and a full gathered skirt. My college roommate, Lillie McKinney Cooley, was matron-of-honor, my only other attendant. She selected a dress of pink embroidered organdy, with a pink under dress to match my choice of the color scheme.

Before I began addressing the wedding invitations, I made a list of all of our family members. When I began making the list of guests in Fitzgerald I made notes of all the people on each street in the colored community. After the invitations were mailed I had an announcement read at our colored churches, Salem Baptist, Mount Olive Baptist, Holsey Chapel C.M.E., and Bethel A.M.E., extending the invitation to everyone in the event that a printed invitation had not been received. We wanted to be absolutely sure that every colored person in Fitzgerald knew they were invited.

By the end of the first week in July, all of the invitations to my family and friends were complete and ready to be mailed. I had not received the guest list from Aldus's parents. Mama called Mrs. Mitchell and asked for it again. She replied that she hadn't sent it because she wasn't sure that the wedding was still scheduled. She said that if it was still going to take place she wasn't sure that she and Dr. Mitchell would be able to come because August 4th was the opening day of the National Medical Association meeting that they attended each year. Immediately after she hung up, Mama quoted what Mrs. Mitchell said and asked me if Aldus had indicated in any way that the wedding plans were off. It was Mama's feeling that if there was any doubt on his part, it would be better to cancel the plans now rather than to wait until the last minute—or worse yet—enter a marriage in a half-hearted manner. I had no doubt in my heart that Aldus was sincere and would be here as we had planned, whether his family came or not. Nevertheless, Mama called Aldus, told him of her conversation with Mrs. Mitchell and asked him what his intentions were. He told her that he loved me and the wedding would take place as scheduled whether his parents came or not. After that, we continued with our preparation for the wedding. About a week later we got a short guest list from Mrs. Mitchell.

After we had been married about a month, I asked Aldus what had prompted Mrs. Mitchell to say that she thought the wedding wouldn't take place. He told me that his parents had offered him an all expense paid trip to California that summer to meet the daughter of one of Dr. Mitchell's medical colleagues. Clearly they hoped for a better match for their son. Aldus told me that he never considered accepting their offer because he had already found the person he loved and wanted to spend the rest of his life with.

A group of Mama's friends had the bright and generous idea of forming a committee to coordinate the gift giving. They were sure that everyone would give me a gift. The problem was that many of the people in our community had very little money. The committee felt that I would receive many inexpensive items from MacCellans Ten Cents Store, because that was all that some individuals could afford. So the group went door to door, suggesting the idea of pooling individual funds to buy gifts that would be of more use to me. The people were very receptive to this idea and happily gave the cash they had planned to spend. I found out later that some donations were as small as fifty cents or a dollar. Even those small amounts were a sacrifice to ladies who earned fifteen dollars a week as full-time domestics for white families. Each person who made a contribution signed the wedding card that was presented with the gifts. One of my most treasured wedding gifts is a medium-sized heavy, deeply cut crystal bowl that had a one scallop broken off when I received it. When I first saw the bowl I felt that it was a gift of love, that the giver had shared one of her prized possessions with me. Even more than forty years later, as I use it I remember this kind generous lady. Because of these wonderful friends I received all of the china in my pattern that Fletcher's Shop had in stock. The following Christmas, when Mama wanted to add cups and serving pieces to my set, she found out that Mrs. Fletcher had omitted an important detail. The pattern,

"Gwendolyn," that I had chosen, was not only discontinued but the company, Pope Gosser, had gone out of business before I made my selection. The only pieces I was able to get were the pieces Mrs. Fletcher already had in stock that summer, so the set was never completed. The other part of the group gift was four, five-piece place settings of silver from Hires Jewelry Store. I received serving pieces from individual friends. Over the years I added other pieces, enough to serve large holiday dinners that became a tradition with Aldus and me.

From these same friends, I had learned years earlier the lesson of expressing thanks. I spent many hours writing personal notes to each person who had contributed to the group gifts.

I placed my order for my wedding cake at Ball's Bakery. My choice was a large, round, three-tiered cake with pink roses circling each tier. For the topper confectionery, I choose pastel flowers instead of the traditional plastic white bride and groom.

My next stop was to Seanors Florist. The bridal bouquet that I chose had one large white orchid in the center, designed to be removed and worn as a going-away corsage. Deep pink rosebuds with cascading tuberoses surrounded the orchid. Alice Rose's and Lillie's bouquets carried out the same design to complement my flowers. On that same visit, we rented an organdy skirt for the cake table, a kneeling bench, aisle markers and ribbons, a white cotton aisle cloth, and two large ferns. We borrowed a record player and speakers from Riggs Funeral Home, one of two colored funeral homes in Fitzgerald. On the day of the wedding the cake table had a white table cloth with the cake in the center and Grandma's two large, silver candelabra on the ends of the table, each with three pink candles.

By the end of the third week in July everything was in place and we could relax a bit. We had mailed the invitations to the Mitchell guest list. When we knew how many out-of-town guests were coming, neighbors and friends who had an available bedroom offered to provide housing and were also gracious enough to serve breakfast. What a wonderful feeling of sharing that was—free bed and breakfast for all of our out-of-town guests. This kind of sharing was not unusual, however, because we always opened our homes to visitors. In Fitzgerald in 1956 there were no hotel or motel accommodations for colored people.

Aldus arrived by bus on Friday afternoon, a day before our wedding, and took a taxi to our home at 516 East Jessamine Street. Or tried to. The white driver drove him around for about twenty minutes. A bit concerned, Aldus noticed that they kept passing the same streets and buildings. Finally, the driver turned around and asked him, "Who you goin' to see?"

When Aldus said, "the Goseers," the driver said, "Oh, that's them colored teachers! Why didn't you tell me that first? I know where they stay."

In less than two minutes they were in front of our house. In this small town, that was originally one mile square and had not expanded a great deal over the years, many of us, including cab drivers, didn't use addresses. We knew the names of people and where they lived so we used expressions like, "over there," "down by the," "near the," or "just ask anybody you see, when you get on the west side"—rarely using even street names. For many years Aldus teased me about this small town where everyone knew each other. When I moved to Chicago I had to develop the habit of learning addresses rather than relying on my memory to get from one place to the next.

That same evening Daddy and Aldus spent some time together walking around the yard talking. It was not until many years later that Aldus told me what they had talked about. The main thing Daddy told Aldus that night was, "I know Erin is tenacious, but don't you ever hit her. If she makes you mad, just walk away until you cool off. I will see to it that she always has train fare home and if you ever feel you must hit her, just send her back home." Then he repeated, "Don't you ever hit her."

Aldus never hit me during the entire thirty-two years we were married, though I'm sure there were many times he went for walks when he felt I was obstinate or unreasonable.

Dr. and Mrs. Mitchell and Aldus's sister, Gwen, did come to the wedding. Around noon, the day of the wedding Dr. and Mrs. Mitchell were walking in our front yard, admiring the pinkish-blue hydrangeas outside my bedroom window. They didn't realize that I was close behind them, in ear-shot of their conversation. I heard Mrs. Mitchell say to Dr. Mitchell, "Oh, by the way, we don't have a wedding gift for them."

Dr. Mitchell's reply was, "I guess we'll have to get someone to take us to town to get a card, and we'll put some money in it."

Apparently they got someone to take them to town because later that afternoon we got a wedding congratulations card with a fifty dollar bill in it. When I got to Chicago I wrote them a thank-you note telling them that I had bought a starter-set of Revere Ware cookware.

The only gift that I got from a white person was from Mr. Pete Roberts, the white store owner, two blocks up the street, where we bought most of our groceries. On the morning of my wedding he came to our house and brought me a gift of a set of six, tall pastel, plastic glasses from his store. I told him thanks and put them on display with the other gifts.

Saturday afternoon, August 4, 1956, was a beautiful hot sunny day, typical of August in South Georgia. A gentle breeze spread the sweet fragrance of white gardenias and burgundy buds of sweet shrubs from the large bushes on the side of the house. Magenta and pink crepe myrtle and rows of purple phlox framed the setting for the wedding ceremony. Soft recorded wedding music played as our guests gathered and stood in our side yard under the shade of the large pecan tree. The ladies and girls were dressed in their Sunday best— hats, gloves, pretty dresses, and ladies in high-heeled shoes. The men wore suits, dress shirts, and ties.

Among the people gathered were Grandma and Grandpa, Aunt Willie, cousins Eryn and Cecil, Miss Ida Cook, my first teacher, Mrs. Hattie Wallace, my first piano teacher, Mrs. Pettigrew, my sixth grade teacher, classmates and playmates from grade school through high school, Elsie Mallory, my other best friend from Spelman, all of the neighbors, and many friends.

At exactly five o'clock the volume of the music increased as Alice Rose and Lillie walked from the front door to the lawn between the posts of white ribbons and joined Aldus and his best man, Franklin Porter, our college friend from Morehouse. After they were in place by Rev. Pettigrew, the music changed to Bridal Chorus from Wagner's Lohengrin. All of Mama's hard work on my dress paid off. We could hear the softly breathed "Ohs" and "Ahs" as I came down the aisle—all ninety-four pounds of me in my exquisite dress of embroidered silk, with its dropped waist, and fitted bodice, scalloped v-neckline, cap sleeves, and very full gathered skirt with its scalloped, ankle length border. My finger-tip veil was attached to a small, close fitting hat. The tuberoses and rosebuds of my bouquet cascaded gracefully down the front of my dress. When I was half-way down the aisle I looked up and saw Aldus standing exactly as I had seen him in my dream the night after I had met him, four summers earlier.

Rev. Pettigrew, a family friend who had known me all of my life was officiating. I had talked with him earlier and asked him to delete the word "obey" from the Methodist wedding ceremony. But he didn't. When he read that part of the ceremony I smiled and shook my head, and there was soft ripple of laughter from my guests. When he asked me to say "I do," I followed his instructions and spoke loud and clearly. I had already told Aldus my feeling about agreeing to the "obey" part, so he knew that I had no intentions of keeping that.

As soon as the wedding was over we formed a receiving line and greeted our guests before they made their way to the punch table. Soon after Aldus and I cut the cake, our guests were served on glass plates with small napkins with our names and the date printed in silver. During the reception a light, brief shower sprinkled while the sun was still shining. Some people went home and others went in the house to continue their visit and see the gifts on display in the living room. Mama had all of the furniture removed from the living room except a small table and lamp. She hired a carpenter to construct stair-step-like stands, three rows high, that she covered with white sheets to display the gifts. I kept my dress on for another hour, then changed to a navy blue suit, white blouse and navy blue, high-heeled shoes that I bought at Rich's in Atlanta on my stop-over from New London. I took the orchid from the center of my bridal bouquet and pinned it to my suit jacket.

Dr. and Mrs. Mitchell left Fitzgerald early evening, after the reception. One of our neighbors drove them twenty-nine miles to the train station at Tifton for their trip to the National Medical Convention.

I expressed my surprise and joy at the outpouring of love to one of Mama's friends who had helped in the collection for the group gifts. She said, "I don't see why you're surprised. You belong to us—all of us—and we're very proud of you." I was indeed a child of the village—raised by my villages of Fitzgerald and Selma. I was loved, encouraged, supported, taught, protected, supervised, and prepared for life by all of these wonderful people who gathered for my wedding. When we boarded the train in Fitzgerald that evening, my family and many friends came to see us off.

• A DIFFERENT SELMA •

I RETURNED TO Selma on Friday, August 20, 1999 to attend Mama's older brother, my Uncle Clarence Blevins', funeral. My sister, Alice Rose, and I flew from Chicago to Birmingham and rented a car to drive ninety miles south to Selma. My earliest Selma/Birmingham trips had been in the back of the Trailways bus that stopped at every town along the way to pick up packages, mail and passengers. Travelers could even flag the bus from the highway to board, or ring the bell and be let off at any point along the way. With its many stops, what could have easily been a two hour drive was often a three and a half hour trip.

As soon as we got to Selma we drove up Broad Street toward the Edmund Pettus Bridge and made a right turn at Water Avenue to the historic St. James Hotel. It was built in 1837 and recently reopened after being authentically restored to its original elegance. This was the first time I had ever walked into a hotel in Selma. It was hard to believe that now, forty years later, *all* people would be allowed to eat, sleep and sit under this same roof. Two young women, one white and one black, who were working at the front desk, warmly greeted us. After we were given our room assignment, we walked along a hallway of gleaming hardwood floors and antique furnishings and took the elevator to our second floor room overlooking the Alabama River and the Edmund Pettus Bridge. That was such a peaceful scene, in sharp contrast to the bloody memory forever etched in my mind. I turned away and suggested that we go downstairs to the bar for a refreshing glass of iced tea before we unpacked our luggage. When we returned to the room, I discovered I had brought the wrong key for my luggage lock. At the front desk, I was told that a locksmith shop was in the rear of the antique mall across the street. The locksmith, a white man, cut off the lock without charging me. With that kind act, my visit to Selma was off to a great start. We took my luggage back to our room but we were not quite ready to face our family and the memories at 1214 Lapsley Street, where we were born.

Mama was already there. She had come from Georgia earlier in the week. We procrastinated and decided to check out the stores on Broad Street. Both Alice Rose and I like jewelry, although I have a preference for antique pieces. There were two jewelry stores next to each other. The first one, Strothers, specialized in antique pieces. The white clerk was patient and polite as we browsed, priced, and asked to try on several pieces. She didn't appear nervous or cautious as she pulled out display cases. I saw a pendant, a gold Nineteenth Century reproduction, that I liked and told her I would think about it and come back the next day.

We left Strothers and went next door to Rogers' Brothers Jewelers, where they had an antique jewelry section in the back. The contemporary jewelry didn't appeal to us, so we went straight to this special section. The clerk introduced herself as "Velma" and engaged us in friendly conversation. When we told her that we were born in Selma and had returned for a funeral, she welcomed us home and offered her condolences. She graciously took everything from the case that we wanted to see or try on. Alice Rose liked a platinum ring with three large diamonds. She told Velma that she would have to think about it and would come back the next day if she decided to buy it. We did go back the next morning and Velma greeted us in her twangy southern drawl with, "Praise the Lord, Alice. I knew you would be back. I talked to Mr. Butler about the piece that you like and he told me that that ring had been in stock for a long time and to let you have it at 50 percent off the price I quoted you yesterday." Velma beamed, almost breathless with joy.

Alice Rose responded by imitating Velma's drawl, and said, "Praise the Lord, Velma. That's a real good price. I'm going to buy it. Thanks for asking Mr. Butler to lower the price."

As the conversation continued Velma told us that she had sold jewelry before, but had been recently hired at Rogers' Brothers. This was her first sale here.

I also went back to Strothers to look at what I had selected the day before. The owner's daughter waited on us this time and told us that her mother enjoyed traveling and shopping for unique pieces. I also saw a gold ring with small diamonds that I liked. Since I especially like rings and it was a perfect fit on my right hand ring finger, I thought that was a good enough reason for buying it. She offered a greater discount if I bought both the pendant and ring. Since jewelry is my weakness I happily accepted what I felt was a good offer.

Our shopping experiences this time were very different from our shopping in Selma during the late '40s and '50s. When I was a child, Woolworth's had "colored" and "white" drinking fountains. It was also a policy in Woolworth's and other stores that we had to wait until all of the white customers had been waited on before we were asked what we wanted. I would often walk around and look in other departments, rather than wait, and come back to the counter when the white customers were gone. I could not have adequately explained my reasons then, but I think my small rebellions kept me from sharing a legacy of bitterness.

After Uncle Clarence's funeral and burial, Alice Rose and I invited Mama to go downtown with us to see the exquisite St. James Hotel. After we had shown her our room with a view of the river and bridge, we went downstairs and sat in the courtyard. She was vocal in her admiration of the black wrought-iron tables, benches and chairs, the water fountain, the wall of banana palm trees, azalea bushes, blooming cannas, the gas lanterns, and the chevron pattern of the red brick flooring. It was if she was storing up details she had never expected to see. We ordered iced tea with fresh lemon like Grandma served with dinner every summer's day. We sat around and talked until dusk and Mama was ready to go back to Lapsley Street. I hoped that these new memories would soften the sharp edges of the old ones that denied her even a glimpse into this forbidden world.

Alice Rose and I came back for a late dinner in the hotel's dining room. Each meal was individually prepared so service was slow. An integrated staff was worth the wait to enjoy fresh, delicious food, crisp linens, silver, and sparkling crystal, all graciously served.

After dinner, we went back to the courtyard and I continued sipping my wine. The flames were flickering as I listened to the soothing, gurgling sounds of water from the fountain. When we had shopped on Broad Street we were treated with respect and dignity. I remembered my Grandma Mabel and my Grandpa Frank and my other ancestors who had lived in Selma all of their lives and could never fully participate in all that Selma had to offer. I remembered how frightened Grandma had been the afternoon the Ku Klux Klan cavalcade drove through Lapsley Street; and the night Carol Moore and I walked through the white neighborhood on our way home from the Wilby theater; and the white taxi driver in Montgomery who doubled the fare when he found out we were colored. I remembered the day Grandma said, "Maybe one day we won't have to go in the back door of the doctor's office."

I remembered Grandpa sitting quietly on the front porch on summer evenings, smoking his pipe and letting out an occasional loud sigh or rubbing his stomach because it was hurting from ulcers. I remembered how he gently stroked and talked to their cow, Alice, as he put the rope around her neck to take her grazing down by Valley Creek. I remembered that he shopped at colored stores when he could, even though he had to pay more. He told me that the colored stores needed our support to stay in business.

Saturday morning Alice Rose and I got up early to explore more of downtown Selma before joining our family to go to Uncle Clarence's funeral. We walked toward Broad Street and the Edmund Pettus Bridge. We walked pass the offices of the *Selma Times Journal*, a paper that I remembered showed pictures of colored men on the front page only if they had been accused of a crime. Next door, one-half block west of the cruelties of Bloody Sunday, March 7, 1965, is the National Voter's Rights Museum, which houses memorabilia of the infamous attack on marchers and other peaceful events of the tumultuous '60s.

I paused just inside the front door of the museum. I remembered seeing pictures flash across the TV as I stood screaming in my living room in Chicago. To the left of the entrance was a wall labeled, "The Honor Roll." There were hundreds of cards, notes, and slips of paper with comments and signatures of heroes telling of their experiences with the tear gas, beatings and other atrocities of that day, and the subsequent successful Selma to Montgomery March.

The Alabama Department of Transportation documented the events of those days and the black and white photos are on display. Alice Rose and I went our separate ways in the museum. I suppose each of us had to deal with our feelings and memories in our own way. I walked slowly through each room, in a rather somber mood. Even though I've seen many of these pictures on TV, in magazines and books, seeing them again in this setting gave me an overwhelming sense of personal history.

There were pictures of the Boyntons, our neighbors across the street, and Mrs. Marie Foster, Grandma's young friend, who were key people in the voter's registration drives. I also saw a picture of "Miss Emma"—Mrs. Emma Vassar, our next door neighbor. Back at the hotel as I sat quietly in the warm night air, memories of the pictures I had seen earlier in the day flashed in my mind. As I gazed into the night skies I felt a strong sense of gratitude for my family, my ancestors, and the dauntless people who made it possible for me to live, eat and sit at this resplendent hotel and be treated with respect and dignity. I sang in my head the words from "Lift Every Voice and Sing" by James Weldon Johnson.

> *We have come over a way*
> *that with tears have been watered.*
> *We have come treading the path*
> *through the blood of the slaughtered.*
> *Out of the gloomy past, 'til now we stand at last,*
> *True to our God, True to our native land.*

I repeated that part of the song again and substituted "I" for each "We". When I did that, I was choked with emotion as these words became real and personal to me and I understood why I have had this compelling force to write about my people in Alabama and Georgia. Our younger generations must know of the determination, creativity, fortitude, dear price, and sacrifices that were paid for us to have the law on our side in our continuing quest for "liberty and justice for all." After this visit to Selma I feel a sense of a circle finally completed. It is my sincere hope that my effort in writing and sharing these stories as a part of our history will be meaningful to readers as they learn about my people who lived in Alabama and Georgia—before Bloody Sunday.

• FREE AT LAST •

I WAS BURSTING with excitement on this hot, sunny Thursday morning in May 2000, as I arrived at the Atlanta airport from Chicago to join my college roommate, Lillie McKinney Cooley. We coordinated our arrival time and other activities in order to spend most of our 45th Spelman College reunion weekend together. Lillie wanted to take a trip to the University of Georgia at Athens before our reunion activities began. She had invited some of her deceased sister's friends to join her for lunch in Athens. Lillie's sister, Dr. Melvin McKinney Bowie at the time of her death, had been a faculty member at the University of Georgia for the past eleven years.

One of Lillie's cousins who lives in the Atlanta area volunteered to meet us at the airport and drive us to Athens. Lillie had made reservations at a restaurant near the campus. Melvin's friends met us there. They were not strangers to me because I had met them almost three years earlier at Melvin's memorial service. Lillie had told me earlier these loving and caring women had taken care of Melvin who, when she knew she was terminally ill, chose to remain in Athens. Her friends in Athens reassured her family in Jackson, Mississippi that they would take care of her needs and supervise her medical care. This close-knit group of friends organized and rearranged their busy schedules so that Melvin received the best care possible. They took her to her medical appointments and did all they could to make her final days comfortable. Melvin was living in a second floor apartment before she became ill. As her illness progressed and she was no longer able to climb the stairs, her friends moved her to the first floor apartment directly beneath. They first set up her bed in the new apartment and got her comfortably situated. By the end of the day everything in her new apartment was in place.

When Lillie called me and told me that Melvin had passed, I told her that I would join her in Athens for the memorial service. Melvin's wishes were to be cremated and her ashes scattered in the garden in the quadrangle on the older part of UGA campus, her favorite place for meditation. A private ceremony was held early in the morning on the day of her memorial service. Her ashes were scattered among the plants behind her favorite bench that faced the fountain.

Melvin's memorial service was held at the Unitarian Church that she had attended. Her department head, fellow faculty members, and friends at UGA, all of whom had become her adopted family, made tributes.

After the memorial service all of Melvin's family, who had come from Mississippi and other parts of the country, were invited to a spacious and beautifully appointed home for a repast. Melvin's friends had prepared all sorts of homemade dishes, and welcomed all of us.

Don't friends and family interact this way in a time of illness and death of a loved one? The great difference for me was that Melvin was black and her adopted family, the support group, was white. This was a new experience for me. The date of the memorial service was July 1997. The date of the luncheon preceding our reunion was May 2000. On both of these occasions, my eyes kept seeing Melvin's adopted family as white people, and me and her Mississippi family as black. I could not help remembering my days of growing up in racially segregated South Georgia in the 1940s to the mid-1950s. My interactions with white people were brief business encounters or unpleasant situations where I had been treated as though I were an inferior person.

Until these visits to Athens and the University of Georgia, my knowledge of UGA was based on news accounts from 1961 when black students, Charlayne Hunter, Hamilton Holmes, and my friend Mary Frances Early entered UGA. They encountered great hostility and prejudice as students there. Mary Frances, a graduate school transfer student from the University of Michigan, was the first black student to graduate from UGA. She received her Master's degree in Music in 1962. Charlayne and Hamilton graduated in 1963. Mary Frances has told many personal stories of being mistreated as she tried to pursue an education in this hostile environment.

Mary Frances and Charlayne were assigned living quarters together in the Center Myles dormitory, separated from the other students, in what was the counselor's office. This was their private suite. One of the hurtful experiences that Mary Frances, a native of Georgia, endured was seeing her classmates embrace female students from India with skin colors darker than hers.

One day Mary Frances came outside and found that the tires on her white car had been slashed and the word "nigger" had been painted on it in red. Another day, as she tried to enter the library, eight football players taunted her and linked arms in an attempt to block her entrance. Even through these hate-filled and juvenile acts she told me that she kept focused on her goal to get an education.

All of the people she encountered were not racists. She recalls that she received encouragement from strangers, both black and white. Students at the Presbyterian Center helped her celebrate her 25th birthday by giving a party. She also remembers a white graduate student in art who registered for classes at the same time she had and walked with her between classes.

When Mary Frances first joined the university choir no one would share their folder of music. When it was time for the concert, her mother was not allowed to see her perform. The dean told her that the university was integrated for students, not parents. Her graduation was different. More than seventy-six people from Atlanta came to see her graduate. These were the things that I remembered in 1997 as I walked around the campus at UGA for the first time.

Almost three years later, I was sitting at a table with some of the women who had been hostesses on the day of Melvin's memorial service. Lillie told us that we were her guests and to order whatever we wished. I ordered a hamburger, which looked more like dinner with the potatoes and large salad. I also ordered "sweet tea" (sweetened ice tea) which is a southern favorite. I was so full when I finished the hamburger that I didn't want to order dessert. The woman sitting directly across the table from me ordered a wedge of hummingbird cake. I had never heard of this although I was told it is popular in the South. It is a rich dark cake with crushed pineapple, mashed bananas, applesauce, and several spices. The frosting is a cream cheese/powdered sugar confectionery. As the woman across from me ate it, she said how delicious it was and suggested that I taste it. At first I refused. She finally said, "This is absolutely too much for me. Somebody please help me finish it."

At that point I was very curious and decided to taste it, so she pushed it across the table to me. It was one of the most delicious cakes I'd ever eaten. I forgot that I was too full, ate the remainder and smacked my lips. I thanked her for insisting that I taste it.

As we left the restaurant, I thought, "I just did a very intimate thing. I just ate the leftovers from someone's plate, a white lady's at that!" By the time I was back in the bright sun and mid-day Georgia heat I was overcome with gratitude to this group of women who no longer appeared white to me. Instead, they were colorless, kind, warm, loving, sincere human beings.

That day at lunch was the last day that my first reaction to a white person was based on the color of their skin. That was the day I was completely freed from the shackles of skin color. Now I am able to look at a person and think how we can relate to each other.

Early experiences make deep impressions on one's psyche. I had been conditioned to be cautious and guarded in the presence of white people. I grew up in Alabama and Georgia where pleasant interactions with white people were rare. After I went to college some of my reluctance to relate to white people gradually began to lessen as I had broader contacts with them. I grew to the point where I was able to relate to white people but I was always aware of the color of their skin first.

I was in a reflective mood as we drove back to Atlanta. That was the day I took another look at myself and realized that racial prejudice is a two-edged blade. I had also been guilty of prejudging people by the color of their skin rather than allowing them to define themselves as individuals.

It has taken me a long time to completely overcome the conditioning of growing up in the South, in a racially segregated society. It is a good feeling to be free of these chains. As the Negro spiritual says, "Free at last, free at last. Thank God Almighty, I'm free at last."

It was this wonderful group of persons in Athens, Georgia, who released me from the last bondage of my seeing a person's skin color before seeing a human being.

· ABOUT THE AUTHOR ·

ERIN GOSEER MITCHELL was born in Selma, Alabama on June 9, 1935, at her maternal grandparents' home. She spent many summers and Christmas Holidays in Selma. With the exception of one school term in Selma, she lived with her parents in Fitzgerald, Georgia and completed elementary and high school there.

She is a graduate of the class of 1955 of Spelman College in Atlanta, Georgia where she earned a Bachelor of Arts degree. During her senior year, one of her professors, Dr. Wilbert Snow, encouraged her to expand her horizons by applying for a teaching position in his home state of Connecticut. She became a fourth grade teacher in Groton, Connecticut and taught one term before marrying her college sweetheart. They moved to Chicago, Illinois where she worked in the Chicago Public Schools for 37 years, taking two brief maternity leaves for the births of her daughters, Audrey and Greta.

When Greta was nine years old, Erin enrolled at Roosevelt University in Chicago and earned a Master of Music degree while continuing to teach full time. When she retired after a 38 year career as an educator, her latent desire to write surfaced with a passion. She began writing what grew into a collection of short stories—memories of growing up in Alabama and Georgia between 1940 and 1956.

An avid reader, pianist and organist, Erin also enjoys traveling, gardening and singing. In addition to two loving daughters, she is the proud grandmother of three young grandsons. She is a widow and resides in Chicago.

· REFERENCES ·

From a work of Ralph Ellison's (pages 9 and 16)

The Rosenwald Schools of the American South by Mary F. Hoffschweller. University of Florida Press. 2006. (page 20)

The Ole Ark's a-Moverin'—Negro Spiritual (page 32)

When the Storm Clouds Gather—Negro Spiritual (page 32)

Blest Be the Tie that Binds by John Fawcett and Hans G. Nageli (page 123)

From *Quotable Quotes of Dr. Benjamin E. Mays.* Vintage Press. New York, NY (page 157)

Be Strong by Maltbie D. Babcock. Reprinted from *American Student Hymnal* (page 162)

Carry On by Robert W. Service. Copyright 1874 by Robert W. Service. Reprinted from *American Student Hymnal* (page 162)

I Would Be True by Harold Arnold Walter (page 163)

From *The Road Not Taken* by Robert Frost (page 181)

Lift Every Voice and Sing by James Weldon Johnson and J. Rosamond Johnson (page 218)